Consciousness and Change

Consciousness and Change

Symbolic Anthropology in Evolutionary Perspective

James L. Peacock

A Halsted Press Book

JOHN WILEY & SONS · New York

Published in the USA
by Halsted Press, a Division of
John Wiley & Sons Inc.,
New York

Library of Congress Cataloging in Publication Data

Peacock, James L
 Consciousness and change.

 'A Halsted Press Book.'
 Bibliography: p.
 Includes Index.
I. 1. Symbolism.   2. Ethnology.   3. Social change.
 Title.
GN320.P42   301.2   75–1349
ISBN 0–470–67452–0

Set in Univers and Linotype Times
Printed in Great Britain by
Western Printing Services Ltd, Bristol
and bound at The Kemp Hall Bindery, Oxford

Contents

Preface

Since beginning the study of anthropology, I have been interested in the relations between symbolic and social structures, a subject wide enough to include studies of myth, ritual, and totemism; analyses of the relations between language and modes of classifying or perceiving; theories of the communicative process; psychoanalytic dissection of fantasies and dreams; works in comparative religion, sociology of religion, sociology of knowledge, and the politics of ideology; the philosophy of symbols rooted in the writings of Cassirer; the pioneer efforts of such anthropologists as Benedict, Mead and Kroeber to abstract themes and plots from culture; sociologically oriented writings in literary and art criticism; and studies in folklore, enthnomusicology, and archaeology.[1] The topic is broad enough to cut across conventional disciplines within anthropology and to unite concerns of both the humanities and the social sciences, but it is specific enough to define a certain focus for study, research, and contemplation (if not explanation) of the history and condition of man.

A chancellor of a rural university in the southern United States was recently challenged by conservative politicians to explain why his professors did not spend as many hours in the classroom as did other state employees in their offices. The chancellor's reply, doubtless the most flattering opinion of an academic he ever expressed, was 'You don't pay a bull for time in the pen but for services rendered.' It is also true, however, that time in the pen

[1] Sources concerning these topics are listed in the 'Suggested Readings' at the end of this book.

improves the rendering of services, and my own perspective on symbolic aspects of social life has been enriched by the experience of teaching a course on this subject in three institutions. This course, in its varied formats, has always been oriented toward the non-specialist, and few of the students have been learned in anthropology. They have come from the disciplines of history, languages, literature, mathematics and sociology, and they have included musicians, actors, ministers of the gospel, collectors of folklore, players of football, housewives (in an evening class for adult education), and, of course, the silent majority whose motives for study are shrouded in mystery. Their interests have encompassed the full range of symbolic forms and systems—myth, ritual, language, cosmology, ideology, theology, drama, the novel, blues and bluegrass, drug experiences, mystic meditation, the fantasies and delusions of the insane, and themselves. The central problem of teaching such a course is to find a conceptual framework which embraces the diversity of interests while preserving the richness of each.

The most satisfactory framework that I have found derives from the European sociological tradition of Emile Durkheim and Max Weber. While other perspectives are invaluable, I have found none so capable of broad, systematic, non-reductionist synthesis capable of inspiring insight into the historical thrust of human consciousness and society. The Durkheimian-Weberian framework fulfills these requirements, though I have found it necessary to stretch and bastardize their tradition in certain respects.

Durkheim and Weber remain massively relevant to contemporary existence, but both were dead long before the Second World War. Such post-war developments as the creation of new nations and the emergence, in old ones, of a counter-culture of drugs and communes, requires, I submit, the addition of a new phase to the Durkheim-Weberian vision of social and symbolic evolution. No contemporary theorist, certainly no anthropologist, has provided a comprehensive and systematic analysis of this new period, and I resort to several popular writers who at least hint at the relevant themes.

The second elaboration of the Durkheim-Weber framework is less theoretical than substantive. In working through the courses on symbols, I have made a practice of encouraging, at the end, 'sensuous presentations' by the students. These are not daring displays of nudity or live sex, but are merely films, tapes, and dramas or exhibitions that we can hear, see, touch, and smell. The performances have usually drawn on the symbolically vigorous local culture in the southeastern United States, and they have included such events as a rendition of faith-healing, a film on pottery-making, and a video tape of what is said to be the last extant medical show, complete with the harmonica playing of Peg-leg Sam and the exhortations of his huckster partner, Chief Thunder Cloud.[2] These little traditions concretize the Great Tradition of classical sociology, resulting in the enrichment of both. Though a book is not built for sensuous presentation, I shall endeavor to enrich the theoretical by the concrete, weaving Durkheim and Weber into the two milieux with which I have enjoyed direct and sustained involvement: the island of Java, in Indonesia, where I have done anthropological fieldwork for nearly two years, and the southern region of the United States, where I have spent most of my life.

The teaching context within which this book developed has resulted in a style of presentation different from that of the orthodox textbook or monograph. The book does not exhaustively survey studies or theories with the aim of summarizing the essence of all. Instead of summarizing, I sketch, hopefully with sufficient detail to preserve flavor, studies of a few scholars selected to illustrate an underlying perspective. After this synthetic portrait of a theory, some of the insights are applied to the cases of Java and the southern United States. A concluding typology formulates a view of the evolution of symbolic forms. Occasionally I cite, where possible verbatim instead of in bland summary, reactions to these materials by students to whom they were recently presented (in a primarily undergraduate course on symbols at the University of North Carolina at Chapel Hill, USA). This semblance of dialogue is meant to affirm the tentative character of the framework set forth.

I intend this book to achieve two objectives. The first is synthesis. Such symbolic forms as those of religion, art, ideology, fantasy, dream, and neurosis are customarily treated as separate

---

[2] This tape was by Bruce Bastin, a student of folklore who, though of British nationality, is doing pioneer research on blues in the US Carolinas. In light of the neglect accorded folklore studies by many anthropologists, I wish to acknowledge the special enrichment provided my own course on symbols by students of folklore working with Professor Daniel Patterson.

phenomena, the specialties of separate fields such as the sociology and anthropology of religion, literary criticism, political science, psychology, psychiatry, and psychological anthropology. I strive to show commonalities and linkages, to set forth a unifying framework capable of synthesizing these several phenomena and fields of study. I am particularly interested, too, in connecting the Durkheimian perspective, which has been influential in anthropological studies of 'simple' societies, to the Weberian view, which is relatively unappreciated even by those anthropologists concerned with complex societies and evolutionary change. To date, the most pervasive and cohesive anthropological approach to symbolism remains essentially Durkheimian; can't we go further?

The second objective, obviously related to the first, is to suggest a schema for treating materials customarily or potentially included in courses on 'symbolic anthropology.'[3] While this book surveys only a fraction of the literature within this vast field,[4] it does position representative studies within a frame. I am aware that the frame is selective and gross, that it slights subtle distinctions and certain remarkable analyses of particular materials. I will be content if the book achieves the objectives mentioned by setting forth, in a manner comprehensible to student and layman, a broad perspective capable or organizing past studies in order to stimulate future thought.

The term 'perspective' warns that this work is only one slant on a study of symbols; and it is only fair to indicate some of the omissions. I have little to say about such discrete but powerful symbols as hair, food, the heavenly bodies, and the Jungian archetypes, nor

[3] As far as I know, this label 'symbolic anthropology' originated with several colleagues and myself, or at least this is the context in which I first recall using the term. In 1965, two of us (David W. Crabb and myself, joined a year later by A. Thomas Kirsch and Martin G. Silverman) embarked on the task of launching a new program in anthropological studies at Princeton University. Sharing interests in symbolic aspects of behavior, we built this focus into the program and labelled it 'symbolic anthropology' as a parallel to such labels as political, economic, and psychological anthropology. Growing out of this program was a projected 'series in Symbolic Anthropology' to be edited by David W. Crabb and published by The University of Chicago Press. The first volume in the series was *Peacock* (1), the second *Silverman*. Recent interest in the topic is evidenced by the 'symbol, myth and ritual' series edited by Victor W. Turner and published by Cornell University Press, and the 1973 appearance of a journal entitled *Symbolic Anthropology*.

[4] The most comprehensive survey of anthropological studies of symbols is *Firth.*

about techniques for the empirical investigation of their meanings.[5] This essay focusses on such *complexes* of symbols as the rite, the myth, and the belief system, and it sets forth a single perspective in terms of which one might organize some notions about the role of such symbolic complexes in society. Owing to my emphasis on the relation between these symbolic complexes and social change, we move quickly from the domain of the primitive and ancient, attending only skimpily to the cults and fetishes so fascinating to the classical ethnologist. Though this field is fundamental, my major concern here is to suggest linkages between these traditional complexes and the historic movement toward modernity. Yet this work is no world history, but merely an elucidation of a perspective which links symbols to history.

Grateful acknowledgment is made to Professor F. G. Bailey, without whose invitation and encouragement this book would not have been written; to Professor Victor W. Turner for gracious interest; to Jon Anderson, Kevin Avruch, Barbara Higgins, Linda Oldham, James MacMurray and George Saunders for indispensable research and editorial help; to teachers and colleagues whose ideas, support, inspiration, and friendship lie behind this volume, and especially to James Boon, Christopher Crocker, Thomas Kirsch, Rodney Needham, William Peck, Steven Piker and Robert Wilson for suggestive commentary on particular chapters. While setting pen to paper, I have remembered the students to whom these materials were presented, and I am grateful for their keenness and their warmth. My wife I thank for tolerance, my mother-in-law for response, and I affectionately dedicate this work to my younger daughters, Natalie and Claire.

J.L.P.

[5] This is the focus of the impressive work by *Firth*, which the reader should consult to fill this as well as other gaps in the present work.

Acknowledgments

W. W. Norton and Co. for permission to quote from Erik H. Erikson, *Young Man Luther* (1958 ed.), pp. 47-8, and Erik H. Erikson, *Childhood and Society* (1963 ed.) pp. 336-7; Macmillan Co. for permission to quote from Ari Kiev, ed. *Magic, Faith, and Healing* (1964 ed.), pp. 260-1; Merlin Press and Beacon Press for permission to quote from Claude Lévi-Strauss, *Totemism* (1963 ed.) pp. 79-81; Jonathan Cape Ltd. and Athenaeum Publishers Ltd. for permission to quote from Claude Lévi-Strauss, *Tristes Tropiques* (1968 ed.) pp. 17-20; Doubleday and Co. for permission to quote from Claude Lévi-Strauss, *Structural Anthropology* (1967 ed.) p. 214 and Bronislaw Malinowski, *Magic, Science, and Religion* (1954 ed.), pp. 101, 146-7.

1
Introduction

Units of Consciousness: Symbols

The Oxford Dictionary gives several definitions of 'symbol', among which are the following:
1. 'A formal authoritative statement or summary of the religious belief of the Christian church, or of a particular church or sect';
2. ' A written character or mark used to represent something';
3. 'A contribution (properly to a feast or picnic); a share, portion' (an obsolete meaning, exemplified by Ben Jonson's 1627 usage 'This reck'ning I will pay, Without conferring symboles' or by Lamb in 1822: 'To have sat down at the cripple's feast, and to have thrown in his benediction, ay, and his mite too, for a companionable symbol').

But the most useful definition, for our purposes, is:

> Something that stands for, represents, or denotes something else (not by exact resemblance, but by vague suggestion, or by accidental or conventional relation); *esp.* a material object representing or taken to represent something immaterial or abstract, as a being, idea, quality, or condition; a representative or typical figure, sign, or token . . .[1]

A symbol 'stands for, represents, or denotes something else', and the symbol is 'material' whereas the something else is 'immaterial or abstract'. Here is a kernel meaning of 'symbol' sufficient to open our inquiry, but some elaboration may be helpful. Let us say that the symbol is a *sensory* form or action—a form or action (such as a gesture, color, musical tone, or verbal slogan) that can be seen, heard, touched, or smelled.[2] We should also remind ourselves that the symbol need not 'represent' the 'something else' by direct duplication; this is shown by the well-known fact that the same image or idea can be expressed by a variety of forms (so that the concept of *horse* is expressed by German *Pferd*, Indonesian *kuda*, English 'horse', and many other words). And the term 'represent' probably denotes too mechanical a relationship between the symbol and its referent. The faithful believe that the wine of Communion actually *becomes* the blood of the Savior rather than merely representing it, and some such feeling of a complex and mystical participation of the symbol in its immaterial referent is part of all the powerful religious, ideological, and artistic or fantasy systems of concern to us in this book. To catch something of this feeling, I prefer the word 'express' rather than 'represent'.

Entertaining little hope of trapping the full range of experiences distilled by symbolic forms, nevertheless I shall hazard a minimal, working definition to serve as an initial indication of the topic. In confronting symbolic forms, we shall focus on sensory forms or actions whose primary and immediate function, in a given context, is to express a configuration of consciousness.

Note the phrase 'primary function'. No form or action is solely expressive in function, but some are primarily expressive while others are oriented toward other functions. Consider the difference between a farmer plowing his field and a drama, say of the socialist proletarian variety known in some nations, which expresses a vision of the farmer plowing his field. The actors might push a plow across the stage, but probably none—not even the most ardent supporters of the party line—would argue that they are actually preparing the floor to grow crops. The farmer does precisely that to his field. The farmer's action is directly oriented toward an end necessary for physical survival, the growing of food. His action is practical, instrumental, technical; his job is to plow. That of the drama is expressive, representational, symbolic: its *primary* function (though not its only one) is to express a conception of consciousness of what it *means* to plow.[3]

What if the drama were also a rite which is believed by its participants to increase the fertility of the field? By our definition, this ritual would apparently be technical rather than symbolic in primary function. But note the term 'immediate' placed before the word 'primary'. Agreed, the ultimate function of the fertility rite may be the growing of food, but the *immediate* function, I would say, is expressive, as when the actors, imitating the primitive, perform interpretative dances to symbolize the plant's growth. One does not normally see the practical farmer don ballet tights and leotards and periodically leap from behind his mule to pirouette among the furrows in a symbolic portrayal of his crop's anticipated growth. While he is plowing, his immediate job is simply to plow, to follow the mule and break the ground.

A given action or form can serve either symbolic or technical functions, sometimes the one, sometimes the other. It depends, as our definition states, on the context. A hammer is usually a tool, serving the technical function of driving a nail. But it can also become a symbol, as in the Hammer and Sickle, the legend of the mighty hammerer of railroad spikes, John Henry, and the song of Simon and Garfunkel; 'I'd rather be a sparrow than a snail; I'd rather be a hammer than a nail'.

Indeed, forms which serve a primarily symbolic function in one society take on a primarily technical function in others, or vice versa. Writing around AD 1150, the great Hindu astronomer and mathematician, Bhāskarā, described two perpetual motion devices. These were designed to symbolize the Hindu belief in the cyclical and self-renewing nature of all things. By AD 1200 the notion of the perpetual motion machine had filtered into the Arabic world, and the Muslims transmitted the concept to the medieval West. Western engineers began to transform the representational into the technical, the symbol into a machine, with which they tried to grind grain and pump water.[4]

A reverse transformation, from West to East and from technical to symbolic, is exemplified by Indonesia's borrowing of the concept of the plan for economic development. The late President Sukarno placed responsibility for drawing up such a plan in the hands of the poet and ideologue, Muhammad Yamin. The result was 8 volumes with 17 sections each, and 1945 paragraphs to represent August 17, 1945, the date of Indonesia's declaration of independence. Sukarno praised the plan for its 'symbolic richness', gleefully recognizing the transformation of a technical instrument into a symbolic form.

The distinction between 'symbolic' and 'technical' functions is arbitrary and relative. A given set of forms and actions will always serve both functions, but stress one or the other depending on the context. In spite of its arbitrariness, our definition of symbol is sufficient to mark loose boundaries, to distinguish a class of phenomena.[5] Such forms as rituals, myths, novels, songs, visions, fantasies, sermons, parables, and slogans are typically symbolic forms. As such, they are a major concern of this book.

Systems of Consciousness: Symbolic Structures

Acts and objects can be distinguished according to whether their functions are primarily symbolic or technical, and so can systems of acts and objects. A system of consciousness, which unites a plurality of symbolic forms into a single structure, tends towards a mode of integration which has been termed 'logico-meaningful'. Logico-meaningful integration can be distinguished from the 'causal-functional' integration of the techno-social system.[6]

The techno-social system is nicely illustrated by a nursery saying:

> For want of a nail, the shoe was lost
> For want of the shoe, the horse was lost
> For want of the horse, the rider was lost
> For want of the rider, the battle was lost
> And all for the want of a horseshoe nail

This saying describes a system connecting objects of technology (the nail, shoe, horse) with social events (war and eventually the loss of a kingdom). The acts and objects composing this techno-social system are linked casually and functionally in that each is a condition or consequence of the other. The condition of the nail's loss sets in motion the consequence of the shoe's loss which in turn is a condition for the horse's loss, which eventually leads to the loss of a kingdom.

In this Mother Goose paradigm, the thrust of causation is one-way—from nail to kingdom—but in real-life techno-social systems, it is circular. The rising enrollment of students prompts a university to adopt computerized, bureaucratized, impersonal methods of administration. Such methods permit still larger enrollment, which necessitates yet more computerization, bureaucratization, and impersonality. The process is a 'vicious cycle'. Whether uni-directional or circular, the techno-social system connects events, roles, groups, tools, and resources in casual-functional relationships.

A system of consciousness is differently integrated. Its units, the symbolic forms, are integrated through their derivation from unified conceptual structure. Consider a theology. Such forms as parables, proverbs, sermons, and ceremonies become meaningful to the believer when they are more or less logically deducible from the premises underlying the theology. With slight adjustment, the same analysis can be made of an aesthetic form. A chord is beautiful to the listener because it is more or less deducible from the rules governing his musical system; a false note, analogous to a false deduction, makes the listener cringe. Even a dream can be viewed as meaningful if the dreamer interprets it in terms of a mental and emotional system. The dream of losing a tooth acquires meaning for the dreamer when he, with the help of the psychiatrist, realizes that it manifests some general theme in his personality, such as fear of castration. Unaware of the underlying schemes, the infidel finds the parable meaningless; the foreigner, the music ugly; the layman, his dream terrifying.

Examples can be found of mongrel systems which employ the logico-meaningful associations as part of a casual-functional network, or vice versa. In the American televised children's show, 'Sesame Street', a character named Ernie explains the chain of mental associations evoked by his cookie. The cookie reminds him of circles; circles recall squares; squares, checkerboards; checkerboards, games; games, an American football helmet; the helmet, brass bands (which play at football games); the bands, bells; and the bells remind Ernie to set the alarm clock so its ring will remind him to eat his cookie. This configuration can be seen as logico-meaningful in that its elements are logically deduced from a central image, the cookie. It is casual-functional in that it links acts and objects in a sequence resulting in the destruction of the cookie that evoked the associations in the first place. As with the classifying of acts and objects as 'symbolic' versus 'technical', the classifying of systems of acts and objects as 'logico-meaningful' versus 'casual-functional' is arbitrary—a matter of emphasis and degree.

Without great difficulty, however, the analyst can characterize most behavioral systems as giving primacy to either logico-meaningful or causal-functional integration. Within a given system, he can distinguish certain aspects as being more strongly logico-meaningful, others as more strongly casual-functional. The distinction helps to delimit the subject of this book. As we are concerned with such symbolic forms as rites, myths, parables, and sermons, we shall focus on those systems which integrate these forms into logico-meaningful patterns: systems of belief, ethics, aesthetics, and fantasy.

Why call these complexes 'systems of consciousness'? The word evokes images of such suspect phenomena as drugs, meditation, mysticism, and Charles Reich's Consciousness III. Alternative terms employed by anthropologists are 'culture', 'belief systems', and 'cognitive maps'. Each has drawbacks. 'Culture' is either too broad (for some anthropologists, it covers all non-biological facets of human existence) or too narrow (for many laymen it denotes only the refined arts). The other terms are too intellectualistic; they fail to encompass the emotions and evaluations which are as important for symbol systems as are cognition and belief. In its vagueness, the term 'consciousness' embraces all of these aspects.

Consciousness must also be considered, for our purposes, to embrace the 'unconscious'. The repressed and suppressed memories, feelings, and motives that psychoanalysts have so powerfully shown to underly the symbolism of their patients may usefully be regarded as unconscious in that the patient cannot verbalize them, at least not before years on the couch. Nevertheless, these unconscious ruminations cannot be entirely outside the patient's awareness, for he expresses them in his dreams, wit, and delusions. The very fact that the unconscious can be so symbolized proves that it is not entirely unconscious. And that part of the unconscious which cannot be symbolized is of no concern to a student of symbols. In sum, I propose that we understand the notion of 'consciousness' to include the 'unconscious', at least until we can find a better term to encompass both the lucidly conscious and the murkily unconscious thoughts, feelings, sensations, motives, beliefs, and memories which are expressed through symbolic forms.

The term 'consciousness' is useful in reminding us that symbolic systems operate only insofar as the actor is conscious, at some level of awareness, of their meanings. Causal-functional chains and networks that we distinguish as constituting the techno-social system can operate without the actor's awareness. Consider the symbols of Christ, Christmas, the Crucifix, and Easter. These symbols have no import for the actor unless he perceives them to be expressing some subjective complex, some configuration of consciousness which may range from a highly articulated doctrine envisioning the drama of Christ's birth, death, and rebirth to a vague sense of pleasure at the prospect of holiday family reunion. These forms, as symbols, are meaningless unless they are linked to some subjective complex. They might have impact outside the actor's awareness, as when someone uses the crucifix to hit him over the head, but in such a case the form is not, to that actor, a symbol.

Consider, by contrast, a techno-social system. The baker may never have stopped to think that he depends on the miller to grind his meal, and that the farmer supplies grain to the miller. The baker's lack of awareness does not in the least prevent his shop from being forced to close if the miller ceases to grind grain because all the farmers have gone to work for a factory. Techno-social forces and relationships are like the 'silent servant' of appliance advertisements: they can operate outside the awareness of their operators. In real life, of course, even techno-social interchanges among people depend in part on their mutual expectations, but it is at least possible to conceive of such operations without consciousness; robots could carry out the miller's, baker's, and farmer's functions. Automation approaches this situation, and in a society of ants, queens and workers allegedly interact through instinct rather than awareness: a society without consciousness. Techno-social relations need not involve consciousness, whereas logico-meaningful relations, by definition, must.

A system of consciousness can be peculiar to a single individual or shared by several. The emphasis of the European sociological tradition has been on shared consciousness, what Durkheim termed 'collective representations'.[7] The classical emphasis will be retained in this book, though we shall also explore the process by which systems of shared consciousness originate in the experience of the individual.

Techno-social Change: Modernization

This book is especially concerned with the interplay between systems of consciousness and techno-social systems that *change*.

Rather than speak vapidly of change in general, which is to say of all existence, I would prefer to focus on change in a certain direction: toward that pattern which is sometimes termed 'modernity'. My concern is to explore the symbolic correlates of man's evolution toward and beyond modernity. This type of techno-social change is 'modernization'.

The simplest definition of modernization is technological.[8] To the extent that a social system employs inanimate sources of power and tools to multiply (or destroy) human efforts, it is modernized. By inanimate sources of power is meant wind to blow sails, gravity to propel carts, and other such rudimentary energies as well as electricity, steam, and nuclear power. By tools are meant primitive digging sticks as well as modern steam shovels. Every society has some technology and precise measurement of differences in amount is difficult, but gross ranking is relatively easy. At one end of the scale would go such societies as Germany, Japan, Sweden, England, and the United States; at the other end, peasant and tribal communities in Asia, Africa, and other places including certain regions of the West.

A variety of social trends correlate with technological modernization. Most of these correlations are subsumed by the statement that with technological modernization, units of the social system become increasingly specialized while the system itself becomes increasingly centralized.[9]

Thus, the more modernized the society, the more its constituent parts specialize in educational, political, religious, recreational, and economic functions. The more traditional the society, the more unspecialized its units, the extreme case being the society composed of units of a single type (the family) which perform all of these functions. In most traditional societies, for example, education takes place within the family, and the family is also the unit of production and worship. With modernity there emerges the school, a unit which specializes in education, and in time the school itself differentiates in sub-types, each specializing in a different form of education until finally we get schools of computer programming, public speaking, and transcendental meditation.

As the diversity of specialized units increases, society co-ordinates then under some central control. Centralization is economic, religious, and educational as well as political. In the United States, charities merge into the United Fund, labor unions join the Teamsters, and the multi-versity centralizes the universities into a single huge educational system.

When units specialize and society centralizes, social relationships change in predictable ways. Among other things, they become more 'functionally specific' and less 'functionally diffuse'. When most of life's tasks are performed within a primitive family, its members cooperate in a number of spheres: economic, political, educational, religious, emotional. Each member's bond to the other is diffuse. In the modern society, no single group performs all functions, and any group's members relate to each other in only a few ways; modern family members may offer each other little more than emotional support so that even family bonds become functionally specific.

Associated changes occur in residence patterns, economic exchange, and social norms. Money, or some equivalent medium of exchange, becomes essential for trade with strangers who replace kinsmen as partners in exchange. Freed of the necessity to serve the family as a productive unit, newly married couples live 'neolocally', in a house separate from those of the parents of either spouse. As relationships based on kinship, on birth, become less important, social norms increasingly censure the evaluation of a person according to his unit of birth, be it a class, race, or caste.

To what extent is world history in the direction of modernization? One analyst argues that the modern pattern is a universal solvent.[10] When a modern society contacts a less modern society, the less modern society inevitably modernizes. The alleged reason is that less modern peoples always recognize the material advantages of modernity. Whether or not this assertion holds universally, it is certainly true that both environmental and motivational factors encourage modernization. Moderns may decry modernity and urge a return to the past, but most of the less-modern societies claim to crave to modernize. In the face of environmental threats such as population pressure and fuel depletion (both of which, ironically, are largely a result of modernization), modernization is probably the most adaptive pattern yet invented for coping. According to the principle of natural selection, those patterns which are most adaptive will be perpetuated, while those which are least adaptive will die out. The principle helps explain why, in spite of occasional reversals such as the Dark Ages, history so far has generally thrust toward modernity.

Whether or not this trend will continue is an issue for debate, especially in light of the ecological crisis and the disillusionment of modernized youth, who endeavor to return to the land and build communal replicas of the simple society. The communal movement may ultimately serve to spread urban values into rural areas, as the 'hicks' and 'hippies' discover the identity between conservatism and radicalism; rejecting the bureaucracy, technocracy, and inhumanity of the industrial state, both laud the rural life. We need not argue that *the* direction of history is toward modernization. Few would assert, after reflection, that the concept of modernization fails to highlight, at least crudely, prominent techno-social trends in world history.

The Interplay between Consciousness and Change

Even if our definitions of 'consciousness' and 'change' were adequate, there remains the enormous difficulty of plotting relations between the two. The problem is partly conceptual. Once reality is sliced into two rough-hewn chunks, it is difficult to glue it back together, and the establishment of a separate discipline to deal with each chunk accentuates the difficulty. But the division would seem to have some empirical basis: human phenomena really do differentiate themselves into some patterns that are more easily conceived as techno-social, others as symbolic. To formulate a framework that usefully illuminates the relationships between such partially but not wholly differentiated patterns is a challenging task which has preoccupied the most profound thinkers throughout the history of social theory. The challenge is not met by a naive empiricism which advises us to abandon conceptualization and simply stare reality in the face. To grasp the relationships of concern to us, we need a systematic and comprehensive theoretical framework. Powerful resources for constructing such a scheme are to be found in the classical sociologies of Emile Durkheim and Max Weber.

Endeavoring to retain at least the rudiments of these classical perspectives while at the same time paying heed to the wealth of insight mustered by recent thinkers in anthropology and other fields, I have resorted to the crude but powerful concept of 'modernization' as an organizing continuum. The argument distinguishes three types of societies, the traditional, the modernizing, and the modern; for each type, a distinctive pattern of symbol and consciousness is elucidated. In considering the traditional type, I draw heavily on the Durkheimian perspective; for the modernizing type, the Weberian perspective; for the modern type, a new and non-classical perspective.[11]

Beginning with the Durkheimian perspective on traditional society and consciousness, our major concern is with rite, myth, and totemism. Here attention is focused on the remarkable Durkheim-inspired, largely Anglo-French studies in anthropology, such as those by Gluckman, Geertz, Turner, Douglas, Malinowski, Leach, Needham, and Lévi-Strauss. Moving to the Weberian perspective as it illuminates the modernizing systems, I am forced to broaden the range beyond main-line anthropology. After a consideration of Weber and certain Weberians, I focus on two areas that would seem distinctively important for an understanding of the symbolic aspects of modernization but which are largely ignored by Weber. These are the fantasies, motives, and ideational processes of the individual experiencing modernization and the aesthetic forms through which these experiences are expressed. Finally, I confront modernity itself, as it is emerging today. Here I abandon the classical perspectives and contruct a makeshift one based on the notion of 'protean man'. These three types and perspectives, the traditional/Durkheimian, modernizing/Weberian, and modern/protean, are recapitulated in considering two illustrative cases and in a conclusion.

Notes to Chapter 1

1. See *Oxford English Dictionary*, Vol. X, p. 363; *Firth*, pp. 54–91, surveys other definitions of symbols.
2. How would the inaudible or the invisible fare in terms of this definition? Is not silence a symbol? Yet it cannot be heard, so is it a sensory form? People say, 'It was so quiet we could *hear* the silence', suggesting that the extreme absence of a sensory form (sound) can evoke perception of its presence. Without great difficulty (but cumbersome wording), the definition could be extended to include consideration of the symbolic meaning of the inaudible or the invisible when they are *perceived* in the same terms as the heard and the seen.
3. 'Function' is not 'purpose'. In judging whether a given action's primary

function is symbolic or technical, we would not simply ask the actor what his purpose is but instead would assess the total context of the action, *including* what it means to the actor, and draw our own conclusion as to the act's function in this particular context. Such a procedure may well be empirically difficult, nevertheless it is theoretically possible.

4. *White*, pp. 130–1.

5. Humanistically and religiously minded students have experienced dissatisfaction with this definition of symbol. They feel that it fails to grasp the sense of intimate participation in the ineffable that is experienced in response to the genuine symbol; I agree that a full description of the symbolic experience must confront this sense of participation in the ineffable, the numinous. At the same time, I am not convinced that this feeling is *always* powerfully present when one perceives a symbol. What I have attempted is a *minimal* definition, a working statement of features that must minimally be present in order to justify labelling a form 'symbolic'. As the African proverb goes, 'To say that a man has a mother is not to deny that he has a father'; I certainly do not deny that a form which fulfills these minimal requirements may also possess the deeper qualities, and with a definition to delimit our investigation we may proceed to explore these. A definition which already included all features of the phenomenon to be investigated would render investigation superfluous.

6. See the distinction as expressed in *Geertz* (1). Geertz links the distinction between 'logico-meaningful' and 'causal-functional', drawn from Pitirim Sorokin, *Social and Cultural Dynamics*, with the distinction between 'cultural' and 'social' (similar to the distinction made here between 'systems of consciousness' and 'techno-social systems') drawn from Talcott Parsons (2). For a more recent statement of Parsons' distinctions, see his Introduction to Parts II and IV, *Theories of Society*.

7. *Durkheim*, p. 22.

8. *Levy*, p. 35.

9. This is a much simplified version of the theory expounded in *Levy*.

10. See *Levy*.

11. Aside from scientific criticism, a number of my students have voiced discontent with such an evolutionary scheme on the ground that it distorts subjective understanding of the self. Several of these students consider any scheme cumbersome and awkward, and they prefer particularized introspection. Other students admit the use of theory but only if (like the archetypes of Jung) it reveals symbolic themes common to humanity; evolutionism unfortunately stresses differences rather than commonalities. A third group clamors for a more sensitive appreciation of differences than that provided by a scheme which categorizes each culture according to 'how far it has to go' along a modernization continuum instead of encountering it 'Where it's at'. Exemplifying this position, Miss Lucretia Pineo 'rejects the idea that each culture will eventually progress out of that stage to a more advanced stage, becoming more complex; Buddhism of the Zen and Tibetan types strives toward, and remains content with, simplicity'.

These criticisms are valid and important. The only defence is to admit that the evolutionary perspective confronts one portion of reality while ignoring others. If the objective of symbolic studies is to reveal the deepest commonalities of the human experience, the evolutionary emphasis on difference and change is unfortunate. If, on the other hand, symbolic studies can also entertain the end of conceptually ordering a range of varied phenomena by classifying both differences and similarities, then the evolutionary perspective is useful. Either approach can enhance self knowledge. Self knowledge proceeds through introspection and classification of similarities and differences between self and other. Classification must place the self within both a scheme of universals and a scheme of differences. One type of scheme of differences is the evolutionary.

2
Traditional Society and Consciousness

The Durkheimian Perspective on Ritual

Emile Durkheim's course of study at the Ecole Normale Super-
ieure was philosophy, his early career was in provincial lycées as a
teacher of philosophy,[1] and his classic *The Elementary Forms of
the Religious Life* had a philosophical aim. Epistemologists since
Aristotle have debated the origins of so-called categories of understanding: conceptions such as time, space, number, substance, and
cause which appear universal in man and without which thought
could not occur. The rationalists believed that these universal and
fundamental categories were inborn in men or even emanated from
the divine. Rejecting such unprovable explanations, the empiricists
believed that the categories were constructed by the individual
after he experienced the external world, but this argument implied
that the categories could be changed at whim, which is not the
case. Durkheim contributed a new position which retained the
virtues of the other two. He believed that the categories were
indeed learned, but not through idiosyncratic experience. Instead,
they were imposed on the individual by society, hence they were
both universal and constraining. Analyzing primitive societies,
Durkheim found that the power of the categories was first experienced through religion, and religion was born from that 'social
being which represents the highest reality in the intellectual
and moral order that we can know by observation—I mean
society'.[2]

In spite of Durkheim's philosophical bent, he was strongly concerned with social and national issues (in this he parallels Marx,
Weber, and other great European social theorists). He even en-

deavoured to apply his notions of ritual to the French war effort. Lecturing and writing during the First World War, he sought to provide what he called 'moral refreshment' for the troops. Among his symbolic creations was a motto 'Patience, Effort, Confidence'.[3]

What, for Durkheim, is distinctive about ritual? Durkheim regards ritual action as of the type we have deemed 'symbolic'. Ritual is not 'technical' since it does not bring about a practical end through a process of causation understandable by natural science. The Australian aborigines, who are the primary subjects of Durkheim's *Elementary Forms*, may claim that they perform the ritual in order to achieve the practical end of making the witchetty grub grow, but the physical scientist (at least in Durkheim's nineteenth century, long before current experiments with the effects of prayer on plants) would deny that the rites achieve that result. Indeed, asserts Durkheim, the stated end is not the real function of the rite. The rite's true function is to solidify and stabilize the society by expressing a collective consciousness, a system of shared representations.

Since the collective representations are sacred, the rites that express them elicit awe and respect. To signify these sacred qualities, the rites are isolated from profane activities. They are restricted to special days when profane activities are prohibited, as on our Sabbath. The participants must be in a special dress and use special decorations which are burned after the rites are finished so that they do not come in touch with the profane. All of these precautions are, from a scientific viewpoint, irrelevant because they do not serve the technical end, such as multiplying the totemic species, at which the ritual is ostensibly directed. But when the rite's true function is considered, the precautions do not seem at all irrelevant. The very impracticality of the ritual arrangements underlines the rite's symbolic and sacred character. Heightening the sacredness of the rite energizes the people's faith in the representations expressed so that society is strengthened and renewed.

Sacredness necessitates segregation. Analyzing the aboriginal totems, Durkheim shows that these objects possess no intrinsic qualities capable of inspiring religious sentiments; indeed, the objects, such as dung, are often dirty and humble. Humble objects become sacred symbols only when men respond to them with emotions of awe and worship. Since the sacredness is not intrinsic to a given object, it can flow freely to others. In Durkheim's metaphor, the sacredness is contagious. To avoid the spread of sacredness, which would dilute its power, the rites and paraphernalia must be quarantined.

When Durkheim speaks of ritual solidifying society, he does not imply the fusion of aggregates of bodies. He means the integration of the social system and its underlying values and beliefs. Reminding the people of their shared values and beliefs, ritual necessarily contributes to their solidarity. Whether the community is unified in a concrete, measurable way is a question Durkheim leaves to the vulgar positivist.[4]

Yet Durkheim's argument is quite specific. He points out that an Australian aborigine tribe is dispersed over a wide desert in tiny family groups that hunt and gather food. During this food-getting period, values and sentiments are obscured in the dust of work. Bands must meet periodically to celebrate their commonalities. In the high excitement evoked by the ritual, the people again become conscious of their shared values.

Noting the emphasis Durkheim places on the effervescence of the natives during such ceremonies, writers such as Robert Lowie accused him of a naive crowd psychology.[5] But Durkheim is not interested in the mob. He emphasizes the discipline of the rite, where, even in funeral ceremonies, which encourage emotional outbursts, every detail is carefully prescribed.

Durkheim is regarded as a proponent of an equilibrium model of society. He is taken to imply that society moves automatically and inevitably toward solidarity. Obviously Durkheim holds no such belief. If he did, he would devote less effort to elucidating that device, ritual, which he regards as necessary for social stability.

In fact, men undergo much suffering to accomplish this end. In his discussion of 'negative cults', Durkheim shows how torture—cutting off one's fingers and burning oneself with sticks red from fire—negates the physical body. Negating the physical body, the individual negates his relationship to the profane and he affirms the power of the social, thus reinforcing the system of sacred representations.

Volumes of scholarly criticism have been written concerning Durkheim's theory of ritual, and many who have just become acquainted with the theory are dismayed at its emphasis on collective rather than individual experience (thus, students frequently wonder whether Durkheim helps very much to explain the mystic or the prophet). More useful than criticism or the search for exceptions is the effort to think out the implications of Durkheim for explaining our own lives. Thus, Durkheim asserted, in a famous equation, that society equals God. Since he seems to believe that ritual is necessary for the survival of society, presumably he would interpret the death of God as rooted in the demise of ritual. And the demise of ritual would seem a necessary and unavoidable consequence of the modernization of society. However this may be, and we shall return to this idea later, let us pass to yet another tactic for assessing the value of Durkheim: the tracing of his influence on the study of ritual since his time. We begin with a brief historical sketch of Durkheimianism within social anthropology.

Durkheimians on Ritual

Crucial in initiating the influence of Durkheim on social anthropological study of ritual was the writing of the English father of social anthropology, A. R. Radcliffe-Brown. Radcliffe-Brown noted that Durkheim's view of ritual as inducing solidarity has been proposed long ago by the Chinese; the *Book of Rites* stated that 'Ceremonies are the bond that holds the multitudes together, and if the bond be removed, these multitudes fall into confusion.'[6] Radcliffe-Brown observed that Plato held a similar view concerning music, and he proceeded to elaborate Durkheimianism with respect to his own materials.

W. Lloyd Warner helped to popularize Durkheim in America. Warner applied Durkheim's theories first to the Murngin tribe of aboriginal Australia, among whom he had spent several years doing fieldwork, then he perceived a similar ritualism in the American celebration of Memorial Day. He argued that these rituals strengthened belief in shared values and inspired a conviction that collective representations can conquer death.[7]

The Durkheimian premise that ritual sustains solidarity has remained essentially intact in the French anthropological tradition continuing after his death. (Thus, Durkheim's nephew, Marcel Mauss, extended the theory through a brilliant exposition of the social solidarity maintained by the ritual exchange of gifts).[8] In other quarters the dictum has been challenged. Among the challengers is Clifford Geertz, who analyzes the way in which a Javanese funeral exacerbates conflict rather than heightening unity.[9] Extending the Durkheimian theory, Gluckman has ingeniously argued that conflict expressed during a rite may still contribute to social solidarity in the long run. Gluckman analyzes 'rituals of rebellion' among the Swazi of South Africa, during which people shout vile insults at the king. Precisely by permitting this expression of conflict, Gluckman argues, the Swazi remind themselves that their social structure is basically so sound that they can permit such outbursts without fear of revolution. The rites of rebellion are ultimately symbols of solidarity.[10]

Ritual of Social Relations

Social anthropologists have begun to move beyond exemplification and criticism of Durkheim to formulate their own theories of ritual which remain within the Durkheimian perspective while substantively and analytically adding to his insights. Among the most influential recent theories are those of Victor Turner and Max Gluckman. Carrying forward the Durkheimian argument, I shall summarize a theory of Gluckman and an illustration from an early study by Turner.

Gluckman postulates that certain social conditions must exist in order that the Durkheimian type of ritual might flourish. Gluckman's formulation is debatable, but it has the merit of formulating a testable generalization and rooting the study of ritual in a theory of social evolution.

Gluckman begins by characterizing what he terms the 'ritualization of social relationships'. Such ritualization has three features: first, the participants' actions within the rite are prescribed according to their secular role in the society; second, their ritual actions are stylized; third, the ritual participants believe that their ritual actions will put their social relationships in order so as to 'secure general blessing, purification, protection, and prosperity for the persons involved in some mystical manner which is out of sensory control'.[11]

Rituals of this type, asserts Gluckman, occurred where people lived in 'largish groups of kin' as in Homeric Greece, early Judea, and perhaps in early Egypt and among the Incas, Aztecs, in China and India, in Saxon and Viking lands, and in pagan Europe in general; such rites survive today in tribal and peasant communities throughout the world.[12]

In such communities, writes Gluckman, the significant units are the village, homestead, and kin-group. Members of such groups cooperate in production and consumption. They hold land and other property in common, or at least subject to claims by each other. They rear their children together, they form a political unit, and they join in worship.

> In short, a man plays most of his roles, as several kinds of productive worker, as consumer, as teacher and pupil, as worshipper, in close association with the people whom he calls father and son and brother, wife and sister; and he shares citizenship with them, that mediated citizenship which is so marked a feature of tribal constitutional law. Moreover, all these roles are played on the same comparatively small stage, of the village and its environs, where shrines are placed about the huts and in the cattle corral, where the baby is born and the dead are buried, where the year's provender is stored.[13]

The relationships among members of such a community are 'multiplex' or 'functionally diffuse'; each interpersonal bond has many dimensions.

Gluckman's argument then develops in two directions. He suggests that when a person plays a multiplicity of roles with the same set of fellows, in the same locale, he is unable to segregate his different roles by locating them in different groups and places. He therefore relies on rituals, rites of passage, taboos, and elaborate etiquette, to signal his movement from one role to another. In a complex, urban community, where the varied roles of the individual are divided among separate groups and locales, elaborate ritual is not required to separate them. Consider, for example, the city child whose maturation is signalled by a shift from one building to another, as he moves from a kindergarten to an elementary, then a secondary school, finally into a university, factory, or office. As an adult, he plays his religious, recreational, domestic, and political roles in separate buildings, neighbourhoods, and groups.

The city dweller, who is unlikely to work with all his kinsmen,

B

live with all his co-workers, or in other ways mix his separate roles, can disrupt interpersonal relations in a given sphere without directly affecting those in another. The tribesman is not so fortunate. Should he disrupt any one relationship in which he is engaged, he threatens the harmony of the others, and indeed the equilibrium of the entire group. Since each of his relationships is so diffuse, so richly multiplex, disturbance of it spills into the natural and supernatural realms, causing sickness and famine, the unrest of spirits and the wrath of gods.

Because disorder among primitive social relations ramifies so widely and deeply into the natural and supernatural realms, the ordering of these relationships carries an equal power to restore harmony in these realms. Such ordering is accomplished by the rituals of social relationships, which express the belief that if participants ritually order their social relationships, mystical and supra-sensory processes are set in motion which bring natural and supernatural order. According to Gluckman's argument, such rituals flourish in the tribal type of society where social relationships are multiplex, but they are incompatible with the unidimensional relations that constitute modern society. Here the rituals decline in power, or die.

Gluckman's perspective can be faulted. One could object that it distorts the reality of tribal existence by dividing it into two aspects (the ritual of social relationships and the multiplex social context of that ritual), whereas the tribesman would see simply a single phenomenological whole. From this standpoint, the so-called theory is really a sleight-of-hand which first gives an illusion that reality is differentiated, then triumphantly demonstrates that it is a unity: Lo and behold, where there exist multiplex social relations there exist also rituals of social relations. The objection is, from a certain scientific viewpoint, fallacious. In order to demonstrate a correlation between two aspects of reality, one must first distinguish and define each, then check a number of cases to see if, in fact, the one is always or usually accompanied by the other. Without first making the distinction, the analyst cannot test the extent of correlation.

A second type of criticism would reject the distinction between primitive and modern. Are the two not more similar than Gluckman suggests? On the one hand, the primitive hoes his garden as well as relying on the mystical processes of fertility ritual. On the other, the modern man engages in congregational prayer which is believed to mystically affect the world. What is the difference?

The difference seems to lie in the method of mystically producing the effects. The primitive ritual seeks to produce these through manipulating the *particular* multiplex relationships that unite the ritual participants. The modern church ritual is relatively less concerned with the particular relationships that bind together the participants (who may well be strangers to each other) and relatively more concerned with entities that entirely transcend the congregation, such as God or the Holy Ghost. Through emotions, thoughts, and ritual actions directed toward such entities the world is believed to be mystically influenced. The modern church ritual has some of the components of Gluckman's ritual of social relationships, but not all.[14]

The best way to explore the viability of a formulation like Gluckman's is to apply it to actual situations asking whether it illuminates what really happens. In the following illustrative analyses, Gluckman's perspective is used to explain why one ritual is effective, the other not.

Ndembu Psychotherapy

In extraordinarily rich and detailed analyses, Victor Turner has investigated the ritual life of the Ndembu of Zambia. As Turner makes clear, the Ndembu community is no closed, primordial village. It is caught between forces of both modernization and tradition. The inhabitants of the particular village of concern here[15] support themselves either by laboring on a railroad three hundred miles away in the industrial towns of the Copper Belt, by shifting cultivation, or by hunting in the bush. But life still revolves around multiplex kinship and communal bonds which provide the social basis for an elaborate repertoire of rituals.

The Ndembu kinship system is based on matrilineal descent and virilocal residence. Ndembu newlyweds go to live with the husband's kinsmen (virilocal residence) who are related to him through his mother (matrilineal descent). From the man's perspective: when he marries he must leave his parents, who reside with his father's matrilineal kinsmen, and go to live with his mother's kinsmen. At least he is expected to do so.

A man whom Turner calls Kamahasanyi had failed to fulfill this expectation. Even after marrying, he has long remained with his father's kin. Here he exists as a kind of parasite, ineligible for the status and duties he should assume among his matri-kin. Kamahasanyi's kinsmen were irritated by his functionless presence, and they kept demanding that he leave. He finally did, when he was in his forties, his father had been dead several years, and he had married his fourth wife, a woman named Maria.

Maria was domineering while Kamahasanyi was effeminate and ineffectual, a man who spent his time gossiping with the women, who had failed to beget children, and who, upon falling into debt, had depended on Maria to sell cassava and bail him out.

Maria was also Kamahasanyi's cousin on his mother's side, which meant that by moving in with his matri-kin, she returned to her natal village. Here trouble arose. Before Maria's marriage to Kamahasanyi, she had enjoyed an affair with a man named Jackson. Returning to her village with the hapless Kamahasanyi, she resumed her liaison. Maria's mother-in-law, Ndono, approved the relationship and treated Jackson rather than Kamahasanyi as her son-in-law.

Suffering conflicts with kinsmen and wife, Kamahasanyi began to display neurotic symptoms—impotence, fatigue, rapid palpitations of the heart—and to suffer delusions of persecution. He withdrew into his hut, and the native healer, Ihembi, was summoned to cure him.

Soon after his arrival, the shrewd Ihembi diagnosed Kamahasanyi's illness as rooted in several causes. The first was his father; Kamahasanyi had dreamed that his father's spirit was trying to bite him in anger at Kamahasanyi's quarreling with his father's matri-kin. The second cause involved Kamahasanyi's wife and mother-in-law, Maria and Ndono. Ihembi accused these women of being witches who wanted to get rid of Kamahasanyi so they could have Jackson. He said that they had sent tiny men to beat Kamahasanyi with hoe handles, resulting in his physical symptoms. The third cause of illness was the total complex of ill wishes toward Kamahasanyi emanating from the community. This general hostility was symbolized by the father's biting spirit.

Ihembi determined to stage a drama in which all the bad feelings would be purged, resulting in the exit of the punishing spirit. Horn cups into which the spirit would come were affixed to Kamahasanyi's body, the community gathered, and the ceremony began. It proceeded by stops and starts. After a phase of drumming and singing, the patient would go into a trembling fit, shaking off some of the horns. Examining them and finding them empty, Ihembi would publicly analyze the social turmoil that must be resolved to drive the spirits out. He would bid the people step forward and confess their secret hate. The cupping horns would be affixed again, the drumming and singing would resume. After hours of this, the people began to yearn for the spirits to appear, and they spoke out to hasten their coming. Maria took ritual action. She spat juice from the mudyi tree (a symbol of 'motherhood', 'matriliny' and 'womanhood') on her husband's temples, feet and hands to give him strength, to affirm her own loyalty and goodwill toward him; and to counteract the witchcraft of which she was accused.

After a time, Kamahasanyi himself spoke forth. He complained that his matrilineal kinsmen had not helped him in his suffering, but he now felt that by venting his ire against them he could release the 'hard thoughts' that had held back the cure. He began to quiver violently, and the cups fell off, one by one. The people felt that animosities were being drawn out. At this point, the witness, Turner, describes what happened:

> ... The whole congregation rose to their feet as one man, and Ihembi fastened on the twitching Kamahasanyi, who fell on his side, writhing convulsively. Kamahasanyi cried out and sobbed when Ihembi removed the blood-dripping horn in a large skin-purse. Mundoyi and Kachilewa (an Ihamba adept from a neighboring village) threw large quantities of medicine over the patient. Ihembi rushed to the small calabash (containing medicine and blood from other cuppings) and threw the cupping horn now concealed by the purse into it. He then spat powdered white clay on the really ugly bulge on Kamahasanyi's neck where the horn had been, 'to cool and purify it'. Kachilewa now held his hand poised over the leaf-concealed calabash while all of us waited intently. He removed the leaves and dredged with his hand in the bloody mixture. After a while he shook his head and said 'Mwesi' ('Nothing in here'). We were all disappointed. But Ihembi with a gentle smile took over. He plunged his fingers into the gruesome liquid and when he brought them up I saw a

flash of white. Then he rushed with what was in his fingers out of the avid circle of onlookers. From the edge of the village, he beckoned to the elders and to me . . . we went one by one to Ihembi. It was indeed a human tooth, we had to say. It was no bushpig's tooth, nor a monkey's.

Jubilantly we told the women, who all trilled with joy.[16]

Turner goes on to say that after the rite enemies shook hands and the village emanated peace. A year later, when Turner returned, he found Kamahasanyi well, Maria still his now-dutiful wife, and Jackson gone. Kamahasanyi had even worked himself into the matrilineal community and was gaining some stature there.

One may wonder how much of Kamahasanyi's relief is due to therapy and how much to change in his situation. Turner mentions that certain inflammatory patrilineal kinsmen who were living beside Kamahasanyi's hut left, as did Jackson, and these improvements in Kamahasanyi's life doubtless helped his cure. But the fortunate departures themselves could have been stimulated by therapeutic transformation of Kamahsanyi's character and demeanor. For purposes of discussion, I shall assume that the ritual was efficacious. We must then seek, within Gluckman's perspective, an explanation of why.

In fundamental respects, the Ndembu psychotherapy resembles that of classical psychoanalysis. Both operate by making the unconscious conscious, by identifying a source of trouble and inducing the patient to share it with others. Abreaction is brought about by heightening the tension in an artificially controlled context; when this dramatized tension is relieved, the real conflict is cured.

The single most striking fact about the Ndembu therapeutic group is that it is apparently synonymous with the entire community. It is Kamahasanyi's political, familial, residential, occupational, and religious group, as well as his therapeutic group. Even modern 'group therapy', in contrast, is *not* the patient's total community; it is not political, residential, occupational groups all rolled into one. Nor could it be, except in rare cases, for few moderns live all facets of their lives within a single group. Family therapy or the encounter group may base their catharsis within a single highly significant group, but it is only one of several in any member's existence, and classical psychoanalysis is deliberately performed on a couch hidden away from any daily group. Because Kamahasanyi's group embodies so much of his existence, it is conceivable that the ritual ordering of relations within that group could dramatically affect his personality within a short time compared to the years required for classical psychoanalysis.

As Gluckman's theory would predict, the Ndembu ritual orders those multiplex relations which form the daily network; within the rite, neighbors relate as neighbors to neighbors, kin to kin, and husband to wife. Also in accord with Gluckman, the ordering of these relationships is believed to affect the supra-sensory world, eventually resulting in expulsion of the biting spirit.

Though the forces are regarded as supra-sensory, the sign of their workings is quite concrete: an actual tooth comes out. Modern psychoanalysis provided a suggestive contrast in that the forces producing the cure are regarded as natural (indeed, in Freud's theory, as quasi-biological and reducible to physical measurement) while the symbolization of their workings is verbal and abstract. A psychiatrist who found it necessary to reveal to a patient the cause of his illness would not draw from him a tooth, but instead verbal insight. Whatever the analytical advantages of the verbal symbolization of psychic process, the tooth doubtless has dramatic advantages. Staging a public drama, Ihembi, the white-haired aristocrat who has the 'throaty voice of the Ndembu hunter' and a 'smile of singular sweetness and charm',[17] must work as an impresario. The modern psychotherapist, permitted the luxury of leisurely exploration in private, is not required to please a crowd by either his charm, his smile, or the dramatic climax of whipping out a tooth.

Freud laid stress on intra-psychic conflict: the tension between id, ego, and superego. For Freud, instinctual desire, repressed because of guilt, was the root cause of neurosis. Psychoanalysis removes this repression and lets the ego recognize the id-instinct. Repressed id-instincts could be imputed to Kamahasanyi. Let us say that an incestuous motive drives him to marry his mother's kinswoman, Maria, and that his effeminacy is a way of identifying with his mother in order to repress his desire to marry her, a replacement of object-cathexis by object-identity. Right or wrong, such analysis is only secondarily relevant to the therapy of Ihembi. Ihembi's therapy is not primarily focused toward the release of repression. The biting tooth does represent a kind of punitive superego derived from Kamahasanyi's angry father, but even this inner pressure is apparently removed by setting the conflicts of the group aright. One may speculate that because Kamahasanyi's group contains so many aspects of his life, his psychic investment in it is almost total. For that reason, re-ordering relations within his group automatically re-orders elements within his psyche, without the need for the verbal surgery of psychoanalysis.

Ndembu therapy offers a way in and a way out. Unlike classical psychoanalysis which leaves it to the society (or the social worker) to define a life role for the cured patient, the Ndembu initiate Kamahasanyi into a new role right there within the therapeutic context itself. The therapeutic group is the community in which the patient will live his life; those with whom he will live are present throughout the therapy, and they bear witness to the cure. Once again, the decisive qualities of Ndembu therapy derive from the multiplex character of the relationships that compose the therapeutic group. In modern, differentiated society, therapeutic ritual of the Ndembu type is rarely if ever possible.

The Javanese Funeral that Failed

Investigating rituals of the Javanese of Indonesia, Clifford Geertz was strongly concerned with a ceremony known as the *slametan*.[18] Though Geertz does not explicitly apply the categories of Gluckman, one could see the slametan as neatly fitting the definition of 'ritualization of social relationships'. The symbolic actions of the slametan are stylized, conventionalized, and rigidly prescribed. Participants sit on the floor in a certain way, only men participate while women prepare the food, a prayer is always given by the host in both Javanese and Arabic language, and the food is not consumed on the spot but is taken home by the guests. Core participants in the slametan play roles prescribed by their daily relationships; they are neighbors, from a radius of eight to ten houses surrounding the host's own, and within the slametan they enact the harmony of neighborliness. The slametan is believed to produce effects in natural, supernatural, and social spheres through mystical and supra-sensory channels: to harmonize relations with the spirits, to order the psyche and the community, and to restore health and well-being to the household.

In the Javanese peasant village where the slametan originated and continues to flourish, the essential bond is territorial. The village is surrounded by fields, ownership of which is ultimately vested in the community as a whole, while rights of use are distributed to individual families by a council. Javanese villagers thus share not only their place of residence, the village, but also their tools of production, the surrounding fields and associated systems of irrigation. They also share responsibility for standing guard against thieves, they exchange labor in harvesting, they form a political unit, and most of the villager's activities take place within his village. The Javanese village community is thus composed of multiplex relationships.

As Geertz observes, the situation is different in the urban neighborhood, the *kampung*. Instead of working at the single occupation of farming, kampung dwellers work at varied occupations, ranging from sidewalk hawker to factory laborer. Though Geertz does not point this out, it is also true that the kampung dweller differs from the village dweller in that the villager shares with his neighbors not only his place of residence but also his place of work, while the kampung dweller shares only his place of residence. Inhabitants of the same kampung work in different sections of town, and the kampung which, like the village, is guided by a headman, has no control over these other places of work. For this and other reasons, relations between co-residents of a kampung encompass fewer aspects than do those between co-residents of a village; they tend toward the unidimensional rather than the multiplex. Following Gluckman, one would predict on this ground that the slametan will not function as well in the kampung as in the village, and Geertz finds this to be the case. But Geertz injects another factor. Kampung dwellers are differentiated by ideological persuasion as well as by occupation. The two major factions are the *abangan* and the *santri*. The abangan are sympathetic to the traditional Hinduistic, animistic Javanese way of life which is centered around, among other things, the slametan. They are merely nominal Muslims who do not practice such pillars of the faith as the fast, the five daily prayers, the pilgrimage, payment of the Muslim tithe, and profession of faith. They are attracted to Marxism or socialism, and they belong to either the proletariat or the civil service. In the town where Geertz was carrying out his research, the abangan were organized into a group known as *permai* which endeavored to revitalize the Hindu-Buddhist-animist traditions in opposition to those of Islam. The *santri*, pious Muslim merchants who faithfully perform the pillars neglected by the abangan, detest the syncretic, Hinduized abangan culture, and they of course oppose permai.

Briefly stated, the incident which Geertz observed happened as follows. A young boy died at the home of his uncle, who fetched a santri priest (*modin*) to administer the funeral rites. The modin refused to do so because the uncle was a member of the abangan organization, *permai*. Without the help of the priest, the uncle did not know how to bury the body. A crowd had gathered, to whom the funeral was highly important as an expression of solidarity, and they grew restive as the spirit of the dead hovered around while the body remained unburied. The boy's mother and father arrived, and the mother, with very unJavanese loss of control, hysterically kissed the boy's genitals. Desperate that the son be buried, the parents finally prevailed upon the modin to perform the rites, and the boy finally was buried in the Islamic way.[19]

Geertz' first point is that instead of harmonizing the community, in orthodox Durkheimian fashion, the funeral nakedly exposed the conflict between factions. Geertz then asserts that a sheerly sociological explanation of the funeral's failure is inadequate. Geertz proposes a more complex level of explanation, one based on the interplay between social and cultural systems or, as he puts it, between systems that are integrated logico-meaningfully and those integrated causal-functionally.

He notes that the slametan, of which the funeral is a variant, is derived from and traditionally associated with the village community. For Javanese, the slametan has come to symbolize the social harmony of this *Gemeinschaft*. Yet in the urbanized *Gesellschaft* of the town, the slametan is a catalyst for schism. 'Slametan' assumes an ambiguous meaning for the participants: is it a traditional embodiment of harmony, or an urban reflection of conflict? Geertz contends, plausibly though without direct evidence, that the ambiguous meaning of a trusted symbol exacerbates the tension and strain for the Javanese. It is the contradiction between cultural meaning and social reality, rather than social conflict alone, that explains such hysterical behavior as the kissing of the genitals.

Margins and Transitions

The studies considered so far have been primarily concerned with the relationship between ritual and the central values or core structure of the group. A complementary relationship, that between ritual and the *margins* of collective and individual life, has been the focus of recent work by Victor Turner and Mary Douglas.

Mary Douglas' *Purity and Danger*[20] treats ritual as creating order by marking the margins which separate the pure from the impure; that which is impure is polluting and dangerous and must be kept outside instead of being permitted to mix with the inside. Douglas considers that this model, derived from the group, applies also to the body. Thus, elements coming from the body's margins, such as excreta, blood, nail clippings, and hair are believed in traditional societies to harm the victim's body by penetrating inside it, and rituals must be performed to counteract such dangers. Douglas suggests that the extent that the person is anxious about such bodily pollution depends on the extent to which the group is anxious about penetration of its social boundaries. Accordingly, a minority group such as the Israelites felt its political boundaries threatened, and, therefore, or analogously, constructed the elaborate Levitical taboos to prevent boundaries of the body from being penetrated by polluting substances. Douglas dismisses efforts by psychoanalysts to explain the concern with excrement and pollution as derived from personal attitudes toward the bowels; she observes that a particular Hindu caste which resembles the Israeli minority group in its fear of pollution by other castes and associated substances is composed of individuals who, in their personal habits of the toilet, are markedly unobsessive.

The marginal areas that yield disorder, pollution, and danger also give power. Persons on the interstices of society characteristically boast powers not held by central figures of the establishment, and the making of a powerful magician in traditional society typically requires the initiate to wander like a madman or in some other marginal state. (Recall how Gandalf, in *The Lord of the Rings*, gained his immense power only after a terrible journey underground). Both persons and objects acquire power from occupying an ambiguous position in society, and under special conditions these powers can be exploited to enhance creativity: Lele initiates eat dangerously taboo foods during their rites, and the Dinka spearmaster voluntarily courts death by permitting himself to be buried alive. In both cases, the dangerous is converted to the creative through its association with some powerfully affirmative value.

Victor Turner touches on similar themes in his writings on 'liminality' and 'communitas'.[21] Liminality is a betwixt and between state of transition exemplified by the position in which initiates find themselves during a rite of passage. Neither remaining in their old status nor yet entering their new, the initiates' condition is both dangerous and fulfilling. They enjoy, among other things, a uniquely intense and warm companionship, a 'communitas' found in groups separated from the central structure of the community. Temporarily sexless, naked, anonymous, silent, and in other ways deprived of orthodox social powers, the initiates possess special mystical powers. The same is true of liminal individuals in general, such as the holy beggar, the mysterious stranger of American Westerns who restores morality, the prophet of millenial movements. The distinctive 'communitas' enjoyed by the initiates is found also in other liminal groups, such as the commune of St. Frances of Assisi and the Krishna Bhakti cult of East India.

In the pilgrimage practiced by so many religious devotees, Turner discovers both the liminal and the communitas, a brotherly passage.[22] Despite its organized quality, the pilgrimage opposes the rigidly ascriptive structure of the hierarchical societies in which it is typically found. Instead of ascribing or prescribing membership, the pilgrimage leaves it up to individual choice: one chooses whether or not to go. Once on the pilgrimage or at the destination, the pilgrims enjoy a striking warm communitas, as has been noted by even so militant an ideologue as Malcolm X. Interestingly, in light of later discussion of Weber's Calvinism as a modernizing force that destroys the traditional hierarchy within which the pilgrimage flourishes, Calvin opposed pilgrimage on the grounds that such rituals are worthless for salvation.

Moving from the center of society to its margins and from structures to transitions, Douglas and Turner remain within the basic Durkheimian framework. Whereas the other studies focus on what Durkheim termed the 'positive' rites that commemorate core values, Douglas and Turner draw attention to Durkheim's 'negative' rites that define taboos and boundaries and to the ambiguously powerful qualities of transition between these boundaries. In their writings so far discussed, both retain the Durkheimian concern with rites within a given (usually traditional) type of society rather than passing to the Weberian concern with the transformation of one type of society into another. Douglas has, however, considered this issue in her theory of 'group' and 'grid'.

Group and Grid

In *Purity and Danger*, Mary Douglas went so far as to assert that 'anthropologists [cannot] do without such general distinctions as "primitive" and "modern"'. She speaks at one point of a 'movement from primitive to modern'[23] that has occurred in history, and she argues suggestively that those who cry for the abandonment of the term 'primitive' are secretly ethnocentric.[24] In short, Douglas in *Purity and Danger* appears to see utility in an evolutionary approach that categorizes societies along a continuum from primitive to modern.

Yet in her later work, *Natural Symbols*, Douglas proposes to banish, 'with one sweep of the arm',[25] the evolutionary distinctions, and to set forth an alternative typology. The divergence between the earlier and later books is clearly illustrated by her statements on 'secularization'. In *Purity and Danger*, she states that 'the European history of ecclesiastical withdrawal from secular politics and from secular intellectual problems to specialized intellectual spheres is the history of this whole movement from primitive to modern'.[26] Here she equates 'secular' and 'modern' and, by obvious implication, 'religious' and 'primitive', and she postulates an evolution from the one to the other. In *Natural Symbols*, she vigorously contradicts this view.

> The contrast of secular with religious has nothing whatever to do with the contrast of modern with traditional or primitive. The idea that primitive man is by nature deeply religious is nonsense. The truth is that all the varieties of scepticism, materialism and spiritual fervour are to be found in the range of tribal societies.[27]

Elaborating this argument, she strives to show that even simple, tribal societies vary from the classical Durkheimian type where ritualism is elaborately developed to reinforce solidarity to a rather secular, anti-ritualist type. We do not need to run the gamut from 'primitive' to 'modern' to see this range of variation.

Douglas' basic variables are 'group' (the experience of a bounded social unit) and 'grid' (rules which relate one person to others on an ego-centered basis). The resulting typology is complex, incorporating variation in family as well as community organization, but some of the major axes are these.[28] Where both group and grid solidarity are strong, the classical Durkheimian situation obtains with the ritual of social relations dominant. Symbolic acts are believed to have magical efficacy such that wrongdoing automatically (regardless of the actor's intent) releases danger, and ritual automatically restores order.

Where group is strong but grid is weak, the social structure still strongly grips the individual but in a less personal and particularized way, so that the individual can squirm loose enough to reflect on society and question its values. This situation gives rise to the classical drama (as opposed to primitive ritual) such as *Oedipus Rex* and *El Cid*. It also encourages a concern with guarding the boundaries of the society and the orifices of the body, especially as these are threatened by witchcraft. This attention to the boundaries follows from the perception of society as an undifferentiated group rather than a grid of particularized relationships.

Where grid is strong but group is weak, people are individualistic. As exemplified by the New Guinea big man, the individual strives to gain power by manipulating particular social networks. In such a society, the classical Durkheimian ritual of solidarity declines, and in its place arises a propensity to millenarian movements such as the materialistic New Guinea cargo cult.

Where both group and grid are weak, the cosmos is perceived as unstructured and unmagical. As both society and network lose their grip, religion becomes personal, and the major ethical problem becomes that of self-justification. Wrongdoing is no more a particular action to be scrubbed clean by a particular ritual, with neither the wrong nor the rectification being dependent on the actor's intent. What matters now is the actor's motive and intent, as in the Christian notion of sin and the modern legal distinction between manslaughter and murder.

Even this brief sketch is sufficient to suggest the power of Douglas' typology, and perusal of the full essay reveals a wealth of systematic linkages between society and ritual. Explicitly denying any evolutionary basis for her scheme, Douglas is able to find a set of 'tribal' examples to illustrate her full range of types. Nevertheless, I believe that a survey of *all* known societies existing in history and today would reveal an evolutionary trend. The primitive or tribal society which is small, supported by fishing, hunting, gathering, or rudimentary agriculture and organized on the basis of kinship, rather than highly centralized and bureaucratized rule as in Kingship, would, I believe, provide the *majority* of the strong group/strong grid cases. The 'archaic' society which is large, supported by highly developed agriculture, and organized into kingdoms, would most likely be of the strong group/weak grid type. The other two types would most likely appear among modernizing (increasingly capitalistic and bureaucratic) societies. History could then be crudely conceived as an evolution from a stage when the 'primitive' (strong group/strong grid) type was predominant to a stage when the 'archaic' (strong group/weak grid) pattern was the most widespread or fastest spreading and then to a stage when modernization was the coming trend.[29]

To the extent that this evolutionary way of classifying societies is valid, Douglas' anti-evolutionism is not, though her typology retains its power. Indeed, I suspect that her typology works even better when applied to the full evolutionary range than when it is restricted to the tribal cases. Her 'classical drama', for example, would seem more characteristic of archaic than of primitive society. However that may be, Douglas reminds even the dogmatic evolutionist of an important principle: patterns which are fully developed only in modern society exist, though in marginal or nascent form, in traditional society as well. Every society can perhaps be said to contain traces of the full spectrum of human potential for social and symbolic patterning.

Ritual in Traditional Society

This survey of Durkheim's theme and the Durkheimian variations certainly does not exhaust anthropological knowledge of primitive ritual.[30] But enough material has been presented to suggest a few propositions and to locate these within the general prospective of this book.

Durkheim's view of ritual as distilling and reviving the collective consciousness proves to be a seminal insight. As Gluckman's theory proclaims, however, ritual of the type based on 'ritualization of social relationships' reaches full power only when its participants are united by multiplex bonds (which occurs when strong group/strong grid are combined), and this condition is fully realizable only in the tribal or peasant community. With modernization, social bonds become more functionally specific, less multiplex, the ritualization of social relationships declines, and ritual may even become a source of conflict as in the Javanese funeral. Where the ritual retains its power, as in the multiplex milieu of the Ndembu, the revival of communal solidarity is believed to work supernatural effects which extend even to the cure of seriously disturbed personalities. In societies of this type, we are likely to find, also, a strong sense of order and of the boundary between outside and inside; accordingly, great store is set on rites that maintain and restore these boundaries, dispelling danger and nurturing purity. Rites and symbolism of transition in traditional societies permit remarkable freedom, power, and communitas, and the anti-structural qualities of these 'passages' ultimately affirm the structures of which they are part.

Gluckman, Douglas, and Turner all imply that if society should revert to the multiplex condition, rites of these types would reappear and regain their potency. It remains to be seen whether, as Durkheimian logic asserts, changing the social structure will automatically restore faith in the mystical and automatic power of the symbolic.

Notes to Chapter 2

1. *Peyre*, pp. 10–12.
2. *Durkheim*, p. 389.
3. *Kardiner and Preble*, p. 111.
4. Three sisters named Peacock, McAllister, and Jolly were at the funeral of their mother. Mrs. McAllister was addressed as Mrs. Peacock, to which she replied, 'Oh, I'm Mrs. Jolly.' The funeral apparently heightened solidarity among the sisters to the point that the one fused her identity with the others. Systematic description of events of this type could usefully document the Durkheim dictum.

5. *Lowie*, pp. 154–63.
6. *Radcliffe-Brown*, p. 159.
7. *Warner*.
8. *Mauss*.
9. *Geertz* (1).
10. *Gluckman* (1). In these studies, 'solidarity' seems to mean both a sense of unity and a harmony of interaction; the term needs to be clarified before Durkheim can be either refuted or defended.
11. Ibid., p. 25.
12. *Gluckman* (2), p. 24.
13. Ibid., p. 27.
14. Which is not to deny that, in the appropriate multiplex social contexts, rituals of the Christian type may take on features of the Gluckman ritual; see *Jules-Rosette* for an illuminating analysis of such a case.
15. The brief account to be summarized here is from *Turner* (1). Additional information is in *Turner* (2).
16. *Turner* (1), pp. 390–1.
17. Ibid., p. 370.
18. *Geertz* (2), p. 11.
19. *Geertz* (1).
20. *Douglas* (1).
21. See *Turner* (2).
22. *Turner* (4).
23. *Douglas* (1), p. 112.
24. Ibid., p. 112.
25. *Douglas* (2), p. viii.
26. *Douglas* (1), p. 112.
27. *Douglas* (2), p. x.
28. The following argument summarizes *Douglas* (2).
29. This view is elaborated, though not with respect to Douglas, in *Peacock and Kirsch*, Chapter 2.
30. For examples of recent refinements, see *Beidelman* (1) and (2), *La Fontaine*, and *Tambiah*.

3
Consciousness and Traditional Society

The Durkheimian Perspective on Mythology and Thought

The rite is enacted, the myth is told. Myth-as-story is literature, and myths can be appreciated primarily for their literary qualities. Durkheimian anthropologists have stressed instead the system of thought that is expressed by the myth. The study of mythology becomes linked, therefore, to the study of other traditional systems of ideas such as totemism, and the investigation of these several symbolic forms leads to a general formulation of traditional thought.

To give some notion of the Durkheimian view of the so-called 'savage mind', I begin with the perspective of Durkheim and Mauss on primitive classification. We pass then to a consideration of three major-figures in the study of mythology: Malinowski, Leach, and Lévi-Strauss. Following Durkheim in linking myth to society, Malinowski deviated in separating myth from thought. Leach waged an epic battle against Malinowskian 'functionalism', which stressed the myth/society linkage, and Lévi-Strauss restored under the name 'structuralism' a renewed appreciation for the relation between myth and thought. After considering the general perspective on primitive thought espoused by Lévi-Strauss, I conclude by suggesting that the notion of homology has underlain the perspective of all these theorists.

Durkheim and Mauss

For Durkheim, myth and ritual are two sides of the same coin: 'Very frequently, the rite is nothing more than the myth put in action; the Christian communion is inseparable from the myth of the Last Supper, from which it derives all its meaning.'[1] Traditional mythology embodies the representations, the system of belief and cosmology of the society:

> ... the mythology of a group is the system of beliefs common to this group. The traditions whose memory it perpetuates express the way in which society represents man and the world; it is a moral system and a cosmology as well as a history.[2]

Only in terms of this system of consciousness do the ritual forms acquire their meaning.

In their monograph, *Primitive Classification*, Durkheim and Marcel Mauss develop the thesis that mythology embodies primitive thought: 'Every mythology is a classification, but one which borrows its principles from religious beliefs, not from scientific ideas'[3] and that classificatory schemes parallel the structure of society: 'Highly organized pantheons divide up all nature, just as elsewhere the clans divide the universe.'[4]

Durkheim and Mauss begin their analysis by examining the classification systems of the Australian tribes. Classifying people into moieties, marriage groups, and clans, the Australians symbolize these divisions by a parallel classification of totems—plants, animals, or other elements of nature, each of which serves as an emblem, spirit, and natural counterpart to the particular social group with which it is identified. The identification is quite intimate; Durkheim and Mauss note that the Bororo feels that he *is* a parrot, though he temporarily occupies a man's body. The scheme of classification which emerges from such emotional identification 'is not the spontaneous product of abstract understanding' since the symbol is not differentiated from the object that it represents; in this view Durkheim and Mauss differ from their descendant, Lévi-Strauss, who prefers to see the primitive as philosophically and analytically composing such identifications. In any event, the crucial point is that the totemic and social systems are parallel in structure.

Durkheim and Mauss see the social divisions as preceding, and giving rise to, the totemic classification. Yet the system of classification may gain autonomy from society: 'What characterizes the latter [the system of classification] is that the ideas are organized on a model which is furnished by the society. But once this organization of the collective mind exists, it is capable of reacting against its cause and of contributing to its change.'⁵ Here Durkheim and Mauss foreshadow the Weberian perspective that with social evolution symbolic and social structures differentiate, and the autonomy of the former stimulates change in the latter.

Durkheim and Mauss then proceed to investigate complex classificatory systems, such as those of the Zuni Indians and the traditional Chinese. They ingeniously argue that everywhere the system of classification is rooted in the structure of society. The role of mythology is to justify both of these structures and occasionally to mediate the discrepancy between them by preserving memory of their ancient parallels. A Zuni myth of the type so familiar to later generations of social anthropologists provides an example of the myth as a charter for the tribe's social organization:

> The first great priest and magician, say the Zuni, brought two pairs of eggs to mankind just after they had been created; one was a marvelous dark blue like the sky; the other was dark red, like mother earth. He said that one was summer and the other winter, and he invited men to choose. The first to make their choice decided on the blue ones; they were delighted that the young birds had no feathers. But when these grew up they became black: they were ravens, whose descendants, veritable scourges, left for the north. Those who chose the red eggs saw the birth of the brilliant macaw parrot; they shared seeds, warmth, and peace. 'Thus,' the myth continues, 'first was our nation divided into the people of Winter and the people of Summer. . . .' Some became 'the macaw and the kindred of the macaw, the Mulakwe; whilst those who had chosen the ravens became the Raven-people or Ka'kâ-kwe'. Thus the society began by being divided into two moieties, one situated to the north, the other to the south; one had as its totem the raven, which has disappeared, the other the macaw, which still exists. Mythology still preserves the memory of the subdivision of each moiety into clans.⁶

Durkheim and Mauss regard primitive classification as based on religious belief, mythical narration, and social imagery which may be taken literally, not metaphorically, and which elicits strong sentiments. According to *Primitive Classification*, the primitive views totems which are within the same class as relatives, in precisely the same sense that kinsmen within the same group are relatives; this identity is apparently the reason why a primitive classification of things evokes the same emotional reactions accorded to a social group of people:

> And in fact, for those who are called primitives, a species of things is not a simple object of knowledge but corresponds above all to a certain sentimental attitude. All kinds of affective elements combine in the representation made of it . . . The pressure exerted by the group on each of its members does not permit individuals to judge freely the notions which society has elaborated and in which it has placed something of its personality.[7]

With modernization, systems of classification become emancipated from the social groupings within which they originated, so that they can serve as abstracted, analytical instruments capable of the precise distinction necessary for reflective thought: 'Thus the history of scientific classification is, in the last analysis, the history of the stages by which this element of social affectivity has progressively weakened, leaving more and more room for the reflective thought of individuals.'[8]

The Durkheimians on Myth: From Malinowski to Lévi-Strauss

The study of myth and the study of classification systems can be distinguished as two major anthropological projects that have grown out of the Durkheimian tradition. Separated for a time, the two have now converged in the effort of Lévi-Strauss and his associates to lay bare the essence of the human mind. Sketching these trends, I follow my customary tack of surveying not a full body of literature, but merely a few representative works to exemplify a central theme. We begin with Malinowski's notion of 'charter', a concept that is embraced by the theory of functionalism. According to Malinowski, myth, like any other element of human existence, can be understood through unravelling its function, its contribution to the social life of the group within which it exists.

The function of myth is to provide a charter, a legitimation for social institutions.

Malinowski

Born in Cracow, Poland, Bronislaw Malinowski received his doctorate in physics. Instead of entering that profession, he converted, during a siege of illness (and, one may suspect, delirium) to anthropology. His inspiration was Sir James George Frazer's *The Golden Bough*, the hallowed and voluminous tome on magic, science, and religion which Malinowski's mother reportedly read to him during a year of recuperation. Whatever the scientific merit of *The Golden Bough* (Edmund Leach has contemptuously dubbed it 'The Gilded Twig'),[9] its rendering of savage rites in elegant prose incited Malinowski to migrate to England in order to study anthropology. In 1925, at the University of Liverpool, Malinowski gave the Frazer Memorial Lecture. He began with a mock eulogy to his idol:

> We are gathered here to celebrate the annual totemic festival of *The Golden Bough*; to revive and strengthen the bonds of anthropological union; to commune with the source and symbol of our anthropological interest and affection. I am but your humble spokesman, in expressing our joint admiration to the great writer and his classical works; *The Golden Bough*, *Totemism and Exogamy*, *Folklore in the Old Testament*, *Psyche's Task*, and *The Belief in Immortality*. As a true officiating magician in a savage tribe would have to do, I have to recite the whole list, so that the spirit of the works (their 'mana') may dwell among us.[10]

In a pattern characteristic of memoriams in British anthropology, Malinowski proceeds subtly to slander the object of memory. Whereas Sir James Frazer had assiduously avoided fieldwork (he reportedly replied, when asked if he had ever seen one of the 'savages' about whom he wrote: 'God forbid!'),[11] Malinowski stresses that his own data is drawn from the field instead of the library. He then heaps ridicule on two schools of mythology which, lacking field experience, postulated that myth is a pre-civilized attempt at intellectual analysis. The first is the school of Nature-mythology which flourished mainly in Germany and maintained that primitive man's interest in natural phenomena is theoretical, contemplative, and poetical.[12] This school includes the 'lunar mythologists' who are so 'moonstruck' that they see no source of primitive myth-making other than 'savage rhapsodic interpretation' concerning the 'earth's nocturnal satellite'. Other scholars of this school specialize in the sun, still others in the wind, weather, and colors of the skies as the inspiration of primitive myth, while others yet 'have a more catholic taste' and admit all the heavenly bodies and processes into their fantasies about the inspiration of primitive mythology. Malinowski blasts this perspective, terming it 'one of the most extravagant views ever advanced by an anthropologist or humanist—and that means a great deal'.[13]

The second school of which Malinowski is critical diametrically opposes the first; the Nature-mythologists saw myth as symbolic poetry drawn from the heavens, the second school regards myth as a 'true historical record of the past'.[14] Malinowski is as critical of this picture of the primitive-as-antiquarian as he is of the view that he is a rhapsodic astronomer. Both views assume that myth is primarily intellectual speculation. Malinowski asserts that primitive myth is more practical. On the basis of his extensive participation in the lives of the Trobrianders of the Western Pacific, he supports Durkheim's view that the primary function of myth, in association with ritual and morals, is to support the norms of primitive society. Religion and morals, he says, have drawn little upon science but depend on an entirely different attitude, that of pious obedience to moral imperatives embedded in institutions. Myth affirms this obedience just as surely as the biblical story of the Creation, the Fall, and the Redemption by Christ's Crucifixion expresses, enhances, and codifies the norms of the Christian.

Exemplifying the role of myth among the Trobrianders, Malinowski shows how they sanctify the custom of annually overhauling canoes, how they relate the cave origins of a Trobriand ancestress, thereby bolstering the Tobriand mode of tracing descent through the mother, and how they testify to the territorial rights of clans and to the Trobriand system of ranking clans. Trobriand myths live, Malinowski suggests, not because they provide entertainment or answer intellectual puzzles, but because

Myth fulfills in primitive culture an indispensable function; it expresses, enhances, and codifies belief; it safeguards and enforces morality; it vouches for the efficiency of ritual and contains practical rules for the guidance of men. Myth is thus a vital ingredient of human civilization; it is not an idle tale, but a hard-worked active force; it is not an intellectual explanation or an artistic imagery, but a pragmatic charter of primitive faith and moral wisdom.[15]

The object of validating the customs and institutions of the community is achieved by depicting them as derived from some ultimate reality.

Myth, as a statement of primeval reality which still lives in present-day life and as a justification by precedent, supplies a retrospective pattern of moral values, sociological order, and magical belief... The function of myth, briefly, is to strengthen tradition and endow it with a greater value and prestige by tracing it back to a higher, better, more supernatural reality of initial events.[16]

After expounding his influential doctrine that 'myth is charter', Malinowski proceeds to ground it in his own fieldwork-oriented approach to anthropology. One may speculate that his personality was a factor. Malinowski was a flamboyant Slav who used to dictate while lying in bed with his pajama bottoms wrapped around his head, who listened to concerts while lying in the aisle, and who kept his London house so crowded with students, colleagues, and strangers off the street that his wife finally retreated to the country. His character seems to have fitted him well for field research and circumstances gave him an unusual opportunity. As a citizen of Austria he was interned in Australia when the First World War began. Rather than sit out the war there, he chose to live among the Trobriand islanders, in whose intimate company he spent the years 1915 to 1918. Supposedly known among the Trobrianders as the Man of Songs, he has reported his personal experiences in rich detail, not only in academic monographs but in a posthumously published private diary. Concluding his Frazer Lecture, Malinowski advocates field research as the proper path to the study of myth.

Folktales, legends, and myths must be lifted from their flat existence on paper, and placed in the three-dimensional reality of full life. As regards anthropological fieldwork, we are obviously demanding a new method of collecting evidence. The anthropologist must relinquish his comfortable position on the long chair on the veranda of the missionary compound, Government station, or planter's bungalow, where, armed with pencil and notebook and at times whiskey and soda, he has been accustomed to collect statements from informants, write down stories, and fill out sheets of paper with savage texts. He must go out into the villages, and see the natives at work in gardens, on the beach, in the jungle.... Open-air anthropology, as opposed to hearsay note-taking, is hard work, but it is also great fun.[17]

Malinowski's polemic was doubtless a jibe against the staid approach of certain British colleagues, but it also follows logically from his doctrine of myth as charter. The anthropologist who interprets a mythical text as an abstracted intellectual theory is less compelled than Malinowski to move from his dusty study into the jungles and on to the beach. He who would link text to context must participate fully in the daily life of which myths are at once expression and charter.

Leach
For decades after the death of Malinowski, his theories of functionalism and myth-as-charter and his method of intimate fieldwork were pillars of social anthropology. While these ideas will doubtless remain useful, their dominance has been challenged by an alternative approach: structuralism. Trained by Bronislaw Malinowski, ultimately (though ambivalently) joining forces with Claude Lévi-Strauss, Edmund Leach is usefully viewed as a transition between these two perspectives, the functionalist and the structuralist. Leach's *Political Systems of Highland Burma*[18] is probably the most brilliant attack on Malinowski's functionalism ever devised, and he has devoted his postwar efforts to the study of the structure of myth with less emphasis on its functions in social contexts.

Leach's study deals with a tribe known as the Kachin, a seminomadic dry-rice cultivating society located in the hills of Burma and carrying on a way of life typical of hill peoples throughout Southeast Asia. Leach views the Kachin as playing a counter-point

to the society adjacent to them, that of the lowland, wet-rice cultivating, Buddhist Shan. Leach's exposition is complex, but those
portions relevant to my presentation can be summarized briefly.

Malinowski saw myth as reinforcing the solidarity and stability
of the entire society, but Leach views it as a weapon deployed by
the individual to affirm his status. Myth is still a charter, but for
personal claims, and Leach stresses that different persons display
different versions of a myth, each choosing that version which best
justifies his claim:

> Many anthropologists have tended to write of myth as being 'a
> sanction for socially approved behavior'; the sort of myth with
> which we are now concerned is perhaps better described as a
> 'language in which to maintain social controversy'.[19]

The Kachin society oscillates between two systems of government, the *gumsa*, which is hierarchical, and the *gumlao*, which is
egalitarian. Much of Leach's analysis concerns the base for a
Kachin's claiming status within the hierarchical system, the gumsa.
Within that system, Leach discovers two major grounds for
claiming status: marriage and descent.

The marriage system is composed of clans known as *htinggaw*,
each of which is composed of persons sharing the same patrilineally-
inherited surname. One clan is perpetually bound to others in that
it receives wives from them or gives wives to them; in any pair the
wife-taking clan, known as *dama*, is inferior in status to the wife-
giving clan, known as *mayu*. Over many generations, each clan
develops a tradition of taking wives from certain clans (their *dama*)
and giving wives to others (their *mayu*). Ideally, women should
always marry into their clan's dama, and it is incest for a woman
to marry into her clan's mayu. Such marriages reverse the
customary direction of exchange, result in a man marrying his
mother's kin, and destroy the whole system of prestations based on
distinctions between inferior and superior. The proscription against
marrying in a reverse direction is usually honored, for reversal is
incest, but the prescription specifying exactly which clan into
which one should marry is not honored by everyone. So long as
elite marriages conform to the rule, the traditional mayu-dama
partnerships endure.

The second means of claiming status is through descent, exemplified by the rule of ultimogeniture: all things being equal, if two clans are descended from two brothers, the group descended from the younger brother is considered superior to that descended from the elder.

These two bases of status, marriage and descent, contradict in particular instances. Thus, in the villages of Hpalang, the clan known as Laga claimed seniority to that known as Gumjye because, in terms of the marriage system, the Gumjye were dama (politically inferior) to Laga. But Gumjye argued as follows. They were superior kin to Nmwe because Gumjye was the youngest son branch line of the ancestral clan, Maran, while Nmwe was only the eldest son line. Nmwe was superior to Laga since Laga was dama to Nmwe's ancestral clan, Maran. Therefore, if Gumjye was superior to Nmwe, and Nmwe senior to Laga, then Gumjye was on the basis of descent superior to Laga, even though Laga was superior to Gumjye in terms of the system of marriage.[20] The dispute reduces simply to this: A is greater than B according to one criterion, but B is greater than C and C is greater than A according to another criterion. Hence B can claim superiority to A just as A can claim superiority to B.

The function of myth in disputes such as this is to narrate genealogies in order to justify claims. For example, each of the five major Kachin clans tells the story of Wahkyet Wa and his sons, supposed founders of all the clans, in such a way as to justify its own claim to be the senior clan on the grounds that it descends from Wahkyet Wa's youngest son.

The ultimate function of myth is to justify a shift from the gumsa (hierarchical) system altogether. A myth is told of a man, Dumsa la Lawn, who went to heaven and was told by the heavenly spirit of the egalitarian gumlao ethos. Returning to earth, he murdered the autocratic gumsa chief and initiated a gumlao rebellion, recruiting his followers from oppressed and discontented clans —a tribal version of the third world revolution.

Leach argues that the Kachin norms are based on contradictory premises. As a result, a community which converts to gumlao ideology is forced by logical discrepancies to revert to gumsa, and vice versa. For example, gumlao (egalitarian) ideology dictates elimination of the mayu-dama ranking, but mayu-dama is the keystone of the taboo on incest, and since Kachin cling to that taboo they eventually resurrect the mayu-dama hierarchy. As they do so, other contradictions force them back to gumlao. For example, gumsa ideology conceives society as a network of ranked but kindred lineages. Kinship implies reciprocity while ranking is hierarchical and exploitative. When the gumsa chief exploits his relatives, the ill-used recall the rules of reciprocity that are supposed to hold among kinsmen but are violated by hierarchy. They revolt, establishing a gumlao type of society, and the cycle continues.

Leach's analysis is a polemic against the Malinowskian (and Durkheimian) viewpoint that tribal society is in equilibrium maintained by myth.[21] Leach shows that Kachin society is composed of groups competing for scarce statuses, each justifying its position mythologically, and that the system as a whole oscillates between two radically different types of organization and ideology. Though Leach's study forcefully refutes the view that primitive society is static, it does not demonstrate that primitive mythology can provoke radical evolutionary change. Kachin society remains kinship-based, dry-rice-cultivating, and mythically-oriented, swinging back and forth between the two ideological oppositions, but not beyond them into a 'modern' type based on law, money, mechanization, mass media, and the like. Leach's study is still Durkheimian; he investigates the role of symbols in maintaining a traditional way of life.

Lévi-Strauss

Claude Lévi-Strauss shares with Malinowski a Durkheimian heritage, yet where Malinowski has distilled from that seminal tradition his functionalist dogma that to understand myth one must unravel its social context, Lévi-Strauss champions the opposing viewpoint of 'structuralism'. He teaches that understanding of the meaning of myth comes from analyzing the structure of the text rather that its function in context. Before delving further into the tenets of Lévi-Strauss' approach, it is entertaining to speculate that his rejection of functionalism, like Malinowski's espousal of it, is rooted in his particular type of experience with fieldwork.

Lévi-Strauss has never lived for a long period in a primitive community. Instead he has confined his field investigations to an adventurous expedition through the jungles of Brazil, which he reports in a sardonic and meditative travelogue entitled *Tristes Tropiques*. The now-classic opening paragraph runs as follows:

Travel and travellers are two things I loathe—and yet here I am, all set to tell the story of my expeditions. But at least I've taken a long while to make up my mind to it: fifteen years have passed since I left Brazil for the last time and often, during those years, I've planned to write this book, but I've always been held back by a sort of shame and disgust. So much would have to be said that has no possible interest: insipid details, incidents of no significance. Anthropology is a profession in which adventure plays no part; merely one of its bondages, it represents no more than a dead weight of weeks or months wasted en route; hours spent in idleness when one's informant has given one the slip; hunger, exhaustion, illness as like as not; and those thousand and one routine duties which eat up most of our days to no purpose and reduce our 'perilous existence' in the virgin forest to a simulacrum of military service . . .[22]

A more direct contrast to Malinowski's enthusiastic 'open air fieldwork' could scarcely be imagined: the bored Parisian opposes the engagé refugee, the sourly reflective existentialist intellectual, the boy scout.

Nor does Lévi-Strauss consider the reporting of exploration to have been fulfilling.

Not many people travelled professionally in the 1930s, and those who returned to tell their tales could not count on five or six full houses at the Salle Pleyel, but on a single session in the little, dark, cold, and dilapidated amphitheatre that stood in a pavilion at the far end of the Jardin des Plantes. Once a week the Society of Friends of the Museum organized—and may still organize, for all I know—a lecture on the natural sciences. 'Lantern lectures', they were; but as the screen was too large for the projector, and the lamp too weak for the size of the hall, the images thrown were intelligible neither to the lecturer, who had his nose immediately beneath them, nor to the audience, who could with difficulty distinguish them from the huge patches of damp that disfigured the walls. A quarter of an hour before the appointed time there was always doubt as to whether anyone would come to the lecture, apart from the handful of habitués who could be picked out here and there in the gloom. Just when the lecturer was losing all hope, the body of the hall would half fill with children, each accompanied by mother or nanny, some delighted by the prospect of a free change of scene, others merely craving relief from the dust and noise of the gardens outside. This mixture of moth-eaten phantoms and impatient youngsters was our reward for long months of struggle and hardship; to them we unloaded our treasured recollections . . .[23]

As a revealing, final comparison, consider the contrast between Malinowski's eulogy of the man who inspired his adventures, and Lévi-Strauss' memory of George Dumas, whose 'slightly perverse whimsies' he credits with fostering his own dreams of the exotic.

Dumas was robustly built, with a body like a billhook and a great battered head that looked like a huge root which had been whitened and pared down by a sojourn on the seabed. He had a waxy complexion that unified his whole face with the white . . . A curious fragment of vegetable matter, one would have said, with its rootlets still adhering to it, had not the coal-black gaze affirmed that it was beyond doubt a human being . . .[24]

In his seminal article, 'The Structural Study of Myth',[25] Lévi-Strauss launched a fundamental criticism of Malinowski's dictum that the way to compehend a myth is to link it to its social context. Lévi-Strauss argued that myths throughout the world are remarkably similar despite the wide variety of social contexts in which they are found, thus myths exist independent of context. He claims that sociological and psychoanalytical attempts to correlate myths with extra-mythic referents are facile or unprovable. He proposes to abandon the endeavour, which is like the philosopher's old quest for particular referents of particular sounds—the theory that big sounds refer to big things, for example. Realizing that the same sound refers to different things in different languages, linguists postulated the dictum that sounds vary arbitrarily with respect to their referents. The futile philosopher's quest ceased.

Recognizing the arbitrariness of linguistic symbols, the linguist recognizes too that these symbols composed independent systems. The sound-system of a language or its grammar could be formulated without worrying about the referents denoted by each word— semantics. The mythologist should learn from the linguist, he should cease to waste time in a fruitless search for linkages between mythical texts and extra-mythical contexts, and he should concentrate on the systemic properties of the myths themselves: their structure. Lévi-Strauss proposes a 'structural study of myth'.

The method is to be illustrated by the analysis of several myths, the first of which is the Oedipal myth of ancient Greece. Lévi-Strauss coyly warns that the demonstration is not to be regarded as scientific but

> ...at best in terms of what is meant by the street peddler, whose aim is not to achieve a concrete result, but to explain, as succinctly as possible, the functioning of the mechanical toy which he is trying to sell to the onlookers.[26]

Lévi-Strauss assumes that a myth is composed of relationships between narrated events. He endeavors to show that these relations fall into 'bundles'. His method is to write each event of the Oedipal myth on a card and then categorize these cards into four columns (see fig. 1, p. 50). In Column 1, for example, are placed the events 'Cadmos seeks his sister Europa, ravished by Zeus' and 'Oedipus marries his mother, Jocasta'. In Column 2 are placed the events 'The Spartoi kill one another' and 'Oedipus kills his father, Laios'. Events subsumed under Column 3 include 'Cadmos kills the dragon' and 'Oedipus kills the sphinx'. In Column 4 is placed not an event but the observation that the name 'Oedipus' means 'swollen foot'.

The earlier an event occurs in the narrative, the closer to the top of its column it appears, so that when the entire chart is read from left to right and up to down, the mythical narrative is reproduced. The rationale for this spatial arrangement derives from a lengthy philosophical discourse preceding the analysis. Discussing everything from the French Revolution to the difference between 'langue' (language system, which has structure) and 'parole' (speech event, which has sequence), Lévi-Strauss arrives at the not-so-startling conclusion that myth, like language, has both sequence and structure. A myth tells a story in time, and it defines a timeless paradigm that makes sense out of the past, present, and future. To take account of both the sequential and the structural properties of the myth, Lévi-Strauss reproduces both dimensions in his chart.

The narrative sequence is entirely irrelevant to his analysis, however, and his interpretation is based solely on the Oedipus myth's

Cadmos seeks his sister Europa, ravished by Zeus			
		Cadmos kills the dragon	
	The Spartoi kill one another		
			Labdacos (Laios' father) = *lame* (?)
	Oedipus kills his father, Laios		Laios (Oedipus' father) = *left-sided* (?)
		Oedipus kills the Sphinx	
			Oedipus = *swollen-foot* (?)
Oedipus marries his mother, Jocasta			
	Eteocles kills his brother, Polynices		
Antigone buries her brother, Polynices, despite prohibition			

Fig. 1. The Oedipus Myth (from *Lévi-Strauss* [4] p. 214)

structure, which he claims to represent by the four columns. Column 1 contains events that 'overrate blood relations' (e.g. Oedipus marries his mother), Column 2 contains events that 'underrate blood relations' (e.g. Oedipus kills his father). Column 3 contains events that 'deny the autochthonous [earthly] origins of man' (the Sphinx is associated with the earth, permitting Lévi-Strauss to assert that killing the Sphinx is a way of denying man's earthly origins). Column 4 contains events that 'affirm the earthly origins of men' (in myths around the world, men are clumsy at walking when they are born from the bowels of the earth, and Oedipus means 'swollen foot', hence Oedipus' very name symbolizes birth from the earth).

Lévi-Strauss asserts that Column 4 is to 3 as 1 is to 2, since a plus is to a negative as a plus is to a negative. Accordingly, 'the inability to connect two kinds of relationships is overcome (or rather replaced) by the assertion that contradictory relationships are identical inasmuch as they are both self-contradictory in a similar way.'[27] Two oppositions make one unity if the two are alike. Lévi-Strauss claims that the posing of oppositions and resolution into identity is a universal pattern in mythical thought.

He then relates the Oedipus myth to tensions within Greek existence. The Greeks claimed to believe that mankind is born from the earth, but they realize that he is born of a union between man and woman. This contradiction between 'theory' and 'knowledge' is reflected in the second opposition within the chart (Columns 3 and 4). The Greeks trace descent patrilineally, in effect asserting that man is kin to only one parent, but they realize that he is, in fact, born from both. This contradiction between overrating and underrating descent relationships is expressed in the first opposition of the chart (Columns 1 and 2).

Lévi-Strauss concludes that by juxtaposing side by side these two contradictions, the first deriving from cosmology and the second from society, cosmology and society are united as though in agreement: 'Although experience contradicts theory, social life validates cosmology by its similarity of structure. Hence cosmology is true.'[28]

By a tortuous process, then, Lévi-Strauss arrives at a conclusion precisely opposite from that of Malinowski. For Malinowski, myth validates society by tracing its cosmic roots. For Lévi-Strauss, myth validates cosmology by demonstrating its social base. Malinowski

c

is sociologistic: he is ultimately concerned with symbolic form only insofar as it functions in society. Lévi-Strauss is intellectualistic: he is concerned with society only insofar as it bears on thought.

Lévi-Strauss and the Savage Mind

To some, Claude Lévi-Strauss is the sublime perfection, the awesome culmination of a thought-mold originating with Durkheim; to others, a disease contracted in that Procrustean French bed. All would agree that Durkheim is a source, though Lévi-Strauss himself terms his relation to the master as that of 'inconstant disciple'.[29] The Durkheimian influences are obvious: the concern with parallels between the social and the symbolic, a focus on stasis, an interest in structure. Most basic, perhaps, is the similarity suggested by similar titles of two tomes: Durkheim's *Elementary Forms of the Religious Life* and Lévi-Strauss' *Elementary Structures of Kinship.* They share an assumption, the master and the disciple, that the study of primitive life unveils those elementary units which compose all systems of human existence, including the civilized. The primitive and modern are essentially one.

One popular review phrases this postulate naively, imputing to Lévi-Strauss the belief that 'Today's philosophies reflect no more brilliant a light than mankind's earliest brainstorms in the dim dawntime of thought.'[30] A more discerning essay regards the postulate as polemic; Lévi-Strauss is characterized as a *moraliste*, one who 'uses primitive cultures, personally experienced or gathered at second hand, as a tuning fork against which to test the discord of his own milieu'.[31] For Lévi-Strauss the postulate does indeed serve as a literary device, a way of shocking the reader by juxtaposing the savage and the civilized. In *Tristes Tropiques*, jungle railroad tracks that go nowhere remind the author of homosexuals on Fire Island, New York, whose sexuality, symbolized by their use of baby carriages to haul bottles of milk, is as lacking in destination as are the jungle tracks.[32] In *The Savage Mind*, Australian aborigines are compared to fat and aging Napoleonic bureaucrats.[33] But more than rhetoric, Lévi-Strauss' postulate of identity between the primitive and the modern reflects a distinctive view of reality. Consider an image he draws from geology:

Sometimes ... on one side and the other of a hidden crevice we find two green plants of different species. Each has chosen the soil which suits it; and we realize that within the rock are two ammonites, one of which has involutions less complex than the other's. We glimpse, that is to say, a difference of many thousands of years; time and space suddenly commingle; the living diversity of that moment juxtaposes one age and the other and perpetuates them.[34]

The ancient and the modern are similarly joined in the savage mind of modern man.

Geology, Lévi-Strauss acknowledges as one of his three 'mistresses', the other two being Marx and Freud. Marx has inspired Lévi-Strauss' view of social life as a set of oppositions and Freud has kindled his desire to uncover the structure of the human unconscious. Drawing on the structural linguistics of Ferdinand de Saussure and Roman Jakobson, on anthropological studies of kinship, and on ethnographic materials from countless societies, Lévi-Strauss endeavors to reveal an unconscious and universal structure that underlies seemingly diverse phenomena: kinship, ritual, language, myth, totemism, and systems of classification.

Lévi-Strauss' view of primitive consciousness (or unconsciousness) is exemplified by his analysis of those socio-symbolic systems known as 'totemic', a subject for which he has a fondness that may seem odd until one remembers that totemism is the most direct attempt to resolve the dichotomy basic to Lévi-Strauss' perspective on existence: nature/culture. Lévi-Strauss' brief volume, *Totemism*,[35] throws into relief, once again, the contrast between the structuralism of Lévi-Strauss and the functionalism of Malinowski, whom Lévi-Strauss quotes as saying:

... the road from the wilderness to the savage's belly and consequently to his mind is very short, and for him the world is an indiscriminate background against which there stand out the useful, primarily the edible, species of animals and plants.[36]

Lévi-Strauss believes, to the contrary, that totemic plants are selected not because they are 'good to eat' but because they are 'good to think', and he musters an impressive example to support his view.

From Firth's work on the island of Tikopia, Lévi-Strauss constructs a chart which ranks Tikopian food plants according to several dimensions: their place in subsistence, the labor necessary to grow them, the complexity of fertility ritual, the complexity of harvest rites, and the religious importance of those clans associated with the various plants: the Kafika clan (yam), Taumako (taro), Tafua (coconut), and Fangarere (breadfruit). The chart reveals that the importance of plants for subsistence does not correlate with their totemic, religious role. Yam, for example, ranks at the very bottom of the ranking of plants according to their importance in subsistence, yet the yam-clan, Kafika, is at the top in terms of religious importance. Coconut is third from the top in subsistence ranking but at the bottom in religious prestige. Lévi-Strauss considers that this analysis refutes Malinowski's notion that totemic classification stems simply from hunger and the need for food.

Lévi-Strauss' own view is that totems are selected because they are 'good to think'. He delights in pointing to similarities between the savage thought and that of the philosopher, Bergson, and he argues that the primitive is a philosopher who utilizes natural materials as metaphors to symbolize the structure of his society. Viewing the natural world as divided into coconut, tiger, and orangutan species, tribesmen construct a metaphor to explain the structure of their society, which is divided into coconut clan, tiger clan, and orangutan clan. The parallel to the argument of Durkheim and Mauss is clear: totemic (symbolic) structures are isomorphic with social structures.

Lévi-Strauss warns that the search for a metaphorical linkage between any one totem and its associated clan is futile: only rarely does one find, for example, that the qualities of a particular totem reflect qualities of a particular group, such as the lion totem for the lion-hearted clan. The search for a direct relationship is rather like the search for language sounds that copy the physical qualities of their referents. Instead, the totemic system as a whole parallels the structure of the society as a whole, or, better, the two together express a model within the mind, a code in terms of which both natural and social phenomena are classified into a system of similarities and differences, homologies and oppositions. An example of Lévi-Strauss' subtle (if not entirely defensible) applications of these principles, very much in the tradition of Durkheim and Mauss, is his discussion of the Nuer of Africa:

In order to characterize twins, the Nuer employ expressions

which at first sight seem contradictory. On the one hand, they say that twins are 'one person' (ran); on the other, they state that twins are not 'persons' (ran), but 'birds' (dit). To interpret these expressions correctly, it is necessary to envisage, step by step, the reasoning involved. As manifestations of spiritual power, twins are firstly 'children of God' (gat kwoth), and since the sky is the divine abode they may also be called 'persons of the above' (ran nhial). In this context they are opposed to ordinary humans, who are 'persons of below' (ran piny). As birds are themselves 'of the above', twins are assimilated to them. However, twins remain human beings; although they are 'of the above', they are relatively 'of below'. But the same distinction applies to birds, since certain species fly less high and less well than others; in their own sphere, consequently, while generally 'of the above', birds may also be divided according to above and below. We may thus understand why twins are called by the names of 'terrestrial' birds: guinea fowl, francolin, etc.

The relation thus postulated between twins and birds is explained neither by a principle of participation after the manner of Lévy-Bruhl, nor by utilitarian considerations such as those adduced by Malinowski, nor by the intuition of perceptible resemblances proposed by Firth and by Fortes. What we are presented with is a series of logical connections uniting mental relations. Twins 'are birds', not because they are confused with them or because they look like them, but because twins in relation to other men, are as 'persons of the above' to 'persons of below', and, in relation to birds, as 'birds of below' are to 'birds of the above'. They thus occupy, as do birds, an intermediary position between the supreme spirit and human beings.[37]

For Lévi-Strauss, totemism is the perfect model of the system of meaning; the point is emphasized in a discussion of the difference between totemism and sacrifice in which Lévi-Strauss draws together a number of his fundamental ideas.

Totemic symbols are 'discontinuous'.[38] Within a totemic system only the species or natural phenomenon from which a given clan draws its name is appropriate for that clan. Neither a beast nor a group can be taken for another; a member of the bear clan cannot belong to the eagle clan or claim the eagle as his totem. The totemic symbols are sharply distinguished, discrete, and discontinuous.

The elements used for sacrifice constitute a continuum. If the required object is missing, the next in line can replace it just so long as the intention (e.g. to placate a deity) persists. A cucumber can be substituted for an egg, an egg for a fish, a fish for a hen, a hen for a goat, a goat for an ox. The series is irreversible, says Lévi-Strauss; it would be absurd to treat the cucumber and ox as equal, to sacrifice an ox for want of a cucumber.

In a totemic system, relationships are reversible. In a totemic system where the ox represented one clan and the cucumber another, the two would be genuinely equivalent 'in the sense that it is impossible to confound them and that they would be equally suitable for manifesting the differentiation between the groups they respectively connote'.[39]

Sacrifice is an event. Occurring in time, it starts and stops. It begins with no relationship between man and deity, and it ceases when a relationship has been established. The direction of the event is irreversible. The victim, once destroyed, cannot be regained; the divine blessing, once granted, cannot be rescinded.

Totemism is a structure. It exists in the mind, independent of time in the sense that its symbolic patterns can be applied to any event, past, present, or future, to classify it and render it meaningful. It is reversible in that it can shuttle forward or backward to classify events at any point in history. History itself, which can only move forward, is irreversible. Lévi-Strauss does not claim that the totemic structures are entirely static, for they are 'lived' as well as 'thought', hence they are in flux. But the natives perceive the totemic structures as constant and eternal. This perception permits them to classify as constant and orderly the ongoing historical processes in whose company the totemic systems 'sail through time'.[40]

Sacrifice is perceived by the sacrificer as a means to an end, a cause producing an effect. Totemism is based on the notion of homology, parallel structures. Sacrifice is merely a technique to achieve a result, but totemism is a genuine system of consciousness, a symbolic structure that permits the interpretation of reality. Totemism enjoys the added advantage of a 'doubly objective basis'. Confining itself to conceiving of the homology between two indisputably existing phenomena, the natural and the social, totemism also correctly perceives the discontinuous character of each; sacrifice is oriented toward a subjective illusion, divinity, and it falsely conceives of nature as continuous. Lévi-Strauss summarizes his admiration of totemism:

> To express this difference in level between totemism and sacrifice it is not, then, enough to say that the former is a system of reference and the latter a system of operations, that one works out a schema of interpretation while the other sets up (or claims to set up) a technique for obtaining certain results: that one is true, and the other is false. Rather, to put it precisely, classificatory systems belong to the level of language: they are codes which, however well or badly made, aim always to make sense. The system of sacrifice, on the other hand, represents a private discourse wanting in good sense for all that it may be frequently pronounced.[41]

Lévi-Strauss remarks further that sacrifice is 'statistical'. This suggests that his comparison of totemism and sacrifice relates to an important contrast he has made elsewhere[42] between 'statistical' and 'mechanical' models. While Lévi-Strauss' original distinction is murky, and commentators[43] have not helped much to disperse the fog, the contrast is significant and suggestive. At the risk of stating too concretely what Lévi-Strauss would prefer to leave abstract, the contrast between 'mechanical' and 'statistical' can be applied to totemism/sacrifice.

In a statistical phenomenon, or a phenomenon conceived in terms of a statistical model, choice is dictated by circumstance. Whether the sacrifice is of an ox or of a cucumber depends on which is available. In mechanically organized phenomena, or phenomena viewed in terms of a mechanical model, there is no choice among objects since the culture dictates the relation between the actor and object. The culture, let us say, dictates that a member of the ox clan employ the ox to symbolize his group membership, and he is not permitted to choose the cucumber as his symbol since that is the exclusive property of the cucumber group.

Given this rigidity of relationship between symbol and group, the group can be described by the symbols. Mechanical analysis of a society is 'emic', i.e., couched in terms of the natives' own symbols. Thus, the analyst of a totemic society presumably could plot social divisions by simply plotting the relations between the totems. Divisions among the cucumber, ox, and egg clans could be described as divisions among cucumber, ox, and egg totems. Exchanges among these clans, such as intermarriage, have cosmic as well as social significance since they unite symbolic categories as well as groups.[44] The pattern is reminiscent of Durkheim's 'mechanical' (as opposed to 'organic') type of society, where relationships between groups are dictated by moral categories instead of by mere utility.

In sacrifice, conceived statistically, circumstance dictates choice; the native categories do not prescribe or predict which object will be chosen. The analyst therefore must construct his own 'etic' or 'analytic' categories. He might, for example, construct measurements for each of the several circumstantial factors that produce the choice between the ox, the cucumber, and the objects in between. Let us say that he decides that the important factors are the actor's color preference (does he prefer green, black, or something else?), his strength (is he strong enough to carry an ox, or so weak that he can carry merely a cucumber?), and wealth (how expensive an object can he afford?). The analyst could score each actor on all factors, let us say on a scale from 1 to 10. Eventually the analyst could set up a statistical table showing the probability for an actor with a given overall score, from 1 to 10, choosing each object. Unlikely as it may be that such an analysis will ever be carried out, it would seem to be what Lévi-Strauss' statistical model, reduced to operations, implies. Owing to the cultural indeterminacy of choices involved in sacrifice, the investigator is forced to resort to his own measurements and calculations of probability rather than relying on all-or-nothing categorizations by the culture itself.

Lévi-Strauss' discussion of totemism and sacrifice, like his discussion of virtually everything else, is fraught with ambiguity because he fails to make clear when he is describing phenomena and when he is expounding models designed for analysis of phenomena. The confusion is, in part, deliberate. It is doubtless derived from a philosophical position[45] as well as from a literary and introspective style which is as much concerned with expounding a point of view, indeed with laying out the author's own 'savage mind', as with viewing so-called reality. Totemism is a model, a metaphor in terms of which any phenomenon can be seen as a reversible, mechanical, discontinuous structure. 'Sacrifice' is a metaphor for looking at reality as an irreversible, causal process, suitable for statistical dissection.

Yet totemism and sacrifice are also phenomena, representing distinct types of existence. Lévi-Strauss' perception of them as such underlines a debate with his rival, Jean-Paul Sartre. For Lévi-Strauss, the totemic system is the shining example of a 'primitive classification system': mechanically organized, meaningful, discrete, and constant. Sacrifice is a symptom of Durkheim's anomic, organic society, statistical in operation, loosely organized, pragmatic, and in flux. Lévi-Strauss' disagreement with Sartre is that Sartre regards the ruling conception of this type of society, i.e., 'history', as universal among men and distinctive of humanity.

Retorts Lévi-Strauss, history is merely one of the many myths for viewing existence. Sartre exhibits his provinciality by imagining that a sense of history has been the possession of all human societies. This historical worldview has come into prominence only in those civilizations of Asia and Europe cursed with the 'totemic void'.[46] These unfortunate peoples have 'elected to explain themselves by history' rather than by totemism. So doing, they have developed a powerful intellectual tool for analyzing both the human and non-human world, but certainly they have not discovered the ultimate model: the 'search for intelligibility' requires abstraction of a structure from historical process. The most sophisticated model for viewing reality, Lévi-Strauss' own structuralism, turns out to resemble the primitive's totemism, while history is only the 'point of departure in any quest for intelligibility': 'As we say of certain careers, history may lead to anything, provided you get out of it'.[47]

Edmund Leach, one of the most knowledgeable and incisive English-speaking interpreters of Lévi-Strauss, has provided a general sketch of his vision which extends the notion of totemism to cover a wide spectrum of systems of thought. For example, Leach describes Lévi-Strauss' insight that roasted foods are party dishes in most cultures, whereas boiled foods are a homely dish. Only in democratic societies are boiled foods highly regarded because

Boiling provides a means of complete conservation of the meat and its juices, whereas roasting is accompanied by destruction and loss. Thus one denotes economy, the other prodigality; the latter is aristocratic, the former plebian.[48]

Animals eat anything their instincts deem edible, but humans classify foods by convention. The opposition of roasted and boiled is totemic in that it classifies the social in terms of the natural.

Why bother with metaphors from nature, why not simply talk directly about the social? For Lévi-Strauss, metaphorical thought confers meaning on the social world. While he does not explain how this is so, he implies that when I perceive that the relationship between A and B (in the social sphere) is analogous to the relationship between C and D (in the natural sphere), the social relationship assumes added meaning for me because I perceive its groundedness in an order larger than itself. Metaphor is crucial in the universal human quest for meaning.

Lévi-Strauss also considers as universal among humans the tendency to perceive continuous nature in discrete categories.[49] Leach illustrates this view by the example of a traffic light. The light is divided into an opposition, red and green, with yellow in between. In nature, colors form a continuous spectrum with each color distinguishable from the other only by measurement of wave length, but culture divides color into a dichotomy. Discontinuous, oppositional structures are created by man because he possesses language. All humans learn to speak by making the same initial series of distinctions, as between consonant and vowel, nasal consonant and oral stop. They are forced to do so because of the architecture and musculature of the human mouth and throat and because of the organization of the human brain.[50] The brain and speech at once reflect and dictate the dichotomous patterning of human thought.

If 'opposition' is the key term in Lévi-Strauss' vision of symbol systems, 'exchange' is the central concept in his view of society, and he regards the two as derived from the same pan-human code. In his *Elementary Structures of Kinship*, Lévi-Strauss demonstrated how cosmological oppositions and marriage exchanges are associated in primitive society. He suggestively classifies these in types which correlate with the varying capacities of society to survive and spread. In a more general formulation, he has proposed that all social and symbolic life be conceived as a neutralization of opposition by the exchange of three elements;

words, gifts, and women. Exchanges involving words, as in conversation, are the most rapid; exchange of women, as in primitive marriage systems, are the slowest; the exchange of gifts is in between.

Lévi-Strauss speculates that exchange originates with the incest taboo. The incest taboo implies a capacity to distinguish between women who are permitted and women who are forbidden, thus generating a distinction between sister and wife. In exchange for giving your sister to an outsider, you receive a wife. The incest taboo insures that this exchange will be made, thus prohibiting the isolation of the family which would occur if its members could marry among themselves instead of engaging in exchange with non-kinsmen. The resulting network of families permits the emergence and the survival of society, which is necessary for that human culture which distinguishes man from the incestuous animals.

The basic opposition within Lévi-Strauss' vision is that between process and structure. Process involves sequence, metonymy (as he defines it, the relation of means to end); it is statistical, irreversible, historical, part of nature, and exemplified by such events as sacrifice and speech (*parole*). Structures involve thought, classification, metaphor; a structure is mechanical, reversible, ahistorical, part of culture, and it is exemplified by such systems as totemism and the linguistic code (*langue*) in terms of which utterances must be interpreted to become meaningful. A great deal of Lévi-Strauss' argument concerns the interplay between these opposing sets of categories or phenomena.

As Leach and others have observed, the non-Frenchman, particularly the empiricist Anglo-American, frequently experiences difficulty in deciding just what metaphysical reality Lévi-Strauss accords to that code which is said to underly all human thought and action. Leach quotes a translation of a particularly mystifying passage:

> We are not, therefore, claiming to show how men think the myths, but rather how the myths think themselves out in men and without men's knowledge.[51]

Here Lévi-Strauss seems to attribute to the system of symbols an existence transcending the process of individual thought. Without passing judgment on this epistemology or even claiming to comprehend it, we still can draw from Lévi-Strauss a suggestive formulation of those patterns (whether they be conscious, unconscious, or transcend individual mental processes altogether) in terms of which myth, society, language, and ritual are created and interpreted by all men.

Traditional Thought

Lévi-Strauss, like Durkheim and Mauss and their disciples,[52] is concerned to elucidate the universal patterns of human thought. His primary materials, however, come from primitive or traditional societies. From these varied studies of myth, totemism, language, and kinship we can draw an impression of the Durkheimian perspective concerning traditional thought.

A central concept is 'homology', the notion that separate systems have parallel structures. None of the Durkheimian-influenced authors whom we have surveyed here empasize that symbolic systems, whether mythical, totemic, or other, find their primary role in such social processes as inspiring activity or providing escape from oppression. This type of process is given little recognition in these authors' conception of traditional society. The relationship between symbol and society which they empasize is one of homology: the symbolic systems and the social systems are considered to reinforce and buttress each other by their parallel structures. Leach and Malinowski may differ in their view of functionalism, but they agree, in their Trobriand and Kachin analyses discussed here, that myth is a charter which, by its symbolic stucture, validates a parallel social structure of groups or statuses. Lévi-Strauss, in his Oedipus analysis, may reverse the emphasis of Malinowski but he concludes by asserting a homology between cosmic and social structure which permits the latter to validate the former. For Lévi-Strauss as for Durkheim and Mauss, totemism is a system of classification which parallels the structure of society. Complex and subtle as Lévi-Strauss' vision may be, a pervasive theme is that traditional consciousness is organized around certain structural principles, such as dualism, which generate homologous patterns in diverse spheres ranging from myth to kinship and language. The relationship between society and consciousness is one of homology owing to their shared code or structure.

The significance of this Durkheimian emphasis on homology is highlighted by contrasting the Weberian emphasis on discrepancy. For Weber, the moving force in history is discrepancy between the symbolic and the social such that men strive incessantly to change the one to fit the other. Certainly it is simplistic to regard Weber as interested only in change, Durkheim only in stability, yet the view of the symbolic and the social perpetuated by each school does reflect this contrast. Homology is possible only when the symbolic and the social are sufficiently stable that the two systems can more or less match.

Lévi-Strauss dubs traditional societies 'cold',[53] because their people classify events in terms of mythical and totemic structures which they regard as eternal. Even though traditional existence may actually change, through birth, death, schism, and migration, it is envisioned as constant owing to its place in the symbolic frame. Without considerable stability of both the symbolic and the social systems, such an illusion, one would assume, cannot long remain.

Notes to Chapter 3

1. *Durkheim*, p. 101.
2. Ibid., p. 420.
3. *Durkheim and Mauss*. See also the excellent Introduction not only to Durkheim and Mauss but to the entire study of primitive classification by *Needham* (3).
4. *Durkheim and Mauss*, p. 78.
5. Ibid., p. 32.
6. Ibid., p. 53.
7. Ibid., pp. 86, 88.
8. Ibid., p. 88.
9. *Leach* (1).
10. *Malinowski* (2), p. 94.
11. *Hays*, p. 121.
12. *Malinowski* (2), p. 96.
13. Ibid., p. 97. Malinowski's polemic unfairly ignores suggestive insights of such erudite scholars as Max Müller.
14. Ibid., p. 98.
15. Ibid., p. 101.
16. Ibid., p. 146.
17. Ibid., pp. 146–7.
18. *Leach* (2).

19. Ibid., p. 85.
20. Ibid., p. 82.
21. In passing, Leach also criticizes the Durkheimian view of ritual: 'If then we accept the Durkheim view that religious rituals are representations of the solidarity of the participating group, we need clearly to understand that the solidarity need exist only at the moment at which the ritual takes place; we cannot infer a continuing latent solidarity after the ritual celebrations are over.' *Leach* (2), p. 281.
22. *Lévi-Strauss* (5), p. 17.
23. Ibid., pp. 18–19.
24. Ibid., pp. 19–20. Here a human is viewed as a totem. See pp. 53–9.
25. *Lévi-Strauss* (4).
26. Ibid., p. 209.
27. Ibid., p. 212.
28. Ibid., p. 216.
29. Ibid., p. vi.
30. *Time* (1), p. 34.
31. *The Times Literary Supplement*, p. 321.
32. *Lévi-Strauss* (5), pp. 143–4.
33. Ibid., p. 89.
34. *Lévi-Strauss* (5), p. 60. Quoted in *Leach* (4), p. 10. See also Beidelman (2).
35. *Lévi-Strauss* (2). A suggestive discussion of Lévi-Straussian and other views of totemism is *Crocker*.
36. Ibid., p. 57.
37. Ibid., pp. 79–81.
38. *Lévi-Strauss* (3), pp. 224–5.
39. Ibid., p. 224.
40. Ibid., p. 233.
41. Ibid., p. 228.
42. *Lévi-Strauss* (1).
43. See, for example, *Nutini*.
44. A classic example of such analysis is provided by *Needham* (2).
45. See *Scholte*.
46. *Lévi-Strauss* (3), p. 232.
47. Ibid., p. 262.
48. *Leach* (4), p. 23. For a Latin version of this theory, listen to Italian movie star, Sophia Loren: 'I call my husband "Invotini" [veal birds] because this is my favourite dish and he is my favorite man. Sometimes I've been known to call him "Eggplant Parmesan".' I call our son Chipi [Carlo, Jr.] "Spaghetti" because he loves it so. Sometimes I even think of myself in terms of food—like a pizza, which I happen to like very much. Being Neapolitan, I see myself as the classic pizza made with tomato and mozzarella. Why pizza? Because pizza is common, and I think I'm a very common housewife.' *Family Weekly*, p. 16.
49. This view of nature as objectively continuous reflects Lévi-Strauss' general view but contradicts his assertion during discussion of totemism and sacrifice that nature is objectively discrete.
50. *Leach* (4), p. 37.
51. Ibid., p. 50.
52. Space does not permit even a cursory survey of the numerous recent

studies inspired by Durkheimian and Lévi-Straussian perspectives, but special mention should be made of the work of Rodney Needham, who is the most significant custodian, defender, and interpreter of the Durkheimian perspective on primitive classification. Not only has Needham translated and interpreted the most significant French writings on the subject, ranging from those of Durkheim and Mauss to Hertz and Lévi-Strauss, but he has also initiated a crucial set of investigations which reveal the dualistic structure of primitive thought and society (see *Needham* 2, 3, 4). It is interesting to note that the American studies of 'ethnoscience', which claim no descent from Lévi-Strauss but have, like his work, drawn inspiration from linguistics, discern in systems of kinship, color, and plant terminologies a 'binary' logic not unlike that revealed by Needham (see *Sturtevant*).

One may discern in *Geertz*'s (3) seminal study of the Balinese cockfight an illustration of the 'structuralist' rather than 'functionalist' mood among contemporary anthropological analysts of symbols. In this essay, as in his earlier one on the Javanese funeral (see *Geertz* 1), Geertz is critical of 'functionalist sociology' which asserts too simple a reinforcing of the social order through ritual. But his alternative view is different now than a decade ago, when he proposed a neo-functionalism to cope with the relation between symbolic and social systems. He concludes that the key to understanding the cockfight is to emphasize (in a way different from Lévi-Strauss) its sheerly symbolic structure, to view it as a 'text'.

53. *Lévi-Strauss* (3), p. 233.

4
Transition to Modernity

The Weberian Perspective

The story is told that theologian Martin Buber was once asked by a student, 'Who was Adam?' Buber replied, 'Adam is you.' This is the Durkheimian perspective. Laying bare the elementary forms of ancient and primitive existence, the Durkheimian claims to lay bare the qualities of modern men as well. Durkheim himself certainly did not ignore history, change, or evolution, but the major thrust of Durkheimian anthropology has been, first, to lay bare traditional patterns and, second, to generalize from these to *universal* human patterns of consciousness and society. Weber's perspective on religion and society was more evolutionary. His primary interest in the primitive was to trace the paths and phases by which moderns have evolved beyond it, and his central concern was with the transition to modernity.

Nor is this the only important difference between the Durkheimian and Weberian perspectives. Each is rooted in a distinctive philosophical and sociological tradition. To simplify, the one is French, the other German. To a degree, the contrasts are still pervasive in the heirs of each tradition.[1]

French sociology is more sociologistic, the German more spiritualistic. Durkheim's dictum was 'society is God', and he sought to reduce spiritual phenomena to the collective life. Weber, like other Germans, deified deities; he took serious account of the special qualities of symbolic forms and systems. Like the German philosopher Cassirer, Weber stressed that each objectification of consciousness, whether myth, science, or the arts, must be comprehended in terms of its own unique laws and attributes. He emphasised that symbolic systems develop according to their own logic and that they cannot be seen as mere reflections of change in the techno-social sphere.

Weber joins other Germans in emphasizing the empathetic, interpretative mode of understanding, the *verstehen*. Weber did not consider a statistical correlation, no matter how well established, to constitute explanation. The analyst must dig beneath the observed relationship and explain it in terms of the motives and purposes of the actors involved. In practice, the French could operate similarly. Thus, Durkheim first established that the incidence of suicide was greater in urban than rural areas, then he accounted for the correlation by subjective factors such as 'anomie' (disorientation arising from a failure of norms to fit reality) and 'egoism' (insufficient commitment to a group). But social psychology was less central in Durkheim's espoused methodology than his sociologism, which was modelled after nineteenth-century physics. Social facts, i.e. norms, are not subjective, Durkheim argued, because they are shared by a group rather than imprisoned within the mind of a subject. As objective phenomena, they are like things. Accordingly they can be analyzed by methods akin to physics.

Such an approach can be seen in Durkheim's search for laws, for example, that suicide increases with urbanization much as pressure varies with volume or volts with ohms. In a more recent analogy drawn from physical science, Lévi-Strauss aspires to construct the equivalent of a chemist's periodic chart, specifying irreducible elements of human culture after the fashion of oxygen, hydrogen, and carbon, which, if combined according to formulae, would generate all possible patterns of social life.

Such sociological laws or schemes are ideally universal. They should hold regardless of the cultural or historical context to which they are applied. Weber was more concerned with the uniqueness of each culture. The question central to most of his work was: what is the distinctive, the unique quality of Western as opposed to Asian civilization? Among the Australian aborigines Durkheim revealed religious principles that hold for all peoples; Weber launched a project comparing the unique qualities of the European, Chinese, Indian, and Judaic civilizations.

In place of the French 'laws', Weber formulated 'ideal types', which classify and highlight significant historical trends and cultural patterns. Examples of such ideal types in Weber's work are the modes of authority (charismatic, rational-legal, and traditional) and the complexes of value such as the Protestant Ethic and the Spirit of Capitalism. The ideal type is not an 'ideal' formulated by the people themselves nor is it a statistical summary derived by averaging a number of measurements in a sample; no society explicitly idealizes precisely those values embodied in Weber's 'spirit of capitalism', nor could one arrive at this formulation by counting and averaging traits of numerous existing economies. And certainly the ideal type has no metaphysical reality like a Platonic ideal. Patterns which are more or less evident in real phenomena are highlighted by the analyst's formulation of the form they would assume if their logic and tendencies could be perfectly expressed. The method is analogous to the novelist's portrayal of a type character, such as Pamela, Crusoe, Rob Roy, or the Artful Dodger, who so perfectly expresses tendencies that exist in paler form among real personalities that we say to ourselves, 'Why she or he is just like so-and-so'. No human brings to total fruition the Spirit of Capitalism or the Protestant Ethic, but once Weber has sketched the perfected pattern it is easy to see its imperfect expression in real people, such as Andrew Carnegie, John D. Rockefeller, or the small-town merchant. Where the French laws summarize statistical regularities or categorical universals, the abstracted clarity of the German ideal type yields acute perception of patterned particularities.

The Germans emphasize the distinction between the symbolic and the technical, as in Max Weber's *Sinn* and *Zweckrational* and Alfred Weber's 'culture' (symbolic) and 'civilization' (technology). They tend to romanticize the primitive as cultivating the spiritual, the symbolic, qualities which modern rationality threatens to destroy. Moderns are therefore encouraged to escape to the *Gemeinschaft*, the cozy and intimate folk community. The idealization of natural man is certainly part of French thought, whether revealed in Rousseau's philosophies or Parisian milkmaid costumes, but it logically could not be dominant in the work of Durkheim or his heirs insofar as they deny the difference between the modern and the primitive.

The German and the French sociologies were rooted in what each regarded as a pressing problem for modern society, but the emphasis of the two traditions differs. Durkheim feared the disintegration of contemporary society and oriented his work toward inquiring how the integration could be restored through solidifying devices, such as rites. The Germans feared not too little integration but too much, as a result of the oppressive rigidity of overly rationalized bureaucratic and capitalistic organization. Weber and Marx were only two of the German sociologists who inquired how these systems originated and developed, and whether a true community could be maintained in their presence.

According to the German philosophical tradition, man and the study of man are divided into two facets. Kant had conceived of a radical dualism between the natural and the spiritual, both of which were embraced by man. Man's physical aspect is bound by laws of nature, but his spiritual aspect is free of them. Accordingly, natural science is sufficient to investigate the human body, but a science of an entirely different type is necessary to study the human spirit. The first type of science is *Naturwissenschaft* (natural science), the second *Geisteswissenschaft* (spiritual or cultural science). Cultural science must proceed by an intuitive understanding of wholes (*Gestalten*) rather than by the analytical dissection into parts. The sweeping historical analyses of Dilthey, Rickert, and Spengler (paralleled in anthropology by the 'holism' of Ruth Benedict and Alfred Kroeber) exemplify the Kantian tradition of intuiting wholes.[2]

Born in Berlin in 1864, reared in cultivated circles and writing historical essays by adolescence, Max Weber was steeped in this German tradition which sharply distinguished the cultural and the natural, the symbolic and the technical. Indeed, Weber's life was divided into two phases, separated by a mental breakdown, the first concentrating on the techno-economic sphere, the second on the *Geist* that lends meaning to the first.

At the age of eighteen, Weber began the study of law at the University of Heidelberg. After a year in the army, he returned to legal studies at Berlin and Goettingen. Dissatisfied with neo-Kantian *Rechtsphilosophie* that emphasized the formal or *Geistliche* facets of law, Weber stressed the importance of economic factors, and his doctoral thesis was a study of medieval trading companies. After completing his doctorate in 1889, at the age of twenty-five, Weber worked as a lecturer in law and also at various practical researches, such as investigations of the stock exchange and of rural labor east of the Elbe. He was also active in politics. In 1894, at the age of thirty, he became professor of economics at the University of

Freiburg. Already recognized as a brilliant scholar, Weber nevertheless craved practical employment. He wrote, 'I am not really a scholar after all; scientific activity is for me primarily an occupation for the leisure hours . . .' Craving to emulate an energetic and ascetic uncle who ran a factory, Weber strove to assuage his guilt about working in the academic world by subjecting himself to a backbreaking schedule calculated to result in scholarly productivity as prolific as that of his uncle's factory.

In 1897, when he was thirty-three years old, Weber fell ill. He resigned his university post, and for four years the formerly robust and forceful man suffered from acute anxiety and exhaustion. He was unable even to read, he would sit picking his nails and staring into space. Eventually, like Germans from Luther to Goethe, he became revitalized and reborn into a new phase of life after a trip to Italy. There he began to read again, but now in the arts and religion rather than economics. As he recovered, he crystallized a focus that was to motivate the remainder of his scholarly life: the study of relationships between *Geistliche* traditions such as religion, art, and worldview, and techno-social systems such as capitalism. Analyzing capitalism as a working system composed of such elements as free labor, rational calculation of profit, and the keeping of books, Weber emphasized that capitalist activity gained meaning only through participation in a symbolic system, such as that embodied in the Protestant Ethic.

After his recuperation, Weber was an enormously productive and inspirational scholar, and he also worked at such practical tasks as administrating army hospitals during the First World War and helping to draft the Weimar Constitution. He was, however, unable to enter the classroom and lecture, a failing about which he felt corrosive guilt. Finally, in 1919 he accepted an invitation to give a series of lectures at the University of Vienna, and after much inner turmoil he accepted a position to teach in Munich. But he died in 1920 at the age of fifty-six.

Weber's intense personality and mental breakdown tempt the amateur psychoanalyst to search for Oedipal factors, and these are readily apparent. His father was the classical German authoritarian, his mother the equally classical sweet, spiritual type, and at least one biographer has portrayed Weber as suffering through thirty years of financial dependence on the father while forced to observe his tyranny over the mother. The relationship came to a head after Weber had married, established his own household, and invited his mother for a visit. When the father came too, Weber angrily drove him away, an action for which he felt deep guilt a few months later when the father suddenly died. The event triggered years of depression into which Weber sank soon after.[3]

Without denying this Oedipal stream in Weber's biography, one may nevertheless emphasize the cultural basis of his dramatic shift after the mental illness at mid-life. The painful transformation from a father-dominated to a relatively emancipated condition was, for Weber, a theme in the larger shift from a focus on the largely technical, *Naturwissenschaftliche* elements in German tradition to a heroic attempt at synthesizing this stream with the *Geistliche*, the symbolic. Noteworthy, too, is the unstable, tense relationship which Weber always postulated between these two aspects of existence. Weber's synthesis, like his life and identity, never resolved into the steady calm of a Durkheim.

In summarizing the Weberian studies of comparative religion, I shall begin with his study of the Protestant Ethic, then proceed to the studies of China, India, and ancient Judaism. The objectives of these studies were two, first to investigate the relationship between religion and socioeconomic modernization, second to highlight the distinctive character of Western civilization and to explore its origin in the prophetic tradition. I then consider a major contribution of the Neo-Weberians, the enrichment of the individualist Weberian framework by stress on collectivism. This collectivism logically leads back to the Marxism that Weber strove to correct, and the Marxist notion of alienation leads, in a second dialectic, back to a concern with the individual as he suffers disorientation owing to modernization.

The Protestant Ethic and the Spirit of Capitalism[4]

For Weber, the 'spirit of capitalism' considered hard work a calling (*Beruf*) which carried its own intrinsic rewards. Such capitalism was distinct from the pursuit of wealth in order to reap hedonistic rewards: to eat, drink, and be merry. Regarding capitalistic activity as a calling rather than merely a means toward riches, the capitalist was an ascetic. He invested his profits in his enterprise instead of spending them on himself, thus expanding his responsibilities and flogging himself to work all the harder. And since the degree to which a person could practice self-denial depended on how much he had available to deny himself, asceticism required profit.

The ascetic capitalist seeks profit through rational calculation, continuous production, and long-range investment. This rationalization of activity distinguished the modern capitalist from the get-rich-quick type who seeks profit by speculation or force, as in piracy, the financing of warfare to gain spoils, and military domination that exploits forced labor. Imposing discipline on the acquisitive instincts, ascetic capitalism harnessed them methodically rather than permitting their immediate expression as greed. Yet the capitalistic spirit imposed no limit on the profit that was ultimately to be acquired, and in this it differed from the limitations of 'wants' characteristically imposed by traditional society. Capitalism violated traditional values, too, in that it permitted an infinite range of means to be employed in relation to the end of profit; anybody and everything could be exploited for profit, or so it seemed to the German who accused American capitalists of making 'tallow out of candles and money out of men'.[5] Finally, modern capitalism operated within a framework of highly bureaucratized society, a rational-legal system, highly organized networks of exchange, and elaborate technology.

Weber admitted that the hedonistic, get-rich-quick capitalism had existed in many periods and places (he mentions Babylon, Rome, China, and India) and that individual capitalists whose enterprise was rational and ascetic could be found in many societies. But he believed that the harnessing of entire societies around the rationalized, ascetic pursuit of profit was distinctive of the modern, primarily Western world. Indeed, he considered capitalism antithetical to traditional society and consciousness as is shown by the flood of mistrust and indignation with which traditional people typically greet the exploitative capitalist whom they combat by spreading rumors of shady past and evil intent. Because the Spirit of Capitalism violates traditional values, Weber was astonished that it had emerged into such prominence in the West, and he decided that its florescence could be explained only by some unusual stimulus.

Weber observed that capitalism had flourished strongly among Calvinistic Protestants, and he noted instances of capitalists who converted to Calvinism, a pattern atypical of the normally unheroic bourgeois who in world history had typically sought pleasure from wealth rather than submitting to so ascetic a religion as Calvinism. Weber could see no obvious economic motive behind the conversion. True, Catholicism condemned such practices as usury, but Catholics were lax in enforcing the rules, and so did not place strong obstacles in the way of acquiring wealth. Indeed, Calvinist preachers condemned the love of riches more than did Catholicism. Why then the correlation between Calvinism and capitalism?

Weber concluded that the Calvinists (more broadly, the Puritans, which included Pietists, Methodists, and Baptists) of the seventeenth century were driven to their frenzied and relentless capitalism by a state of terror derived from the doctrine of predestination. Fearing an eternity of hellfire, they sought a means to prove irrefutably that they were of the elect rather than the damned. All traditional means of insuring salvation had been rejected by Calvinism. Membership in a church could not assure or prove one's destiny for salvation, for some congregations were believed doomed. No bond to a priest could help. Sensuous elements such as sacraments, ceremony, and magic were worse than nothing for they promoted idolatry and superstition. What could prove one's destiny for salvation rather than eternal hellfire?

The Calvinist finally came to believe that he could prove his destiny for salvation by planned and systematic, disciplined and continuous work at his calling. Only the saints, the saved could so vigorously serve God; hence work at one's calling was proof of one's fortune. Waste of time was the deadliest of sins, for only unceasing activity avoided temptation by the Devil. Idle talk, contemplation, ornamentation, the arts, sports, or any sensuous and undisciplined impulse were condemned as distracting from the central commitment. Friendship was an irrational act, for the saint should trust only God; as one preacher advised, 'Each morning one should think of going among people as of going into a wild forest full of dangers.' Even family ties were hindrances to the quest for assurance of salvation. In *Pilgrim's Progress*, John Bunyan's wife and children cling to him as he receives the call to travel to the holy city, but he stops his ears with his fingers and staggers forth across the fields crying, 'Life, eternal life!'

In Calvinism, writes Weber,

There was no place for the very human Catholic cycle of sin, repentance, atonement, release, followed by renewed sin... The moral conduct of the average man was thus deprived of its planless and unsystematic character and subjected to a consistent method for conduct as a whole... The life of the saint was directed solely toward a transcendental end, salvation. But precisely for that reason it was thoroughly rationalized in this world and dominated entirely by the aim to add to the glory of God on earth... Only a life guided by constant thought could achieve conquest over the state of nature.[6]

The Calvinist created conviction of his own salvation by systematically hewing the line, carrying out his plan, deterred from relaxation by the knowledge that 'at every moment [he] stands before the inexorable alternative, chosen or damned'.[7] Even though Calvinist sermons might explicitly condemn the pursuit of wealth, Weber believed that the total system of Calvinist belief instilled in the believer psychological drives (*Antrieb*) which found expression in rationalized work in the vineyards of the Lord. In this fashion, the Protestant Ethic promoted the Spirit of Capitalism which, in turn, resulted in highly successful capitalistic activity.

Here, then, was a set of symbolic forms—doctrines, sermons, parables, exhortations, visions—composing a system of consciousness, the Protestant Ethic, which, Weber believed, was a necessary condition for the genesis of a techno-social system, the capitalistic society. Weber realized that the capitalistic activity that maintained this system was symbolic as well as technical, that it was a *ritual*, an ascetic discipline which properly expressed the underlying *Geist*. In analyzing the Protestant Ethic and the Spirit of Capitalism, Weber synthesized into a single framework the spiritual and technical perspectives on human behavior.

Weber agreed with Marx that once capitalism got going, it was self-sustaining; he called it an 'iron cage' from which society could not escape. But he challenged Marx in arguing that the genesis of capitalism depended on such non-economic factors as religion. He opened his argument by taking note of statistical correlations between Protestantism and capitalistic-oriented education in Germany, but his central stress was on the logical similarity of the values underlying Protestantism and those underlying capitalism. He regarded this logico-meaningful correspondence as too strong to be accidental, and he considered, but rejected, the possibility that capitalism developed first, after which the capitalists created Protestantism in order to give religious justification to their activity. Weber concluded that the Protestant Ethic developed first, motivated by theological dilemmas which prompted the faithful to define new paths toward salvation. Through its own dynamics, the symbol system was transformed, and it then assumed a critical role in the transformation of the techno-social system.

Much controversy has surrounded the Weberian thesis that Calvinism fostered capitalism. Though some of the criticisms are legitimate, many of the most popular ones misrepresent Weber's views.[8] Summarizing several of the simplest and most popular criticisms of this type, I cite first each criticism (C), and then an answer to it (A):

(C) Weber is wrong since many successful capitalists today are not Calvinist.

(A) Weber explicitly denied that Calvinism is necessary for capitalism today. Instead, he argued that Calvinism helped inspire the creation of the *first* capitalistic societies. (Also several studies suggest that, in spite of the numerous exceptions, an overall trend can still be seen for the most capitalistic nations and individuals to be Protestant).

(C) Weber is wrong since even in earlier times, many successful capitalists (for example, the great merchants of Italy) were not Calvinist.

(A) Weber recognized the achievements of these individual capitalists, but his argument was not that Calvinism was required to spur each individual to capitalistic feats; instead, he felt that Calvinism was the revolutionary force required to drive entire societies to reject traditionalistic values and modes of organization, replacing these with values and organizations harnessed to the practice of capitalism. In Weber's view the difference between traditional and capitalistic societies was qualitative, not quantitative. Numerous great merchants may have been present in pre-capitalistic societies, but they had to work against the grain of the social order. In the capitalistic societies, law, government, education, science, labor and, indeed, the culture as a whole, were organized so as to facilitate capitalism.

(C) Weber is wrong, since before Calvinism entire societies (e.g. medieval Italy and Flanders) practiced capitalism on a grand scale.

(A) The reader must decide for himself by examining the historical record whether such societies really fit Weber's conception of a society organized around rational, ascetic, bourgeois, bureaucratic capitalism. Weber's own verdict was that they did not.

Weber is frequently misconceived as arguing that Calvinistic doctrine fostered capitalism because it approved it, while Catholic doctrine disapproved. The linkage Weber postulated between the symbolic and technical orders was not nearly so simple as this. He did not believe that religion commanded 'Thou shalt', or 'Thou shalt not', and the businessman simply obeyed. Weber went to great pains to show that Calvinist preachers explicitly spoke against the pursuit of wealth, and he states that Puritan writings did so much more frequently than did late medieval religious literature. He speaks of the 'undoubted capitalistic backwardness' of the preaching of Calvinistic preachers such as Baxter. Critics such as Samuelsson, who triumphantly display the 'anti-capitalist' preachings of Calvin, Baxter, Wesley, and Penn in order to argue that Weber was wrong in claiming that Calvinism approved capitalism, have simply failed to read Weber or to appreciate his psychology. Weber argued that, in spite of its explicit disapproval of capitalism, the powerful theological dilemmas posed by later Calvinism created a 'mood' (*Stimmung*) and a 'peculiar atmosphere' (*eigentümliche Luft*) which incited an 'impulse' (*Antrieb*) to go out and do capitalism .The result was an *unintended* affluence, which Weber contrasts with the relative poverty flowing from certain religions that explicitly favored the pursuit of material comfort.

Lest it be thought that Weber postulated a one-way direction in the interplay between religion and economics, it should be noted that in writings other than *The Protestant Ethic and the Spirit of Capitalism*, Weber analyzed socioeconomic influences on religion. Thus, he postulates that urbanization and commercialization encourage a Protestant-like ethic. Commerce and industry require calculation of means in relation to ends to an extent greater than is true of traditional farming. Before the day of mechanization and flood control, natural forces played a strong part in agriculture, rendering abstract planning more difficult than in commerce, which is alienated from nature in that it is practiced year 'round and indoors. The merchant's and artisan's conditions of work encourage him to develop or accept a doctrine that salvation depends on calculation and planning. Merchants and artisans should also find the notion of payment or punishment for virtue or sin compatible with their experience, for they are accustomed to work for direct recompense. The means of livelihood of lord and peasant discourage these ways of thinking, for they live by neither work nor planning but by either oppression or submission. As a result, they have not, in most of world history, rivalled the urban middle class in piety or ethical systematization. Instead, they typically worship gods notable for their cunning or daring.[9] Weber's 'existential psychologizing' (generalizing from socioeconomic situation to probable psychological response) is more abstract than his specific argument regarding Protestantism and capitalism, but it demonstrates his awareness of multiple directions of influence.

Because *The Protestant Ethic and the Spirit of Capitalism* is published in English translation as a separate volume, many English-speaking readers and most of Weber's critics treat it as a unit in itself, failing to realize that it was merely a section in his much broader comparative study of the sociology of religion.[10] In Weber's comparative study, he moved from similarity to difference, attempting to show that in China and India, capitalism did *not* flourish in periods when material conditions were quite favorable for it, that the missing element was the Protestant Ethic, and that indigenous religious ethics stifled the rise of capitalism.

From the standpoint of neatness in experimental design, the ideal method would have been to discover societies which resembled the West in all respects save the religious, and which, lacking this crucial element, failed to develop capitalism. Unfortunately, the major Asian civilizations differed in their total configuration from the West, and Weber's task became the larger one of setting forth the major goals and premises of Hinduistic, Buddhist, and Confucianist culture, then linking these configurations to the total structure of Indian and Chinese society. This tack did not merely deviate from experimental methodology, but it fulfilled Weber's ultimate purpose of demonstrating the distinctiveness of Western civilization, in economic, social, and psycho-cultural facets, by comparing its entire configuration with that of Asia. As part of his study, he shows that capitalism was not as compatible with the civilization of traditional Asia as with that of the post-reformation West.

Religion and Society in China and India[11]

China

In its strongly familistic orientation, traditional China contrasts strikingly with Western society. The patrilineal exogamous clan, broadly coterminous with the local village community, is the basic unit of Chinese society. The principles of parental authority and filial piety are very strict, and women are subordinate within the patrilineal, patrilocal complex.

Outside the family, traditional Chinese society was open. There was no caste system as in India or Japan. Regardless of origin, a man was ideally free to enter any occupation: occupational mobility in China certainly equalled that of the feudal West.

Government in China was intertwined with the religion of the elite, though separate from the religions of the people (by comparison with the West, where religion and state were separate but elite and masses shared the one religion of Christianity). In the state cult, the emperor was the 'Son of Heaven', the principle intermediary between the divine order and human society. He alone was entitled to offer sacrifices to heaven, and disorder could be blamed on his ritual failure.

Though the emperor was at the center of the state, he was not surrounded by an hereditary priesthood as in other archaic societies. Instead, under the emperor was a special class of bureaucratic administrators, the mandarins. Their training was literary and they gained entry into the bureaucracy by passing a series of examinations which tested their knowledge of the classics. Favoritism was confined primarily to selection from those who had passed the examination.

The principle of bureaucratic impartiality was carried through to an impressive degree. An official could not be stationed in a province where his patri-clan lived, and his term in a given office was restricted to three years in order to prevent the creation of local ties that would encourage favoritism. In early periods of Chinese history there were princes of domains, who had codes of chivalry much like those of the knights of medieval Europe, but no feudal families were able to appropriate as their personal property any segment of the bureaucracy, and appointment of local officials depended on central authorities.

Because the mandarins were, considering the vast area they had
to administer, few in number, the bureaucracy did not penetrate
deeply into local communities. Between the kinship unit and the
central government there existed considerable freedom for the
development of groups independent of either bureaucracy or clan,
and there did indeed develop strong craft guilds. In spite of these
and China's impressive array of technological inventions, nothing
on the order of the Western industrial capitalistic organizations
emerged in traditional China, and industry remained largely on a
handicraft basis.

Remarkably early in history, then, China achieved conditions
that would seem, at first glance, to encourage the development of
capitalism: a society relatively open to individual mobility and
the formation of new organizations, bolstered by a rationalized
bureaucracy that maintained peace over an almost unprecedented
period of time and expanse of space. Nevertheless, these factors
did not, in Weber's opinion, overcome the obstacles imposed
by the patrimonial state and the extended family, institutions
reinforced by the Chinese consciousness, which Weber characterized as the ethic of the literati, centrally inspired by Confucianism.

The central notion of Confucianism was order. The social order
mirrors the cosmic. To live in accord with both was the object of
the educated man. The Confucian gentleman, the Mandarin
bureaucrat, should avoid the lack of propriety that comes with
loss of self control and the expression of passion. He must be polite
and refined, properly observing the proprieties of each situation.
He is obligated to maintain harmony with those persons to whom
he has particular relationships, such as kinsmen or subjects, but he
is not, like the Calvinist, obligated to show concern for the entire
society, to act as his brother's keeper, or to 'love thine enemy as
thyself'. He is a cultured man rather than a functionary, he is no
instrument of God or anyone else, but a perfected being who 'does
not implement anything'. He should not become overly involved
in economic affairs, for such work violates his station and his
ethos: as Confucius says, 'the educated man must stay away from
the pursuit of wealth, though not from wealth itself, because
acquisitiveness is a source of social and personal unrest'.

The cosmic-social order with which the gentleman sought to live
in harmony was most concretely the state, and ritual was among

the duties of public office. The Confucian should accept these duties as sacred. He should not reform them, neither need he justify them ethically or theologically. The ideals of the social order were embodied in the classics which, like the state rituals, were sacred and unchangeable. The cultivated gentleman should not indulge in magic and superstition, but such habits were regarded as given in the lives of the masses, and the Confucian, unlike the Calvinist, was not exhorted to drive them out.

In sum, the rationalism of Confucianism was worldly: the Confucian should accept the order of the world, whether manifested in the state, the classics, or ritual. The world was given, a good and orderly place; the gentleman need not reform the world in the name of some abstract and otherworldly ideal. The Calvinist ethic was revolutionary in that it instructed the believer to transform the world in the image of transcendant ideal, the Kingdom of God. To the Calvinist, filial piety would be idolatry, ritual an impious superstition; both must be purged. Confucianism sanctified tradition, Calvinism relentlessly destroyed it.

India

If the most striking social feature of China was the clan, that of India was the caste. Castes are rigidly endogamous (in-marrying) localized groups in which membership is hereditary. Each caste has a governing council, and they are categorized into supra-local strata, such as the Brahmin (priests), Ksatriya (warriors and statesmen), and Shudra (artisans). Whether local or supra-local, each caste is associated with a particular occupation.

The most important factor dividing the castes is an extraordinarily complex and rigid set of rules and rituals that prevent pollution of upper by lower through prohibiting their contact and commensality. Brahmins will not take food from lower castes, but any caste will accept food from the Brahmins, and similar rules cover inter-marriage. The extreme Indian emphasis on ritual purity has permitted the Brahmins to maintain their elevated position through centuries; their high rank is quite extraordinary since they are not particularly wealthy or powerful, and they have not organized themselves into a religious association such as a church.

The Indian caste system is supported by what Weber has termed the most conservative ideology in history. Each caste has its *dharma*—duties appropriate to its own station and unique to it.

('In principle there could be a vocational *dharma* for prostitutes, robbers, and thieves as well as for Brahmins and kings.').[12] Loyalty to the dharma is insured by the doctrine of *karma*. Karma postulates that each act has permanent effects on the fate of the soul. According to whether one does good or bad acts, one is reborn in a higher or lower caste in the next life. Excessive evil may even result in rebirth as an animal, and among the sins is violation of the dharma by moving out of one's caste altogether. The dharma/karma ideology blocks social mobility.

Only through the twin paths of asceticism and mysticism could the Indian escape the cycle of rebirth. When the Brahmin is still young, he is encouraged to study with a guru, a teacher whom he venerates even more than his own father. Here, in a remote retreat, a small group of noble youths would study autohypnotic practices such as temporarily ceasing to breathe in order to be more receptive to God. In later life, the Brahmin could hope to achieve the ideal of withdrawing from the world after seeing the son of his son. Through ascetic meditation, the adept can ultimately escape the wheel of rebirth and achieve Nirvana, a fusion with the ultimate stream of the universe. Weber contrasts the Indian asceticism with that of Calvinism, terming the former 'other worldly' and the latter 'inner worldly': the purpose of Calvinistic asceticism is to hone the body into a sharper tool so that it can be more efficiently used by God for his action in this world, while Indian asceticism aims merely to deny the flesh in order to prepare the spirit for escape into the otherworld.

The ethic of the caste system, embodied in Hinduism, and mysticism/asceticism, most fully elaborated in Buddhism, are logically opposed. The first advocates complete conformity to the established social order, the other radical withdrawal from it. Yet the two stances can unite, as is illustrated by the Bhagavad Gita, a scene in the Mahabharata epic. The hero, Ardjuna, and his divine charioteer, Krishna, are engaged in a dialogue. Ardjuna expresses his unwillingness to kill his kinsmen in battle, but Krishna advises him that he has no choice but to do so since, as a Ksatriya, he must conform to the dharma of the warrior. His only solution is to abandon all desire for the fruits of his action, and in this way remain mentally detached even while fighting. He conforms to the objective ethic while maintaining subjective peace.

Put tersely, Weber sees Asian religion as dominated by two

streams exemplified in the Bhagavad Gita: the desire for mystical withdrawal from the world (as in Taoism, Buddhism, and Hindu Yoga) and the obligation of ritualistic conformity to it (as in the Confucian doctrine of the gentleman's obligation to the government and the Hindu concepts of obedience to dharma). Neither ethic drove the individual to change the world through elaboration of a universalistic and transcendent system in terms of which it could be made over. The seeds of this worldview were sown, in Weber's view, by the prophets of ancient Judea.

The Hebrew Prophets[13]

Beginning with Elijah in the eleventh century BC, the prophets of ancient Judaism began to receive commandments from the voice of God. These messages inspired the prophets to militantly exhort the people to change. Extolling the glories of the Judaic confederacy of the past, they prophesied doom in the future if current abuses continued. Receiving the message in solitude while given to fits, trembling, and hallucination, the prophets were stormy, tortured, and tragic figures, with whom the troubled Weber himself identified. They felt their calling a burdensome vocation, he wrote, and none of them enjoyed the

> tranquil, blissful euphoria of the god-possessed, rarely the expression of a devotional communion with God and nowhere the merciful pitying sentiment of brotherhood with all the creatures typical of the mystic. The god of the prophets lived, ruled, spoke, acted in a pitiless world of war and the prophets knew themselves placed in the midst of a tragic age.[14]

Weber recognized the traditionalistic legalism of Judaic society, but he believed that the Judaic prophets, inspired by transcendental elements in Judaic religion and the harsh sufferings of the Jewish people, created the religious basis for an ascetic rationalism which would later find expression in the reformation and in Puritanism.

The prophets looked to the future rather than the past, by comparison with the Asian religions which stressed conformity to dharma and worship of ancestors or some other eternal order. The prophetic tradition assumed that the world of men is historical, that in time it will be replaced by an entirely different world of God. With the coming of paradise, the sinful will meet their doom, but the faithful remnant will receive their just rewards.

Innerworldly (*innerweltliche*) or, more simply, worldly asceticism was characteristic of the prophets, by contrasting to the otherworldly (*weltablehrende*) asceticism of the Asians. The Jews believed that man is God's instrument by which He accomplishes His design in this world. Though working in the world, the faithful must avoid succumbing to worldly temptations, for these distract from single-minded obedience to God. The Jew must also reject the otherworldly asceticism, an emptying of the self of the mundane in order to achieve emotional ecstasy. When an otherworldly ascetic turns to prophecy, wrote Weber, he becomes a guru or a millenarian, gathering his pupils into a retreat or awaiting the millennium. The worldly ascetic becomes a revolutionary reformer.

Unlike the Brahmin priest or the mandarin official, the Judaic prophet did not enjoy established status or bureaucratic authority. He spoke directly from God, he led the people through his personal, heroic charisma, and he justified his exhortation by claiming a special mission, a calling. He provided a model for the Protestant reformer who, centuries later, would oppose the traditions and kingdoms of Europe by claiming a calling to save the sinful children of the world.

Neither Hinduism nor Confucianism conceived of radical sin, as in the Fall of Adam and Eve. Nor did they conceive an agent of radical evil, such as the Christian devil, or a radical punishment of evil, such as the judgment day when all sinners suffer total and eternal damnation. In Asian religions, specific errors would be greeted with specific disadvantages, but the punishment was not total or eternal: no reincarnation is forever. Sin for the Jew, as for the Christian, was the violation of a totalistic and rationalized scheme that derived from one God, to whom obedience must be absolute and unceasing. Punishment was equally absolute.

Summarizing Weber's view of the prophets, Reinhard Bendix writes

Free of magic and esoteric speculations, devoted to the study of the law, vigilant in the effort to 'do what was right in the eyes of the Lord' in the hope of a better future, the prophets established

D

a religion of faith that subjected man's daily life to the imperatives of a divinely ordained moral law. In this way ancient Judaism helped create the moral rationalism of Western civilisation.[15]

In sum, Weber's thesis was that Protestantism, rooted in the prophetic tradition of Judaism, saw a stark hiatus between the ideal and the actual, the Kingdom of God and the Kingdom of Man, and the drive to actualize this ideal incited reform, change, and the 'rationalized' way of life embodied in the Protestant Ethic and the Spirit of Capitalism. Asian religion did not, in Weber's opinion, motivate reform, rationalization, and modernization. Instead, it served either to sanctify the traditional order or to provide mystical and ascetic escape from it.

Neo-Weberians: The Collectivist Perspective

During the postwar years, a number of social scientists have discovered in Weber's perspective powerful resources for the understanding of societies that did not come into Weber's ken or were marginal to his concerns. Running through these neo-Weberian studies is one strikingly pervasive theme: religious modernization is as much involved with collective processes, with social and political structures, as with the rationalization of the life style and *Geist* of the individual. Selecting a cross-section of neo-Weberian studies to illustrate this theme, I consider a theory that the Reformation itself is rooted in political organization; that Asian religions do engender modernity in its collective aspects; that the ideologies of the New Nations are analogous to the Protestant Ethic except that they serve not so much to transform the individual conscience as to mobilize collective sentiments.

Roots of the Reformation

Paying little attention to the origins of the Protestant Reformation, Weber was much more concerned with the consequences. Among the theories that do attack the question or origins, probably the most ingenious is that of Guy Swanson.[16] Swanson argues that whether a community became Protestant or remained Catholic during the early phases of the Reformation depended on its political experience which, in turn, influenced its religious dispositions.

Swanson's central idea is 'immanence'. Immanence he defines as the embodiment of the spiritual in the material. Thus, for a Catholic, God is present ('immanent') in the wine and the wafer, and He is embodied in the visible church as the body of Christ. For the Protestant (except for Lutherans), neither the church nor the sacrament *is* God, though they symbolize His spirit. According to Swanson, Catholic doctrine places greater emphasis on immanence than does the Protestant: for the Catholic the spiritual *is* the material, instead of merely standing for it. One is reminded of Durkheim's Bororo who supposedly felt he *was* the totem, the parrot. As Swanson notes, Weber believed that a crucial difference between Catholics and Protestants was their belief in immanence. More generally, Weber saw modernization as a process of declining belief in immanence, as the symbolic separated from the social.

Political as well as religious systems vary in degree of immanence. In an absolute monarchy, the king's wish was the people's command; no opposing political bodies competed with him. In a federal government, any wish is translated into action only through a complex process such that legislation is always a compromise between the will of the leaders and that of the constituencies that elect them. Swanson considers immanence to be greater in the monarchy than the federation since the monarch's wish, his 'spirit', is closer to the material implementation.

Earlier cross-cultural researches by Swanson had led him to believe that experience with politics determines religious belief, specifically belief in immanence.[17] With these studies in mind, he formulated the following hypotheses concerning the Reformation: first, that Protestantism was more likely to replace Catholicism in early modern Europe when political immanence was less, and, secondly, that if Protestantism was adopted, it would more likely be Calvinistic than Lutheran or Anglican if political immanence were less. In sum: religious immanence varies with political immanence. One could hardly ask for a more Durkheimian Weberianism, since here the social order is considered to determine the symbolic order, but in the specific sense that the amount of discrepancy between social and symbolic order in the political sphere determines the amount in the religious sphere.

In order to test his theory, Swanson examined the central government of every major sovereign society of Europe that had been Catholic until AD 1500. He categorized these regimes as follows:

Commensal The regimes lack a central figurehead, and individuals who exercise power do so only as representatives of the group of all politically enfranchised people as a whole, i.e., they do not represent special interests. In the Swiss canton of Glarus, for example, all adult males met once per year and were responsible for passing laws, levying taxes, formulating foreign policy, and electing a council to carry out its decisions. In addition to Glarus, Swanson classifies as 'commensual' Poland, Venice, Florence, and the Swiss cantons of Appenzell, Schwyz, Unterwalden, Uri, Zug, and Fribourg.

Centralist All legitimate power stems from the government (defined as a single individual or a small group whose membership does not exceed ten percent of the population). Countries with regimes of this type prior to the Reformation include Austria, France, Bavaria, the Rhenish dynasties of Jülich and Berg, Ireland, Scotland (Highlands), Portugal, Spain, and the Swiss cantons of Lucerne and Solothurn.

Limited centralist The central government has sole authority to determine policy, but its power in administering that policy is shared with local authorities. Officers of the regime boast no independent power to determine formal policy, nor do they have a role in choosing the polity's leader. They do, however, have considerable discretionary power in the administration of policy. Countries characterized by limited centralist regimes include Denmark, England, Saxony, Württemburg, Brandenburg, Prussia, Hesse, and Sweden.

Balanced The ruler shares his power with constituent bodies (e.g., a parliament or a diet). Instances of balanced regimes include Bohemia, Cleves, Mark, Hungary, Transylvania, Scotland (Lowlands), and Geneva.

Heterarchic Representatives of constituent bodies determine policy and exercise power. Heterarchic regimes include those of Zurich, Basel, Schaffhausen, Bern, and the United Provinces.

According to Swanson, all heterarchic or balanced societies became Calvinist, the most anti-immanent of the Protestant faiths. All limited centralist societies became Lutheran except England, which became Anglican—Lutheranism and Anglicanism being generally the most 'immanent' of the Protestants. All centralist societies remained Catholic, as did all commensal societies except Appenzell and Glarus. In short, the less immanent the polity, the less immanent the religion.

Swanson believes that his theory explains the rise of Protestantism better than do the standard explanations, which include the rise of humanism (nowhere greater than in Rome) and of commerce (greater in Catholic than in Protestant countries prior to the Reformation). Reinterpreting the Weber thesis, Swanson suggests that both religious reformation and economic rationalization expressed the attitude of anti-immanence, which in turn derived from a distinctive type of political experience.

Buddhism outside India

Some of the most suggestive neo-Weberian scholarship has concerned the Buddhist-influenced countries outside India. Revealing a modernizing potential neglected by Weber's analysis of Buddhism in India, all of these studies focus on collective processes.

Robert Bellah has dealt with the strategic case of Japan, a Buddhist-influenced nation which has managed one of the most remarkable economic and social transformations in history.[18] Bellah concludes that a complex of values rooted in a syncretic Buddhist-Confucian-Shinto religion of the Tokugawa period was harnessed in the service of modernization. All of these religious ethics converged to emphasize loyalty to the superior, be he lord, emperor, or industrial boss. In the extreme instance, devotion to the superior became a mystical union which rivalled the otherworldly salvation of Calvinism in motivating relentlessly rationalized and ascetic labor. At the end of the Tokugawa period, the Japanese government exploited this loyalty ethos to develop a national cult where worship of the emperor was through devoted work—certainly one factor in Japan's remarkable economic surge.

Theravada Buddhists of Thailand make a very different type of linkage between Buddhist religion and economics. According to A. T. Kirsch,[19] the Thai Buddhist is strongly concerned with 'making merit'. By meritorious acts, the Thai bids to set in motion processes within the universe that permit him rebirth in the next life into a status higher than his status in this life. Ultimately he can even attain Nirvana, release from the cycle of death and rebirth. The best way to make merit is to become a monk, which is a very exalted status in Thailand, ranked in many respects even above the position of king. Being a monk is, however, difficult. Monkhood demands abstention from food, sex, and other worldly pleasures. For that reason, many men remain laymen. These laymen make merit in the second best way: joining the civil service. To serve the king is to serve the Buddha, for the king is Defender of the Faith in the Buddhist State of Thailand. The worst way to make merit is to enter business, for business is materialistic and worldly, hence sinful in the eyes of Buddhists. Few men take this route, but many women do. The reason, Kirsch suggests, is that women are regarded as so worldly anyway, by virtue of their babies, cooking, and other material concerns, that they cannot make much merit no matter what they do. They might as well go into business. Unlike Calvinism or Tokugawa religion, Theravada Buddhism does not encourage capitalism, and most Thai who are capitalists —the women—are such by default.

What Weber's individualistic-oriented analysis did not predict, however, is that Theravada Buddhism will encourage governmental service. Within the governmental, as opposed to private sphere, Buddhism could conceivably inspire development and change. Ames, studying Theravada Buddhism in Ceylon, concludes that this is precisely what is happening there; recent religious changes unite Buddhism and politics 'thus raising material and mundane ends of economic development . . . to the level of the sacred, by making allegiance to civil authority a question of religious morality'.[20]

Generalizing from studies like these, Bellah has proposed in his 'Reflections on the Protestant Ethic Analogy in Asia',[21] that Weber's insights be generalized within the Asian context to elucidate not merely the personal and economic implications of religion, but deep-seated changes religion can bring in the structure of society and government. Interestingly, this collectivist perspective on Asia has inspired at least one new look at the Weber thesis in Europe. W. F. Wertheim, in a volume devoted to comparisons of the East and West,[22] suggests that bureaucrats rather than businessmen were responsible for the economic rise of the Netherlands during the age of exploration. Wertheim argues that it was rational and efficient bureaucrats associated with the Dutch ports who were responsible for the florescence of sea trade and colonialism in the Netherlands. Wertheim suggests, too, that the religion of these

bureaucrats was not Calvinism, but another Protestant sect, Armin-
ianism, the ethic of which inspired their bureaucratic efficiency
just as Calvinism bolstered capitalism.

Political Religion
The logical extension of the collectivist neo-Weberian perspective
is past the realm of conventional religion and into the domain of
symbols which are directly harnessed to political processes. In an
analysis indirectly indebted to Weber, David Apter theorizes about
the role of such 'political religions' in the new nations that have
gained independence after the Second World War.[23]

A political religion is a system of politically oriented symbols
which resembles conventional religion in that it promises immortality, provides a sense of identity, and defines meaningful purposes. Conventional religion promises salvation in the next world;
political religion promises a this-worldly salvation, a secure social
future rooted solidly in the nation's proud social past. Conventional religion gives a sense of place in a cosmos; political religion
provides a sense of identity with mighty social forces. Conventional
religion defines such exalted purposes as salvation; political
religion defines similarly exalted, though worldly purposes, thus
creating what Apter terms 'political puritanism'; the individual feels purified as he disciplines himself to postpone immediate pleasures in order to efficiently struggle toward the future
utopia.

In the new nations, political religion is associated with a 'mobilization system', which Apter distinguishes from the 'reconciliation
system' typical of Western societies. The reconciliation system is
grounded in conventional religion, but separates state from church
and laws from men. As a result, government is stripped of religious
and personal overtones. This situation, combined with the decline
in conventional religion, can leave the citizenry emotionally
starved, but it encourages the free operation of the private capitalism. Apter regards the reconciliation system as optimal for well-
established, highly complex, industrial societies.

The mobilization system merges charismatic personalities, ideology, and government, rooting politics in transcendental symbolism
able to inspire struggle in the collective sphere as surely as the Protestant Ethic once encouraged work in the private sector. Apter
asserts that 'the most effective ideologies of modernization ... have

been the Protestantism of Calvin and Marxism'.[24] He considers the mobilization system optimal for societies on the verge of industrialization.

Mobilization systems characteristically have a single 'party of solidarity' which helps to generate power through unifying the various factions. The party is composed of three elements: a militant vanguard, which is an instrument of the founder or leader; a set of functional auxiliaries such as trade unions, youth organizations, and agricultural cooperatives; and a geographically organized general membership. The founder is charismatic, and the party, inextricably linked with his life and consciousness, may even bear his name.

Utopian ideology and a sense of urgency encourages central planning oriented toward radical reform. In the mobilization system, action is necessary, passivity suspect, and all of life is politicized. In the end, the state has primacy over everything. Political entrepreneurs rather than businessmen are the dominant figures, for the state accepts the burden of economic development. Key careers are in the party and the bureaucracy.

The youth and the army are crucial to the mobilization system. The youth are vulnerable emotionally, caught up in dreams of the future and holding little allegiance to the past. Possessing little property, family, or occupational commitments to divide their interests, the youths stress solidarity, and they scorn the egoism, pettiness, and opportunism of their elders. Bound to the youth through paramilitary organizations, the army, boasting weapons, uniforms, and parades, is less an instrument of war than an inspiring symbol of the new order.

By its very structure, the mobilization system is necessarily subject to destructive forces. In order to get enough done to remain in power, the mobilization system must merge ideals with techniques. Moral metaphors must be translated into laws, regulations, office buildings, and party organizers. The Great Society becomes the back room and red tape. With less idealism, there is more opportunism. With more opportunism, there is less moral excitement. With less moral excitement, the state must coerce. With coercion, political religion begins to lose its charisma. The youths are the first to feel disaffection.

This depressing socio-symbolic dialectic is reinforced by organizational difficulties. Even youthful leaders grow conservative and coercive as they stay in power, and this process disillusions each new generation. Another problem is the party of solidarity which breeds factionalism, intrigue, and purge. Energies turn inward to party affairs, away from the needs of outlying communities. With the decline in both government and party, there is less achievement of announced economic goals. With the failure to achieve goals, the people become cynical and disloyal. The government must become increasingly coercive to remain in power. Coercion diverts resources from development to pay the added military cost. Mobilization systems reach their maximum capacities quickly. Their best use is to mobilize energies for rapid change. In later phases, they tend to transform themselves into more stable types such as the reconciliation system. As Weber put it, in a theory much like Apter's, the charisma becomes routinized.

The Weberian and Neo-Weberian Perspective on Symbolic and Social Modernization

Weber's studies of Protestantism, Hinduism, Buddhism, Judaism, Confucianism, and Taoism were published as sections in his *Gesammelte Aufsätze zur Religionssoziologie*. The closest that Weber came to a synthesis of themes underlying these comparative studies appears in an unfinished essay known as *Religionssoziologie* (Sociology of Religion) composed as a portion of a tome entitled *Wirtschaft und Gesellschaft* (Economy and Society). A summary of the central argument of this synthesis suggests the evolutionary direction that Weber saw religion taking and the place in his evolutionary framework occupied by the various religions that we have considered so far.[25] We can then proceed to take note of the contribution of the Neo-Weberians and to suggest some additional elements which could usefully enrich the Weberian perspective.

For Weber, the dominant process in the evolution from primitive to modern religion is 'rationalization'. Rationalization begins as soon as primitive man perceives the homologous type of symbolic-social relationship postulated by the Durkheimians; as soon as he recognizes the dualism between the ordinary and the sacred, *mana*-filled, extraordinary aspect of existence, the primitive comes to see the ordinary as symbolizing the extraordinary: a tree has mana, a ritual expresses the mythic order, a totem reflects a cosmology. In highly traditional society, which includes not only Durkheim's 'primitive' type but also layers within the great civilizations of India and China, the sacred order is regarded as static; accordingly, that which symbolizes the sacred is a stereotyped and rigid ritual. The slightest ritual departure from the fixed pattern has terrible consequences or loses efficacy.

Once men perceive profane acts and objects as symbolic of sacred realms, they become increasingly preoccupied with the question of the meaning of these acts and objects: what do they truly express? Specialized priesthoods systematize cosmologies and pantheons in order to explain the acts and the objects. But not all customary rites and taboos can be subsumed into a single coherent system, therefore custom must be rejected or modified. Each rejection and each modification forces the innovator to rationalize his scheme further, for he must now explain his innovation.

When the rationalizing innovator claims sacred authority for his reform, he becomes a prophet. Weber distinguishes two types: the ethical prophet (of the Judaic type, but also Jesus or Mohammed) and the exemplary type (Buddha). The ethical prophet believes himself an instrument of the divine will, called by God to bring in His name a command with which the people should comply as an ethical duty. The exemplary prophet simply shows the way through example. The ethical prophet creates revolution, the exemplary prophet, harmony. Both exhort disciples to adopt a more rationalized stance toward the world, to seek meaning rather than merely follow tradition. Both are necessarily in conflict with the world; in Weber's view no traditional order can be made to conform completely to the requirements of *any* fully rationalized conception of the meaning of the world.[26]

Since the world cannot be accepted, the prophetic movement must be either ascetic or mystical. The mystical type, exemplified by the Buddhist, rejects worldly things and embraces the transcendent as embodied within the self. The ascetic type, who derives from the Judaic prophetic tradition and is exemplified by the Calvinist-capitalist, neither withdraws from the world nor succumbs to its temptations, but instead struggles to master it. His method, like his theology, is highly rationalized (in Weber's sense of *Zweckrational*, efficient linking of means to ends). Thus proceeds the process of rationalization, relentlessly innovative in the interest of both efficiency and logical conformity of practice to ideal.

This paradigm, which summarizes much of the framework in terms which Weber conceived his comparative studies, is cast from the viewpoint of the individual actor. As the actor increasingly rationalizes existence, he shifts from primitive to priest to prophet to mystic and ascetic Calvinist-capitalist. The Neo-Weberians break out of this individualistic frame. They Durkheimize Weber, a tendency derived, perhaps, from the fact that many of them were heavily influenced by Talcott Parsons, who endeavored to synthesize the orientations of these two seminal figures.[27] Durkheimizing Weber, the neo-Weberians emphasize the collectivity as the agency through which a rationalization must proceed. The explanation for this neo-Weberian viewpoint must be sought both in theoretical trends (exemplified by the sociologists' Durkheimization of Weber and by the psychologists' socializing of Freud) and in history: modernization outside the West has been collectivized, and theory must adapt to fact.

The collectivization of Weber suggests a radicalization as well. Weber balanced Marx not only in recognizing the power of the *Geist*, but also in stressing those aspects of modernization which the liberal would deem positive: increased efficiency, industrialization, and rationalization of life. Marxism and radicalism stress instead that alienation and exploitation flow from modernization in its capitalistic phase. Weber was intensely aware of these noxious consequences and he was pessimistic about the future of modern society (he predicted, before his death in 1920, the rise of a fascist-like movement in reaction to German over-rationalization). Nevertheless, a balanced perspective would have to give more recognition to these unpleasant aspects of modernization than either Weber or the neo-Weberians include in their sociology of religion.

Such a theory would have to recognize that the modernization and the rationalization of life disproportionately benefit certain classes, such as the entrepreneurial (in the individualistic type of modernization in early modern Europe and America) and the bureaucratic (in the East European, Russian, Chinese, Latin American, and New Nations),[28] that modernization exploits the proletariat and disrupts the peasantry, and that it leads to colonization of the weak by the strong. In terms of systems of consciousness, the result of these patterns is typically either a mass movement or personal disorientation. Oppression and fragmentation of life result in cargo cults, ghost dances, pursuit of the millennium, and peasant revolt. Psychiatric studies repeatedly show Indians, Asians, and others caught between indigenous and modernizing Western influences, the former represented by parents and community, the latter by some outside agency such as a school. The mental symptoms range from alcoholism and drug addiction to apathy and psychosis.[29]

Industrial capitalism pulls ever more people and institutions into its orbit. Governmental and educational institutions, social classes, and charitable agencies all are harnessed to the goals of capitalism and the welfare state. Depriving local communities of their autonomy and distinctiveness, centralization dehumanizes. As Durkheim so powerfully demonstrated, localized communities foster a firm awareness of traditions, beliefs, and symbols perpetuated by authentic ritual. With the loss of these localized and kinship-based institutions comes alienation, anomie, meaninglessness, and ultimately despair, violence, and destruction—unless society manages to reconstitute itself at a higher level.

What, in sum, is the thesis of Weber and the Weberians? Weber himself believed that a transcendental yet activist belief system like that of Calvinism was necessary to incite the painful break with tradition necessary for the modernization of the West. Because the Asian civilizations lacked such a belief system, they remained traditionalistic in spite of their marvelous complexity. The neo-Weberians qualify this conclusion by recognizing that Asian religions and non-Western ideologies do have modernizing potential, especially in the collective and political realms. The collectivism leads naturally to a more 'radical' and less 'liberal' perspective on modernization. The result may someday be a Weberian Marxism, or a Marxist Weberianism that gives full recognition to both the alienation and the creativity spawned by modernity.

Pondering the implications for symbols and consciousness, the reader may have been struck by a shift in focus associated with the passage from Durkheim to Weber. Durkheimianism kept its eyes on symbolic forms, such as rites, myths, and totems. From these, the Durkheimians infer underlying systems of consciousness. Weberianism bases itself less concretely on such forms, but moves directly to formulate such abstract and comprehensive systems of consciousness as the Protestant Ethic. Without denying the power of the Weberian abstraction, the next two chapters endeavor to enrich it through the study of these sensuous forms that emerge through modernization, both Oedipally rooted fantasy and in the arts.

Notes to Chapter 4

1. Some of the following contrasts are drawn from *Aron*, pp. 107–17.
2. This analysis is largely taken from *Parsons* (4), p. 475.
3. These facts on the life of Weber come from *Bendix*, the 'Introduction' to *Gerth and Mills*, and *Mitzman*, a Freudian analysis of Weber's life which contains much useful information together with some far-fetched interpretation.
4. In addition to *Weber* (3), this section has drawn some points from *Parsons* (4) and *Bendix*.
5. *Weber* (3), p. 6.
6. Ibid., pp. 117–18.
7. Ibid., p. 115.
8. Many of these criticisms are summarized in *Samuelsson*. See especially pp. 12 and 27–42. The defenses are elaborated in *Peacock* (3).
9. *Weber* (4).
10. This comparative study, originally published as *Gesammelte Aufsätze zur Religionssoziologie* has been translated as follows: a *section* of Vol. I as *Weber* (3) on Protestantism, an additional section of Vol. I as *Weber* (2) on China, Vol. II as *Weber* (5) on India, Vol. III as *Weber* (6) on Judaism. Additional essays from Vol. I are translated in *Gerth and Mills*. The most accessible German edition is *Winckelmann*, Vol. I, which includes all of Weber's writings relevant to the Protestant Ethic.
11. These summaries are drawn from *Weber* (2) and (5).
12. *Weber* (5), p. 144.
13. *Weber* (6).
14. Ibid., pp. 312–13.
15. *Bendix*, p. 256.
16. *Swanson* (2).
17. *Swanson* (1).
18. *Bellah* (1).
19. *Kirsch*. For an interesting comparison, see the seminal work by *Spiro*.
20. *Ames*, p. 70.
21. *Bellah* (2).
22. *Wertheim*, pp. 147–63.
23. *Apter*.
24. Ibid., p. 322.
25. *Weber* (4), pp. 1–59.
26. *Parsons* (4).
27. Ibid.
28. A useful typology documenting these types of modernization is *Eisenstadt* (1).
29. For a general bibliography of anthropological analysis of acculturation see *Keesing*. On peasant movements as a result of destructive force of foreign capitalism, see *Wolf*. On the psychopathology of acculturation, see *Wintrob*, *Graves*, and *Chance*.

5
Transition to Modernity

The Oedipal Aspect

*. . . instead of defining man as an animal rationale,
we should define him as an animal symbolicum*
Ernst Cassirer[1]

Weber gave little attention to Freud. He was a social scientist, not
a psychiatrist, and in any case he harbored doubts about both the
methodology and the morality of Freudianism.[2] Whatever the
reasons, Weber's analysis of modernization completely ignored the
'Oedipal' aspect, by which I mean the psychological dynamics
revolving around the relationship between parent and child,
especially father and son. Whether for good or for ill, precisely
this aspect has come to the fore in numerous American-based
postwar studies of the transition to modernity. These studies have
drawn on the talents of anthropologists, sociologists, psychoanalysts, psychologists, economists, and political scientists, to suggests a direction for the enrichment of the Weberian framework.

Few of these analysts have explicitly defined their task as
Weberian. Yet all are concerned with the relation of Oedipally-
rooted imagery and symbolism to those processes of history which
Weber sought to elucidate. Consider the themes of studies we shall
survey here. Psychoanalyst Erik Erikson explores the Oedipal
basis of that unique Protestant Ethic created by Martin Luther.
Psychologist David McClelland treats a pattern of fantasy which
he labels the 'achievement motive' and considers it at once parallel
to the Protestant Ethic and crucial in economic change. Anthropologists Anthony Wallace and Weston LaBarre investigate

Oedipally-rooted imagery of visions experienced by prophets in movements toward radical change. Sociologist Philip Slater's suggestive if speculative extrapolations from research on small groups hypothesize an Oedipally-grounded imagery that underlies both revolution and evolution toward modernity.

The Roots of the Reformation: Young Man Luther[3]

Erikson's Luther differs radically from Weber's Calvin, or better, Calvinism, since Weber focused on the movement rather than the man. Luther formulated no rationalized life plan through which to build anew the collective life or the individual life cycle. He built no Geneva or New England. After a brief, if decisive eruption, he became a fat, belching, constipated, middle-aged, bourgeois patriarch, who enjoyed the pleasures of food and domesticity and composed a hymn which expresses the rocklike sturdiness of pious conservatism: 'A mighty Fortress is our God, a bulwark never failing'.

Luther did, of course, rationalize Christianity in ways consonant with the Protestant Ethic. He dispensed with many of the ritualized and sacralized practices and institutions of pre-Reformation Catholicism, such as indulgences, the monastic life, and the priestly hierarchy. And, as Eric Erikson makes plain in his analysis of the 'The Meaning of "Meaning It"',[4] Luther cut the fluff of ceremonialism in order to say bluntly through the vernacular what was in his heart. Once the Reformation was under way, however, Luther became conservatively authoritarian. Luther believed that the laws of heaven and the laws of the earth are separate and distinct; therefore, the establishment is justified in crushing the unruly peasants through earthly force. This position was obviously less revolutionary than that of the Calvinist: the kingdom of man must be remade in the image of the Kingdom of God. It is in accord with Weber's opinion that Lutheranism is generally more traditionalistic than Calvinism.

For Erikson, Luther's contribution is not the Calvinist's streamlined rationalizing. Luther's calling was to do the 'dirty work' of dissecting the inner life, to confront the punishing conscience and corrosive guilt which crippled medieval man and which Erikson sees as derived from the authoritarian father, in Luther's case the bourgeois, ambitious, and possessive Hans Lueder. Luther's mother is virtually absent from Erikson's analysis, ostensibly because little is known of her (though we might note that Erikson's analyses of German character always focus on the father, whereas his studies of America star the 'mom'). Summarization is inadequate for an analysis as supple as Erikson's, but a sense of his insight comes from tracing, phase by phase, his perception of the unfolding of Luther's life. Previewing his analysis, Erikson states:

> We will therefore concentrate on this process: how young Martin, at the end of a somber and harsh childhood, was precipitated into a severe identity crisis for which he sought delay and cure in the silence of the monastery; how being silent, he became 'possessed'; how being able to speak, he not only talked himself out of the monastery, and much of his country out of the Roman Church, but also formulated for himself and for all of mankind a new kind of ethical and psychological awareness; and how, at the end, this awareness, too, was marred by a return of the demons, whoever they may have been.[5]

Erikson notes that Luther's father fits the classical psychoanalytical formulation which links suspiciousness, obsessive 'scrupulosity', and a preoccupation with dirtying and infectious thoughts and substances. Erikson hypothesizes that the devil and his association with feces and the recesses in which they originate all came to be associated in Martin's consciousness (or unconsciousness) as a 'common underground of magic danger'. He feels that these tendencies may have been encouraged by the experience of sleeping naked with his family, which led Martin to associate half-waking perceptions of sexual intercourse, birth, sickness, death, and the body with sinister dealing of the devil.

His father, Martin could not fully hate; and the father, though raging at the son, could not completely let him go. The father beat him self-righteously, and from the father, Erikson believes, Martin absorbed a sensitive, indeed morbid, conscience. Theologians helped, too, by teaching that man is inescapably sinful. As a pupil in an all-male school, Martin was taught by the endless 'drumming in' of knowledge by rote, and a pupil would be secretly appointed to keep a ledger of his fellow's 'sins', such as speaking German instead of Latin. Progressing diligently through the various educational levels, Martin entered a college in Erfurt at the age of seventeen, to be trained as an official in the medieval hierarchy. Erikson imagines that by this time Luther was 'a deep-down sad youth',[6] who did not permit himself the boisterous behavior of his peers, and who already felt compelled to account for his as yet untried life.

In 1505, just after he had graduated from the college and prior to his entry into the faculty of law, Martin was hiking back to school when a bolt of lightning struck near him, inciting him to call to none other than his father's saint, 'Help me, St. Anne . . . I want to become a monk.'[7] He then entered an Augustinian monastery, renouncing his obedience to his enraged father—whom he had cheated out of both a son and, through his celibacy, a grandson—in favor of his obedience to God.

Erikson regards this period as the beginning of Luther's 'moratorium', a time of isolation and neurotic suffering that the genius experiences prior to breaking through into creativity. Erikson compares Luther to Freud, both of whom endured such a period for some ten years before working through their crises to forge identities that would define a direction not only for themselves but for an epoch. Erikson sees Luther's particular moratorium as lasting from the age of twenty-two to thirty, a period of nervous disease and inhibition, followed by a manic productivity in his thirties, then severe breakdown in his forties. During the thunderstorm, Erikson notes, Luther claimed to feel 'walled in' and he literally walled himself up in the monastery. But eventually he was to break out.

'In the first year of the monastery', Luther remarked, 'the devil is very quiet.'[8] Erikson suggests that the monastic routine relieved Martin of the necessity for decisions concerning marriage and career that had tormented him just before he encountered the lightning bolt. Through communal confession, Luther could transform his lonely, personalized anxieties into a collective and militant repudiation of a well-defined enemy. As in other types of thought reform, the monastic life removes the person from family and community. Restricting sensory intake while magnifying the power of the word, the monastic life dims memory of personal past and enhances commitment to a transcendent ideal. The monastery is a natural breeding station for reformation.

The moratorium, at least in its benign aspect, ended when

Martin had to celebrate his first mass. His father, whom he now met for the first time since his seclusion, led a delegation of proud home town citizens to attend the ordination. Luther was obsessed with a feeling of his unworthiness to manifest God on earth, and he was disturbed by divided loyalties—toward the God above him and the father who sat in front of him as he prepared the Eucharist. His performance was hardly heroic. He suffered from an attack of anxiety and later spoke childishly to the father, asking 'winningly' whether his 'dear father' was not now proud of the son. The father responded to this entreaty with coarse and brutish fury, cursing the monks for their theft of his son.

Increasingly tormented by his yearning to gain justification, to feel legitimate in the eyes of God the Father, Luther came to neurotically exaggerate the mechanisms of atonement provided by the monastery. He would confess for hours but mistrust the forgiveness that was promised at the end. He finally rejected altogether the hope of achieving grace through works that were motivated by the desire for forgiveness, and he formulated the idea that one must first have faith in God's grace, then perform the works in gratitude.

Travelling to Rome, Luther was peculiarly oblivious to either the grandeur of the Vatican ceremonialism or the free spirit emerging with the Italian Renaissance. Erikson suggests that Luther's reformation resembled the Renaissance but was psychologically of a different order. The Renaissance freed the body and the senses to serve the mind, but it did not create for the ordinary man a 'sturdy style of life' or a 'new and workable morality'.[9] Through struggle with his conscience, Luther undertook the burden of this 'dirty work', thus contributing in his own earthy way to modernity. His methods were like those of the Renaissance: return to original texts, determined anthropocentrism, and affirmation of the vernacular.

Working through the scriptures while preparing theological lectures Luther pondered anxiously the question of justification. The break-through came, characteristically, as he was seated on the toilet; while he relieved his bowels he released his inner self. In Luther's new affirmation of the voice and the word as instruments of faith, his recognition of God's 'face' in the passion of Christ, and his redefinition of the just life, Erikson sees parallels to cures experienced by psychiatric patients. Permitting himself a certain resignation, Luther had allowed a theology to emerge from his soul, imbued with his inner emotions, and he could now mean what he preached. God, for him, was not external, but a force working inside. Work is good only if it is more than 'works', meaningful activity done with feeling instead of mechanical ritual.

At the age of thirty, Luther began lecturing on 'justification'. At thirty-four, he nailed the ninety-five theses on the door of the Castle Church in Wittenburg. By age forty-five, he had provoked a reformation and a revolution. Craving to speak to God 'directly and without embarrassment', he had, in God's name, opposed pope and emperor—both of which rebellious acts stemmed, in Erikson's analysis, from Luther's stormy relations with his father. Leaving the church, Luther married, an affirmation of virility which he publicly stated was performed 'to please my father'. The next year his wife bore him a son, named for his father, Hans.

At this point, Erikson believes, Luther developed a new source of ambivalence: the pope and the devil. A compulsive and anal defiance of both became a central theme in his emotions. At the same time, he cultivated a richly intimate style of life centered around the home and nursery, as he sought relief from the loneliness and isolation of a lifetime.

Summarizing the life of Luther in terms of his theory of crises, Erikson suggests that Luther's mother, obscure as she may have been, gave him sufficient 'basic trust' to sustain him through his first crisis, the oral period of early infancy: 'Nobody could speak and sing as Luther later did if his mother's voice had not sung to him of some heaven.'[10] The second crisis was, in Freudian terms, that of anality, and here Erikson believes that Luther was driven prematurely from his mother by the jealous and demanding Hans. Ever after Luther was nostalgic for the lost trust of early infancy, which he finally rediscovered through returning to faith from which all doubt is removed. The third crisis, the genital, posed the choice of 'initiative' versus 'guilt', and Luther, beat down by a punitive father, chose the latter, sadly envisioning a drab life of scholarly duty and eventually secluding himself in the moratorium of the monastery. The next stages, identity, intimacy, and generativity, were postponed until early after this moratorium. Now Luther could make his mark, marry, and procreate. The final stage, integrity, challenges the mature individual to consolidate the failures and successes of a lifetime. This crisis goaded Luther into a new phase of neurosis and, Erikson suggests, calls for a study of the aging Luther.

Erikson's analysis is speculative, based on skimpy data which the psychoanalyst frequently interprets not by demonstration of relationship but by assumption of relationship based on his wide experience with patients on the couch. The sympathetic reader is nevertheless left with a strong impression that the interplay between Hans Lueder and Martin Luther was, indeed, a major source of the extraordinary development of consciousness that culminated in the Reformation. An appropriate response to *Young Man Luther* is perhaps not an acidly analytical critique, but a suspension of disbelief sufficiently lengthy to permit us to explore the method, to think along with Erikson. As an example of this type of exercise, I shall attack the psychology of several of Luther's predecessors while armed with a few of the Eriksonian insights.

The figures of concern are mystic monks who were leaders of a movement known as the Gottesfreunde (Friends of God) in fourteenth century Germany: Meister Eckhart (1260-1327), Henry Suso (1300-1366), Rulman Merswin (1307-1382), and Johannes Tauler (1300-1361), this latter being recognized by Luther as a direct inspiration of his own thought.[11]

The Rhine Valley in which the movement centered was, during this period, a place of population growth, commercial development, and social change. German towns were emerging as centers of capitalism north of the Alps, and studies of such communities as Strasburg reveal that wealth was replacing birth as a means to social status. The feudal hierarchy was crumbling as a bourgeois society and culture rose in its place, and the hierarchical establishment was quite aware of the threat posed by the rise of the bourgeois style of life.

The Friends of God flourished in these same commercial towns. Though remaining formally within the church, they were regarded as threatening it through their mysticism: 'He who closed his eyes in pious meditation ... looked no more upon the stately building of the Church.'[12] The mystic monks were not persecuted like the later Protestants, but they were, to a degree, resisted, and the writings of the greatest of them, Meister Eckhart, were condemned at his death.

Sharing a commitment to a system of values which threatened

the medieval hierarchy, the mystics and the merchants were also thrown into association through their common residence in the towns. This was the point when Gottesfreunde mysticism began to flourish, its popularity among the burghers revealed by the spread or sermons in the German vernacular (Luther was not the first to preach in German): the sermons were transformed into manuals for devotion that were copied, recopied, edited, and passed from town to town. The mystics also served as confessors to the burghers, as in the relationship of the mystic Tauler to the merchant Merswin (the latter eventually shifting from the status of merchant to mystic, when he joined the Gottesfreunde). In sum, the merchants and mystics enjoyed a relationship, and reconstruction of admittedly skimpy evidence suggests some of the psychological aspects of this relation.

The simplest psychological service that the mystics may have rendered the merchants was religious approval of their nascent spirit of capitalism. Though the church did not roundly condemn commerce, it was negative toward many of its aspects, and some evidence can be found of the merchant's feeling guilty about his activities. One can imagine that he appreciated hearing from Eckhart his praise of commercial asceticism and enterprising spirit, and that he welcomed such remarks as Tauler's: 'Know that if I were not a priest . . . I would consider it great if I could make shoes!'[13]

More complex was the inspiration that, one may suspect, was given the merchants through the sermons, devotionals, and counseling of the mystic monks. The Friends of God taught that mysticism led toward rebirth and a spiritual growth, and Meister Eckhart endowed this process with Oedipal symbolism. Eckhart describes his spirit as leaving his earthly family and hurrying upward in the sky to join his father, God, whom he enters and becomes. But 'God is not sufficient for me', declares Eckhart, and he is thrust out: 'Man's last and highest parting, is when, for God's sake, he takes leave of God.' This break is a leap, an eruption, a breaking through to the void. From that desert of silence, the mystic is reborn into a condition of remarkable independence and power:

I was myself, I willed myself and knew myself as Him who made this man. Therefore am I the cause of my own self according to my eternal and to my temporal nature. And hence was I born and can never die because of the manner of my birth, which is eternal ... In my eternal birth all things were born. I was the cause of my own self and of all things. If I had not so willed neither I nor all things had been. Were I not, neither would God be.[14]

Whatever the meaning of such imagery, and without profound knowledge of the underlying theology any interpretation is hazardous, it does seem to preach transcendence of a father-figure. Paucity of information prevents a full-flown Eriksonian analysis of Eckhart's Oedipal situation, but one may suggest resonances with two general social processes occurring as he spoke. On the one hand, the imagery parallels what was happening in the changing society: sons were identifying with fathers but then transcending them as they moved upward to new statuses and occupations. On the other, the participant in such imagery is carried through a process analogous to psychoanalysis. He experiences a 'transference' of affection and identity to an authority figure, God the father, but then he transcends Him as he is reborn into a new identity as creator and innovator. Like Luther, Eckhart transcends symbolism of the mother, but, also like Luther, Eckhart provides a substitute image: a rock-bottom, elemental base of identity (the void), from which the believer is born into an activity of creativity and meaning. Whatever its Oedipal origins, such imagery must have contributed to the working through of Oedipal conflicts and problems of identity that Germans other than Luther, indeed most men living in a feudal structure, would likely have experienced as a result of their society.

Yet another type of Oedipal emancipation which may have come from the monk-mystics was a certain atonement for sins of the merchants. Without presenting the evidence, which is patchy though fascinating, the process can be summarized thus. The generally authoritarian structure of feudal society was embodied both in the father's harsh denial of the son's rights to his own feces (some may wonder why he wanted them anyway, but note Freudian observations of the child's delight in playing with his excreta and his sorrow at losing it) and in the church's denial of the merchant's right to accumulate money and goods; in the minds of the merchants, the 'filthy lucre' came to be identified with feces, and his quest for wealth evoked Oedipal as well as religious guilt. The guilt was relieved by passing the money-feces to the mystic monks in the form of alms. The mystic monks, who made their own sin against the father (illustrated by the confessions of Suso), then proceeded to atone for both the merchant's and their own Oedipal sins, undergoing horrible tortures that purged all parties of guilt. The Oedipal undercurrent would not fully account for the rite, but would give it a dramatic inevitability and emotional richness; the sin of trade leads naturally to atonement at several levels, theologically, economically, and Oedipally.

Whether or not the particulars of such an analysis are accepted, the general theme of an Oedipal grounding for the medieval religious movement seems clear. A dimension added to the Eriksonian is the relationship of the religious figure and his lay clientele. The Oedipal drama looms not merely as an expression of the life experience of a single giant individual, but as a symbolic interchange between merchant and monk. A similar dynamic could have been explored in the genesis of the consciousness of Luther, but a comparison of the Reformation and the Gottesfruende suggests also a difference between the medieval and the modernizing society and consciousness. In medieval society, the division between mundane layman and religious virtuoso had not yet collapsed; every man had not yet become, in Luther's idiom, a monk, nor the whole world a monastery. Accordingly, the sinful man could not, like Luther, cure himself through introspection, nor, like Weber's Calvinist, through work. He must seek a specialist, a religious virtuoso especially trained in the art of atonement. Calvinstic doctrine, in Weber's analysis, caused the guilt that work cured; medieval merchants sought religious therapy to cure the guilt that work caused.

A Global Neo-Weberian Psychology: McClelland's n Ach[15]

In-depth study of a particular reformer, such as *Young Man Luther*, obviously generates insights and hunches. Yet the basis of social science is generalization, and at least one method of generalization is through statistical analysis of correlations among measures derived from a large sample of individuals and societies. Though bruised by a variety of criticisms, David C. McClelland's

The Achieving Society remains the most comprehensive and ingenious attempt to statistically demonstrate, across cultures and through history, correlations between Oedipal patterns, fantasy imagery, and the religious and economic complexes of the type expounded by Weber.

McClelland has proposed a characterological configuration uniting elements of the Spirit of Capitalism and the Protestant Ethic as the crucial factor explaining the economic growth of societies. Rejecting commonplace explanations such as race, climate, population growth or decline, and the amount of capital poured into an economy, McClelland endeavors to demonstrate that none of these account for the presence or absence of growth. Instead, the crucial factor is the 'need to achieve', which McClelland abbreviates as 'n Ach'.

Years ago, as an experimental psychologist, McClelland began to use the analysis of fantasy as a means of asesssing the strength of motivation. Utilizing a set of cards, each of which depicted a life situation centered around work, he showed pictures to his subjects and asked them to compose stories concerning them. A picture of a boy seated at a desk, for instance, might evoke fantasies of the boy struggling to do his best, overcome obstacles, and achieve a goal. Measuring the amount of such imagery, McClelland developed a scale to assess the strength of the achievement motive n Ach.

McClelland then became aware of parallels between n Ach and Max Weber's Protestant Ethic and Spirit of Capitalism. Calvinist-capitalists and high n Ach subjects were both strongly motivated to do a job well for its own sake, regardless of extrinsic rewards, and they shared other traits as well. Inspired by the Weber thesis, McClelland elaborated a neo-Weberian psychology of history. He felt that the relation between Protestantism and Capitalism was not as direct as Weber had thought, that other variables intervened. Finally he arrived at a model showing Protestantism as the initial condition, which encouraged childrearing practices inculcating mastery of the environment and independence from others. Such childrearing would foster a strong need to achieve, and individuals, especially males, with this motivation would express it through the spirit of capitalism and in economic activity yielding growth.

McClelland musters statistics to demonstrate the validity of each link in this hypothetical chain. He produces evidence that nine of twelve Protestant countries did better in economic growth than would be predicted on the basis of their economic resources, while only three of thirteen Catholic countries did so; thus, he supports the relation between Protestantism and economic growth in the modern world (a relationship which Weber did not claim since he maintained only that Protestantism contributed to the *genesis* of capitalism).

Moving to the next link in the chain, McClelland discovered that in Connecticut, USA, active (church-going) Protestant mothers tend to stress self-reliance training a year earlier than do active American Irish Catholics, and two years earlier than do active American Italian Catholics. In Germany, he found that Protestant boys tend to have higher n Ach than do Catholic boys. Back in the United States, he found support for the last link: boys with high n Ach share interests with entrepreneurs more often than do those with low n Ach.

Once formulating this association between n Ach and economic growth, McClelland decided to test it on a global scale. Drawing a sample of numerous contemporary nations, he measured the n Ach of each by applying his story-analysis scales to the imagery appearing in story book readers used in the schools of each nation. To measure economic growth, he assessed the amount of energy each nation produced, as in output of electricity. The results of this survey did indeed show a correlation: high n Ach predicts *subsequent* economic growth, but not past or present growth. Through a study of three historic nations—Ancient Greece, Medieval Spain, and England, 1400–1830—an increase in achievement imagery of literary works of a given period forecast economic growth in a subsequent period, as in England where high literary n Ach predicted a gain in the importation of coal eighty years later. These discoveries led McClelland to a theory of psychological determinism reminiscent of Weber: first comes the psychological change, then the economic change, rather than vice versa.

McClelland then asked what conditions give rise to his mysterious n Ach, with its power to predict the rise and fall of national economies. He argues that conditions are not simply the social, economic, and political ones favored by historians; if they were, historians could continue to ignore motives and concentrate on objective factors. Instead, the conditions that give rise to n Ach are Oedipal: they concern family life and childrearing. McClelland agrees with the psychoanalysts that the inner concerns of fantasy have their roots in early child-parent relationships and that they persist relatively unaffected by the experiences of adulthood.

Drawing on the huge aggregate of correlations which McClelland supplies, we can abstract a recipe for the Oedipal creation of n Ach: nondominant fathers, or fathers who are absent after age eight or so but not before (for the mother-child household during early childhood, whether in slum America or polygynous Africa, has been found to produce low n Ach), so that the father does not stifle the son's initiative; and a warm, rewarding mother with high standards of excellence who requires her son to be self-reliant (but not too early, as in the lower class home where the mother, trying to get the child off her back, pushes it out of the nest before it can fly).

McClelland then explores the relationship between religion and childrearing. He finds that in Kaiserslautern, Germany, Protestant families more often buy walking harnesses, Catholic familes play-pens; the Protestants stress independence training, the Catholics, control and circumscription. In general, though, McClelland does not find that whether one is a Protestant or Catholic consistently predicts a difference in n Ach, and he rejects such gross institutional labels in favor of a type of religious orientation present in numerous religions. This orientation he terms 'positive mysticism'; the positive mystic, be he Jew, Quaker, or Jain, tends to reject traditional religious authority in favor of his own choice of religious action according to whether it contributes to his eternal salvation or his reverence for life. According to McClelland, positive mysticism fosters alertness and high n Ach, whereas the ritualist unthinkingly conforms to prescriptions of tradition.

Admitting that family life is a complex phenomenon and that wide-scale changes in childrearing are difficult to engender without brutal social engineering, McClelland believes that the religious movement is most likely to accomplish such deep-seated changes. Providing no evidence to support this hypothesis, he does offer one striking if apparently trivial example in a description of two Mexican villages, one of which converted to Protestantism while the other remained Catholic. Eight years after conversion, the Protestant boys showed more n Ach as measured by such tests as the game of throwing rings at a peg. McClelland cites precise statistics to show that the Protestants took moderate risks most frequently, starting at middle distances from the peg and moving in gradually until they reach a position which is challenging yet offers a chance of success. Catholic boys never budged from the position assumed for the first throw.

McClelland thinks that the religious reformist has higher n Ach not because of the content of his reformist belief but because he feels superior to the folk around him, whom he regards as ignorant and blinded by tradition. As reformist zeal dies, so do the feelings of superiority and presumably the n Ach. In one of his rare considerations of the social effects of n Ach, McClelland laments that such a motive is unfortunately associated with the zealot and fanatic who incites war and bigotry as part of his movement toward change.

McClelland's theory has been criticized on virtually every count. Some studies have shown n Ach to correlate less strongly with independence training than with other factors, other studies have shown a low correlation between individual n Ach scores with the collective scores derived from national readers, and still other studies have failed to find n Ach stronger among businessmen than others. Researchers have wondered whether valid measures of economic growth have been used and whether n Ach measures a motive which impels toward activity or simply a fantasy wish fulfillment.[16]

A general difficulty with McClelland's theory is its global scale, which forces him to rely on statistical correlations based on diverse samples and measures. A correlation between A and B is established for sample X, between B and C for sample Y, and between C and D for sample Z; from these varied samples, instruments, and correlations is postulated a single complex linking A, B, C, and D. Given the scope of the theory, such methodology is difficult to avoid, but the correlations could be usefully supplemented by Erikson-style studies exploring the dynamics uniting these various factors in the life of a particular individual in a particular historical situation. The case study could explore *how* Protestantism encouraged n Ach, how n Ach encourages entrepreneurial activity and so forth.

McClelland's measuring devices unfortunately preclude discovery of those patterns which Weber emphasized as most distinctive of the Protestant Ethic. In Weber's view, the Calvinist-capitalist *rationalized* his total life action, systematizing the relations of means to ends so that the entire life cycle thrust relentlessly toward a single ultimate goal. Doubtless owing to the mass of assessments that his study required, McClelland did not ask his raters to score the total 'rationality' of a character's actions within a story but instead to count the discrete achievement images composing that action. In spite of his inability to assess the total structure of action, McClelland does discover in his high n Ach stories a pattern strikingly like that emphasized by Weber's Calvinist-capitalist configuration: a strong concern with the means rather than the rewards of a given activity.

The Oedipal configuration in which McClelland roots the achieving personality differs strikingly from that Erikson attributes to the religious reformer (and, as we shall see later, the political revolutionary). The achiever, who is occupationally most likely to be an independent entrepreneur, derives from a demanding mother and a non-authoritarian father; the reformer from a highly authoritarian father and a nondescript mother. The reformer is apparently struggling to get free of his father, the achiever to gain the affection of his mother. The configuration is certainly not so simple, but we may have here the rudiments of an Oedipal typology of modes of social change.

Revitalization Movements

In Weber's classic work on types of authority,[17] he laid the groundwork for analysis of any movement, whether of the reformation or revolutionary type. According to Weber, such a movement always begins with a charismatic phase. Traditional authority is replaced by the charismatic leader, a magnetic and innovative figure with whom people feel a strong emotional bond in a situation of flux and excitement. When the excitement dies down, the charismatic leader is replaced by a bureaucratic organization which divides the leader's talents into several bureaucratic specialities. Though Weber's typology gives fundamental insight into the psychology of movements and the leader-follower relationship, he did not explicitly relate this phenomenon to the Oedipal pattern evoked by Freud in explaining charisma as the transfer to a leader of one's feelings about his parents.[18] Among several attempts at incorporating this Oedipal perspective, the most balanced and succinct is Anthony Wallace's theory of 'revitalization movements'[19] to be discussed shortly. The great importance of a theory

ike that of Wallace which attempts to relate individual consciousness to collective movements is that such movements offer an
unparalleled opportunity for the personality to impose its peculiar
fantasies, symbols, and values on large populations for long
periods. Think of the impact on history, on living men, on all of us
that the personal imagery of Christ, Buddha, and Muhammad
have had through their radical and revitalizing movements. The
revitalization movement demonstrates the relevance of individual
psychology to history.

Whether erupting in relatively primitive societies (as have the
American Indian Ghost Dance and the Melanesian cargo cults), in
archaic civilizations (as have Christianity, Buddhism, and Islam),
or in relatively modern states (as have such movements as Communism), revitalization movements typically occur when the
traditional social order is breaking down. Tribal clans are disinte-
grating, serfs are cutting feudal bonds and moving to town,
peasants are selling their lands and becoming proletarian. Traditional authorities fall, be they village headman or feudal lord, and
the disoriented people typically come under the guidance of some
outsider such as a travelling artisan. The resulting movement
endeavors (but usually fails) to establish a new system of consciousness, what Wallace terms a 'mazeway'. Under the best of
circumstances, the new mazeway can resolve chaos into order and
provide orientation and meaning while inspiring sudden and radical
change.

The revitalization movement is viewed by Wallace as proceeding
through several predictable phases. Initially the society is at a
'steady state' in that its cultural design, its mazeway, successfully
orders its member's lives. The steady state is interrupted by internal
contradictions or by some external force, such as colonization,
conquest, or the intrusion of capitalism, culminating in disruptions
of the type we have described.

This phase is followed by phases of 'cultural distortion' and
'individual stress'. Failing to find meaning and direction, the
people become indolent, alcoholic, depressed, guilt-ridden, corrupt,
and violent. In time, they may despair of rejuvenation and endeavor
to extinguish themselves. Death rates increase, birth rates decrease,
and the society is defeated in war or dispersed.

But the revitalization can come to the rescue. It formulates a
new 'mazeway', a system of ideas, values, and symbolic forms

which promise to inspire, validate, and render meaningful a new and better life. Wallace asserts that the mazeway is typically conceived in one or several hallucinatory visions by a single individual. The visions always have Oedipal content; a wish for a satisfying parental figure in the form of a spiritual symbol. They also include an apocalyptic fantasy of the world's complete destruction, a feeling of personal guilt about one's own conduct or that of one's society, and a longing for a new and utopian order that provides a stable and satisfying life.

Wallace emphasizes that the visionary, the prophet, is not mad or psychotically out of touch with reality. Unlike the psychotic, he does not believe that he *is* the deity about whom he dreams, only that he enjoys some peculiarly intimate bond with him. Nor does the visionary suffer the mental disintegration of the psychotic. Indeed, through his vision he may gain renewed mental health, a he becomes a more effective and integrated person and is cured of addictions and maladies.

Given that the vision typically defines a calling, an exhortation to reform and revolutionize, the visionary is disposed to seek followers. His preaching always contains, according to Wallace two fundamental motifs: first, 'that the convert will come under the care and protection of certain supernatural beings', and second 'that both he and his society will benefit materially from an identification with some definable new cultural system'.[20] Once the movement is rolling, the visionary becomes a charismatic leader who stands in relation to his followers much as the supernatural stands to him. The movement usually encounters resistance from the society. If it becomes accepted by a wide or controlling segment, it becomes institutionalized and some 'organized program of group action' ensues, sometimes with radical reforms. In time, the reforms become established institutions and the movement church responsible for the preservation of rites and doctrines. With the new 'steady state', a viable pattern of social life is instituted legitimized by a new scheme which, though Wallace does not say so, would seem to be characteristically more rationalized and abstract than the old and capable of subsuming a more complex and modern techno-social system.

Examples to fit Wallace's theory are not difficult to find; in fact Wallace himself supplies an extended case study. Handsome Lake was inspired by a vision to rise from his sickbed where he had lai an invalid, to become leader of a Seneca movement which eventually provided a rationale for an adaptive modernization. His vision justified men's performing farmwork, a feminine task in traditional Seneca hunting society, but requiring the strength to push the plow in the American farm economy.[21] Margaret Mead has reported an even more vivid modernization as a result of a movement under Paliau among the Manus of the Admiralty Islands of the South Pacific. Upon returning to this 'stone age' group which she had researched twenty-five years before, Mead was 'greeted by a man in carefully ironed white clothes, wearing a tie and shoes' who explained that he was one of the officials of the community council that was systematically planning a new society; later Mead was asked to provide a list of rules for modern child care to guide the planners in their social engineering.[22] Movements, of course, have not always ended so rationally. The anabaptist Jan Bokelson strove to organize heaven on earth in the city of Münster, Germany during 1534–5. Inaugurated with parades honoring Bokelson in the role of exalted king, the city of joy and free love became a hell when the bishop's besieging forces cut off supplies. Some of the starving populace escaped outside the walls to crawl about gobbling grass as they were captured by soldiers, while others were forced by Bokelson to perform exhausting athletic games for the glory of God. In the end, Bokelson's Queen, Diavara, was beheaded and he himself was led like a performing bear around Europe on a chain until the authorities mercifully tortured him to death with red-hot irons.[23]

Emphasizing the irrational and infantile character of the revitalization movement and, indeed, religion in general, Weston LaBarre's *The Ghost Dance*,[24] polemically stresses the Oedipal aspect which in Wallace's theory is merely an element. Taking up only a thread of LaBarre's rich and complex analysis, we may summarize as follows. All religions derive from fantasy which, in turn, is rooted in the distinctively human Oedipal complex that is derived from features of human prehistory such as sexual divergence encouraged by hunting, the father's remaining home as the child matures, and the long dependency of the child. In the womb, the infant feels himself omnipotent in that 'every subliminal wish, every organic need in that perfected environment is in fact accomplished instantly'.[25] Life from that point is uphill; discovering progressively less omnipotence in the self, the individual seeks it in the not-self, the omnipotent God, which he still secretly hopes to control or persuade. Worshipping God, then, is regression to an infantile mentality.

LaBarre's argument ranges through the entire Sibero-American sweep, uniting the ethnography of Europe, Asia, and America, and tracing linkages back to paleolithic and ancient Judaeo-Hellenic times to conclude that religion originated with shamans, who were depicted in the earliest Stone Age caves as masked dancers. The Oedipal underpinning of shamanism is revealed among the American and Siberian Indians. Transvestite shamans offer frightened people a child's vision of manhood, as he approaches the father, becomes ambiguously himself a father to the people, and even serves as 'the first "god"', only in a very little world'.[26]

Heirs of these shamans are the visionaries of the Ghost Dance, the revitalization movement. Such movements originate with the juxtaposition of indigenous and foreign cultures, a situation which sets in motion a new Oedipal conflict as the visionary is paralyzed by fear of abandoning his parentally-derived traditions (as LaBarre puts it, 'defenses') to accept alien innovations, even if the innovation is objectively adaptive. Whereas Wallace stressed the difference between these figures and the psychotic, LaBarre states baldly that any psychiatrist would deem them psychopathological.

LaBarre then traces the Ghost Dance as it has emerged in the two root sources of Western civilization, the Greek and the Judaic. LaBarre blames Plato, 'the direct father of fascism in Europe',[27] for destroying the original Greek's trust in the body and fostering instead the soul-hypothesis which elevated a spiritual father above the mother 'materia', who was then blamed for all troubles. This patriarchal theme, LaBarre laments, is found also among the Hebrews, whose prophets were unstable figures pathologically dependent on a father-figure. The culmination of the two Ghost Dances, the Hebraic and the Hellenic, is St. Paul, whose contribution to civilization LaBarre tersely summarizes as follows: 'Paul, another vatic with inchoate ego boundaries, achieved only paranoid identification of the divine Hebraic father with the divinized Hellenized son ... he aids us very little in understanding human fathers and sons'.[28] The aftermath of Paul, in LaBarre's opinion, has been a destructive and repressive Christianity which is one of the several traditions from which man must be emancipated. LaBarre pleads:

Can man now know and accept his nature and his limitations with equanimity, and receive with cool confidence and gladly the legacy of his manhood, without any antic self-cozening ghost dance?[29]

LaBarre regards the religious movement, the Ghost Dance, as a pathological acting out of Oedipal fears and desires. Irrational in its origins, religion is also maladaptive in its consequences, for it generates false or untestable hypothesis about reality. LaBarre asserts: 'the soul hypothesis has never generated a single demonstrable truth; the matter hypothesis however has made man the most magnificently adapted mammal in the history of evolution'.[30]

This view diametrically opposes Weber's. To begin first with fact, the full weight of Weber's comparative studies and *Religionssoziologie* document the argument that without the soul hypothesis the magnificent matter hypothesis never would have come about at all. Only through formulating a spiritual order differentiated from the visible order was man able to regard the visible order as objective and secular, hence exploitable by capitalism and manipulable by science. Civilizations such as China which were extremely worldly failed to de-sacralize the world sufficiently to rationalize it. Calvinism with its transcendental metaphysic achieved this momentous step in evolution,[31] and the Calvinist metaphysic derived from the prophetic tradition and the reform movement, in a word, from the Ghost Dance. In light of the massive historical argument of Weber, LaBarre's is myopic.

LaBarre does succeed brilliantly in suggesting the infantile and irrational *origins* of at least some religious themes and movements, but elementary logic forbids the argument from origins to consequences. As Weber's studies remind us, irrational reasoning could have adaptive results (Calvinists reasoning logically from the premise of predestination would have become fatalistic ritualists rather than activist innovators). We can doubtless salvage hypotheses from the Oedipal argument, for example, that the greater the Oedipal and the less the rational content of the prophet's vision, the more likely his movement will be maladaptive. But proof of maladaptive consequences requires an analysis entirely separate from that of Oedipal origins. Such an analysis is the Weberian, to which the brilliant but biased synthesis of LaBarre adds a fundamental dimension.

E

With regard to the question of the adaptiveness of religious movements, then, Weber is at one extreme, LaBarre at the other. Wallace is closer to the position of Weber, but for different reasons. He takes account of the Oedipal origins of the vision, but he nevertheless stresses its rational content and adaptive consequences. And he explicitly denies that the prophet is psychotic. Indeed, Wallace fears that with the loss of psychotherapeutic benefits from religious movements the world incidence of neurosis may increase. If not that, the populace seeking therapy for stress may create a substitute for religious faith by deifying the state, resulting in tyranny and a new threat to reason. Some might consider Wallace's view of religion too rosy, in that it does not take account of the numerous movements which have, indeed, had noxious consequences. Bizarre figures like Bokelson, highly respected reformers such as Zwingli and Savanorola, and scores of Asian, Amerindian, Melanesian, and other non-Western visionaries have met bad ends while their movements dwindled into passivity or violence. On the other hand, others might consider Wallace's theory to be too mechanical. Burridge provides more of an inner view when he analyzes the movement's potential for achieving more than the 'steady state' of Wallace. By resurrecting cultural values through identification with charismatic prophet the revitalization movement can provide what Burridge terms 'redemption'.

Whatever the adaptive consequences of the movement, it offers a unique opportunity for a single personality to impose its qualities on history. The charismatic leader's uniquely personal vision, whether autistic or rational, can powerfully influence the course of history for millennia. Great world religions such as Christianity and Islam originated as revitalization movements in marginal areas. Spreading widely, they have endured long, incalculably influencing history to the present, and still capable of affecting its future. The convergence of personality and history that is accomplished by the movement calls for psychological analysis in order to illuminate this aspect of the evolution of consciousness.

The Legend of Hitler's Youth

Norman Cohn considers Communism and Nazism to stem from the great tradition of millennial movements in Europe. Communism and Nazism, suggests Cohn, endow conflict and aspiration with transcendental significance, in fact with all the mystery and majesty of the final eschatological drama.[32] According to Cohn, the medieval millennial movements gained transcendental significance by their claim to express the Will of God, the modern ones by expressing the Purpose of History and, one might add, by their use of symbols as mystical as those of medieval Europe—the swastika, goosestep, and prayers directed to Der Führer. Certainly Nazism rivals and foreshadows the new nations in harnessing political religion to a mobilization movement. Erik Erikson's analysis of 'The Legend of Hitler's Youth'[33] is a companion piece to his *Young Man Luther*, providing suggestive (if speculative) insight into the Oedipal factors underlying collectivist, revolutionary movements.

As in his analysis of Luther, the key figure in Erikson's study of Hitler is the German father. Erikson portrays him as authoritarian and demanding. When the father comes home from work, 'the walls seem to pull themselves together',[34] so oppressive is the atmosphere. The children hold their breath and the mother hastens to fulfill the father's whims in order to avoid angering him. The father speaks curtly to both mother and children, expecting immediate obedience. He seems bitter over the intimacy mother and children have enjoyed during his absence, and the German boy, in particular, feels that his affectionate bond with the mother is a thorn in his father's side. The boy comes to sense that he can win the mother's love only without the father's knowledge, and the mother reinforces this sense of collusion by keeping some of the son's mischief from the father, but revealing enough so that the father punishes the son. The father does not trouble himself to inquire about the details of misdeeds; he seems to assume that sons are always bad, so punishment is always justified.

In reaction against the authoritarian father, German sons have long made a tradition of rebellion. In the old days they would embark on the *Wanderschaft*, the 'wandering', through marvelous forests or from city to city and from one artisan master to another. More recently the boys have amused themselves by ridiculing the stodgy burgher-father, who had betrayed youth and idealism to become a philistine employed in the civil service. Going to the other extreme, the youths would ecstatically enjoy the romantic life of the student or join movements that stressed physical culture and union with nature, and were led by young men whom Erikson calls 'professional' and 'confessional' adolescents. The young individualist might write diaries and poems, dreaming of immortality while fearing early death. Erikson notes that all those activities exclude the true father while appealing to some abstract and impersonal substitute, such as Nature, Fatherland, or Essence.

Since the son has identified with the father since early childhood, he is not entirely comfortable with his rebellion. In time, he becomes a stodgy burgher like his father before him. But he is left with a feeling of regret that he has sacrificed his freedom by throwing away his youth.

Erikson believes that this German dynamic contributed to the rise of Nazism, that Hitler has a special appeal for Germans nostalgic for their youthful rebellion against their fathers. In their hearts, as well as in the souls of youth who were still in the process of rebelling, chords were struck by Hitler's defiant words in *Mein Kampf*.

> No matter how firm and determined my father might be ... his son was just as stubborn and obstinate in rejecting an idea which had little or no appeal for him. *I did not want to become an official*.[35]

States Erikson:

> This combination of personal revelation and shrewd propaganda (together with loud and determined action) at last carried with it that universal conviction for which the smoldering rebellion in German youth had been waiting; that no old man, be he father, emperor, or god, need stand in the way of his love for his mother Germany ... Both fathers and sons now could identify with the Führer—the adolescent who never gave in.[36]

Hitler was a symbolic youth, a man who refused to become a father, or, for that matter, a Kaiser or a president. He was simply Der Führer, the 'unbroken adolescent who had chosen a career apart from civilian happiness, mercantile tranquility, and spiritual peace: a kind of gang leader'. The gang that he led was, in the widest sense, the German nation. Most specifically, it was the Hitler Youth. Inspired by Der Führer, the *Hitlerjunge* proclaimed their independence of parents, tradition, past:

All those who from the perspective of their "experience" and from that alone combat our method of letting youth lead youth must be silenced ... An entirely fresh, newborn generation has arisen, free from the preconceived ideas, free from compromises, ready to be loyal to the orders which are its birthright ... Let everything go to pieces, we shall march on. For today the enemy is ours; tomorrow, the whole world.[37]

Believing that a basic theme in adolescence is the search for identity, Erikson tries to show that Germany as a whole was particularly troubled by the problem of identity. Overrun by an encircling combination of Paris, Rome, London, and Moscow —Latin from the South, Slavic from the East, Anglo and Gallic from the West—the German has found it difficult to define his national identity. He oscillates wildly between the 'too broad' cosmopolitan, whose hope is to be mistaken for English or French, and the 'too narrow' chauvinist, who, 'wherever he went, made himself at home, and, gritting his teeth, remained a German'.[38] The ambiguous national identity exacerbated adolescent ambiguity of personal identity, strengthening the linkage between adolescence and nationalism.

Particularly threatening to identity is an alien minority, especially one with the characteristics of the Jew. The Jew combined 'defensive rigidity and opportunistic adaptability', suggests Erikson, a dualism exemplified by the image of the 'bearded Jew in his kaftan and Sammy Glick'.[39] Rigidly traditionalist in dealings within their group, the Jews threaten indigenous values through their opportunism toward the natives. Erikson points out that historically Jews have originated theories of relativism; Einstein's theory relativizes the physical world, and Marx and Freud developed a relativistic view of culture; they argued that belief varied relative to class or familial pattern rather than standing as an absolute verity. Such a relativistic orientation (expressed, by the way, in anthropology through the doctrine of 'cultural relativism', of which the best-known exponent was Melville Herskovits) necessarily threatens an adolescent-like search for total commitment to some absolute good. If the Jews threatened identity, the purge of the Jews would re-establish it.

Erikson has elaborated, then, a psychologically plausible argument to explain the relations among symbols composing the ideological complex known as Nazism. Reared by an authoritarian father, sons romantically rebel to seek their own identity, but upon becoming adults they grudgingly accept the traditional father role. Their smoldering rebelliousness is later inflamed by the symbol of the adolescent who never gave in, and this adolescent leader mobilizes a nationalist movement. The adolescent imagery of the movement intensifies feelings of personal identity diffusion which resonate with a diffusion of national identity. Given this diffusion of identity, it is natural to seek a scapegoat in opposition to which coherence of identity can be affirmed.

Anyone who reads Erikson's original essay will, I suspect, feel intuitively that he has put his finger on German qualities, the German character. My own favorite supporting documents are the wonderful German student songs. Consider these words in which a youth depicts the traditional 'Studentleben' (student life): First the youth describes the fun:

> ... in die Kniepen laufen
> und sein Geld versaufen,
> ist ein hoher, herrlicher Beruf ...
> (... running into taverns
> drinking up your money,
> is a high and glorious calling)

Then he recalls the voice of his father:

> ... Vater spricht: 'Das Raufen
> und das Kniepenlaufen
> nutz dir zum Examen keinen Deut';
> doch dabei vergist er
> dass er ein Philister
> und dass jedes Ding hat seine Zeit
> (Father speaks: 'Those fights and those bouts of drinking will not help you with your examination'. But he forgets that he is a Philistine, and that everything has its time ...)

Listening to a standard repertoire of German student, drinking, and military songs, one can literally hear the themes of Erikson's essay: authoritarianism and rebellion, romantic wandering, lusty adventure, intense male comradeship, and deep-seated, almost religious, loyalty to father and nation, as in the hymn 'Mein Vater-land'. Hearing these stirring songs bellowed in a German beerhall, it is easy to imagine that Nazism could mobilize so charismatically such themes. What is more, notable German lives do follow Erikson's pattern; Goethe had a warm mother, an authoritarian father, romantically rebellious student days, and then a bureau-cratic post in a provincial court. Max Weber fit this pattern per-fectly, and he cherished dueling, nationalism, and heroism. Erikson synthesizes qualities that really do seem part of the German experience.

But as David McClelland once put it, in social science you may first exclaim 'Gee Whiz!' but then you must ask 'So what?'[40] Even if Erikson's analysis does lay bare the German soul we must view his methodology critically.

An obvious question is whether the elements in Erikson's com-plex are unique to Germany; if they are not, is their affinity so strong that where one appears in a non-German context, the others do too? Striking parallels appear in ideologies of other nationalist systems. Indonesia, for example, equals Germany's ambiguity of national identity, derived from a history of being overrun by a diverse set of civilizations: Hindu, Chinese, Islamic, European, and Japanese. Indonesia also had the Nazi-like abundance of youth imagery during its revolution: even streets and famous buildings were named after callow youths. And it had a revolutionary hero, Sukarno, who enjoyed an extraordinarily charismatic and intimate bond to his people. Sukarno was often called father (*bapak*), occasionally even mother (I have interviewed one mental patient who suffered delusions of being suckled by Sukarno). But the revolutionaries knew him as 'bung' (comrade). Like Hitler, Bung Karno was a kind of pal, a leader of the gang composed of the small nationalist elite who had been boyhood friends and who, like a teenage club, made their own language, costumes, flag, and songs. Like the Germans, they desired to exclude the paternalistic invader from the motherland: as Sukarno put it, 'We will move heaven and earth until . . . there is not one single imperialistic louse left in the fold of our motherland.' The Indonesian national identity was, like the German, threatened by a mercantile minority which enjoyed an in-group solidarity oriented relativistically toward the wider society. These Chinese, the so-called Jews of the Orient, dominated Indonesian trade and had the reputation of opportunistically sacrificing traditional values for the sake of profit. Indonesian nationalism occasionally bursts into Chinese massacres, but without the devastation of gas chambers.

Sukarno's Indonesia, then, created a complex symbolically similar to that of Hitler's Germany, though lacking an equivalent efficiency in military expansion and minority pogrom. Nor were the songs so lusty or economic mobilization so vigorous, suggesting the possibility that Sukarno's Western-derived nationalism never fully caught the Indonesian mentality. In spite of these differences, the similarities are striking. Such parallels support Erikson's view that the symbols composing such a cluster share a psychological core.

Another parallel is the 'Authoritarian Personality' investigated by Adorno and his colleagues.[41] The authoritarian individual, hypothesized Adorno, would overappease his super-ego (his father) in repressing his aggression, but he would express it against scapegoats such as the Jew. This basic configuration could take several variants, one exemplified by the Nazi stormtrooper, Ernst Roehm, a swashbuckling nihilist who rebels against his identification with the father; another by the affectionless, efficient Himmler, who stereotypes the world as a diagrammatic field for administrative manipulation and who prefers the gas chamber to the pogrom. The counterpoint to these unsavory types is the genuine liberal, who is supposed to achieve the balance between superego, ego, and id that Freud deemed ideal. The difficulty that confronted this theory of 'The Authoritarian Personality' was rather crippling: in questionnaire interviews designed to check the extent of correlation among these various attitudes, they did not highly correlate. Any single authoritarian trait did not consistently predict another, and the liberal revealed unsuspected rigidities and prejudices.[42]

Adorno probably attributed too much strength to sheerly psychological associations, and took too little account of the cultural and historical basis of such an ideological complex as Nazism. Erikson makes the same mistake. Consider his argument that the German is authoritarian because he lacks the 'true inner authority'[43] that comes from a well integrated system of ideals. Treating authoritarianism as a compensation for inner doubt, Erikson ignores the obvious, that German authoritarianism is also buttressed by well-entrenched cultural ideas and symbols. One thinks of Luther's doctrine that the power of the state is not bound by the laws of heaven, Nietzsche's notion of the will to power, the heroic myths of

Siegfried, and the operas of Wagner. Such cultural models cannot be ignored, and a virtue of the Weberian methodology, as opposed to the psychoanalytical, is that Weber carefully takes them into account; his analysis of the Calvinist personality begins with the Doctrine of Predestination.

Reminiscing about his youth as a wandering artist, Erikson admits that he sometimes paints pictures instead of analyzing data. To learn the most from Erikson's studies, as from similar 'culture and personality' and 'national character' studies in anthropology,[44] we need to develop a methodology that can sensitively elucidate intuitions. Since Erikson's statements are frequently difficult to translate into orthodox, testable hypotheses of the 'if X, then Y' type, probably our best strategy is simply to compare his portraits with our own experience and judge whether the elements plausibly hang together. Erikson certainly demonstrates enough Oedipality in reformation and revolution to render suspect any attempt to deny the Oedipal aspect altogether.

Oedipal Rebellion in a Small Group

Cognitive psychology is *prima facie* more convincing than the psychology of the unconscious. No great logical leap is involved in postulating that a mazeway 'orders' behavior. It stands to reason that one system of order can subsume another, hence it is immediately plausible that insofar as people begin to order themselves in terms of a cognitive order their behavior becomes more orderly. To predict that affectionate mothers encourage n Ach or that authoritarian fathers engender Nazism is not so obviously plausible. These linkages depend on two types of relationships, neither of which can be rendered even plausible without intricate analysis: first, relationships among unconscious images, and, second, relationships between childhood and adult experiences.

Adding insult to injury, I shall now discuss a study which not only suffers from the difficulties besieging every study in depth psychology, but which also risks a taboo extrapolation: from the small group to the larger society. Over the course of several years sociologist Philip Slater and his associates taught a small seminar at Harvard University, the subject of which was the participants themselves. Each seminar group, composed of a dozen or so students, would spend the term discussing their own relationships and perceptions. What emerged strikingly was an evolutionary process, such that during the course of the semester the group would go through phases of consciousness resembling those that human society itself has undergone. I do not give here the details of Slater's studies, but summarize the parallels he discovered between the phases of evolution of his small group and those of the larger society, particularly as each bears on Oedipal dynamics.[45]

Primitive phase

Slater sees in primitive consciousness a relative lack of differentiation between environment and self. 'Everything inside is outside', as when motives are seen as commands from a medicine bird, and 'everything outside is inside', as when the earth is perceived as sacred. Social bonds are relatively unconscious (we would say multiplex) in that they are traditional instead of pragmatic. Social unity derives from a projection outward of shared fears.

In its earliest meetings, Slater's seminar group parallels the primitive consciousness in the broad sense that its members fear submergence into the group resulting in a lack of differentiation between self and other. Struggling to differentiate their roles from the group perceived as an amorphous mass, individual members report

> the fantasy of merging with, or being devoured by, the mother, which in turn is associated with loss of consciousness and death.[46]

Archaic-historic phase

As the group continues to meet, it deifies and becomes dependent on the teacher-leader. As one student put it, this leader is 'a sort of spontaneous fountain that will bring forth and all we have to do is sit and drink'.[47] For Slater, this situation is parallel to the emergence of archaic kingdoms associated with deities and rulers whose favors the people seek through prayer and sacrifice. Slater emphasizes that some glorification of the leader is necessary at this phase to encourage the self to seek autonomy from the group by relating to the differentiated leader.

Revolution and Modernization

Slater's observations of numerous seminar groups indicates that deification of the leader is inevitably followed by revolt. The movement may begin with a student's fantasies of murdering or expelling the leader. It culminates in action, such as seizing the leader's chair and asking him to leave. Slater claims that any leader who has worked with several such groups can sense when the moment is coming.

The leader's teaching has been perceived, Slater claims, as an erotic irritant: 'In and out! In and out!' as one exasperated student described the process.[48] The leader's phallic potential is appreciated during meetings preceding revolt, for the male students talk enviously of the male leader seducing female students. As revolt approaches, the girls alternate between trying to seduce and to reject the leader. After the revolt, sexual interest among the members increases. Slater's explanation for this phenomenon is that the libido is decathected from the leader and spread among the members.

Following the revolution, the members of the student group become more conscious of their bonds and they worry about the group's future. Eventually they develop messianic hopes that the group will endure for eternity, and they may even dream of idyllic meetings in the distant future. This hope for the future is expressed in a concern with sexual reproduction. The group comes to center its discussion on a 'sacred couple', such as some couple within the group which is actually planning to marry. Slater notes that sacredness is now abstracted from a particular entity, such as the group or the leader, so that it can become immanent in anyone including the sacred couple.

According to Slater, this pattern resembles those of modernizing reform movements which everywhere emphasize immortality and rebirth at the expense of dependency. With modernization and emancipation, group relations are consciously understood and based on unrepressed sexuality and cooperation rather than hierarchy. The dominant emotion becomes guilt instead of fear, coupled with a sense of loss and an anxiety about isolation and death.

To generalize from Slater's small group to the psychosocial evolution of mankind is obviously risky and not simply because of the discrepancy in size. How many archaic societies had the opportunity enjoyed by one of Slater's groups to read Freud's *Totem and Taboo*? That book, which portrays revolt against the father, could suggest revolt against the leader. Granted, seminars which did not read that particular book still held the revolt, but the broader issue remains: how much of Slater's observed evolutionary process was intrinsic to the structure of the small group and how much was a product of the culture (American, Harvard-Radcliffe, 1960s) shared by members of the group? Even though Slater did consider evidence from small groups at other institutions, they were all American colleges; and the anthropologist would certainly demand cross-cultural observations before accepting the idea that a small group represents in microcosm the pan-human forces of social evolution.

On the positive side, Slater's use of the small group permits certain observations that the anthropologist cannot normally make. A major issue in the study of the evolution of societies is whether the forces of change are psychological and social, or whether as the so-called 'cultural materialists' claim these processes merely mirror technological and economic changes.[49] Unlike the real society, Slater's laboratory group is isolated from problems of production and consumption, and it undergoes no marked technological or economic development. Nevertheless, it evolves socially and psychologically. This observation supports the hypothesis that social evolution is motivated by psycho-social as well as techno-economic factors.

Freed of practical problems faced by the true society, Slater's seminar was free to express openly its unconscious fantasy life. Constraints necessary for the functioning and survival of society prevent such expression in real life. Slater's study was useful in uncovering unconscious fantasies that may accompany societal evolution. Among the dominant fantasy themes is the Oedipal.

The Oedipal Theme

The studies surveyed in this chapter cover a wide range of types. In terms of samples, they include a single historical individual, a student group, religious and ideological movements, and a set of nations. Methodologically, they include the psychoanalytical, questionnaire survey, clinical testing, small group observation, and historical documentation. These diverse approaches converge on a single theme: the Oedipal conflicts involved in the transition from tradition to modernity. The studies by Erikson, Slater, Wallace, and LaBarre locate the conflict and symbolism in relation to a father figure. McClelland's study sees the mother as the motivating stimulus, but McClelland's 'recipe' implies, and parallel analyses by Hagen assert, that this stimulation can occur only when the father has been reduced in authority.[50] One may also take the distinction between McClelland's study and the others as implying that the type of modernization featuring the private entrepreneur is more influenced by the mother, while that taking place in collective movements (the reformation, the revolution, the revitalization, and the small group rebellion) derives more from the father.[51]

The anthropologist, who is aware of the diversity of family life, will naturally hesitate before entertaining such a typology. As Malinowski pointed out long ago, the Oedipus complex takes a different turn in a society where the mother's brother rather than the father has authority over the son.[46] Nevertheless, the fact remains that except in cases of artificial insemination, everyone is born of a mother and a father. Certainly every human child must depend for a long period on some kind of parent or parent surrogate. This parent is necessarily older than the child. Accordingly, any transition from the old to the new would seem to evoke logically the distinction between parent and child. A reasonable hypothesis is that this relationship, the Oedipal theme, is necessarily involved in any transition toward modernity.

Notes to Chapter 5

1. *Cassirer*, p. 44.
2. *Gerth and Mills*, p. 20. *Mitzman's* analysis would suggest also that Weber rejected Freud due to his own Oedipal conflicts—an interpretation that insufficiently respects Weber's ability to analyze objectively in spite of personal torment.
3. *Erikson* (1).
4. Ibid., Chapter 6.
5. Ibid., pp. 47–8.
6. Ibid., p. 83.
7. Ibid., p. 92.
8. Ibid., p. 130.
9. Ibid., p. 194.
10. Ibid., p. 72.
11. This analysis is detailed in *Peacock* (2); the symbolism of the mystics is extraordinarily rich and suggestive.
12. *Pinnow*, p. 138. An equally dangerous attack by the German mystics on the secular hierarchy is described by *Benz*, pp. 509–16. Benz reports

Eckhart's argument that a hierarchy based on spirituality is more significant than that based on hereditary status.

13. *Peacock* (2), p. 53.
14. *Otto*, p. 185.
15. This summary is drawn from *McClelland*.
16. Criticisms of *McClelland* are surveyed by *Brown*, pp. 461–3.
17. *Weber* (1), pp. 324–82.
18. *Freud*, pp. 90–100.
19. *Wallace* (1).
20. Ibid. (1), p. 273.
21. *Wallace* (2).
22. *Mead* (2).
23. *Cohn*.
24. *LaBarre* (2).
25. Ibid., p. 17.
26. Ibid., p. 198.
27. Ibid., p. 528.
28. Ibid., p. 603.
29. Ibid., p. 610.
30. Ibid., p. 390.
31. Note the studies by *Merton* which show that a strikingly large number of early English scientists were Calvinists.
32. *Cohn*, pp. 281–6.
33. *Erikson* (2).
34. Ibid., p. 331.
35. Ibid., p. 336.
36. Ibid., pp. 336–7.
37. Ibid., p. 343.
38. Ibid., p. 349.
39. Ibid., p. 355.
40. From a lecture given by McClelland at Harvard University, Fall, 1959.
41. *Adorno, et. al.*
42. *Madge*, pp. 377–423.
43. *Erikson* (2), 'The Legend of Hitler's Youth', p. 336.
44. Such as *Benedict* (1) and (2), *Mead and Bateson*, and *Mead*.
45. *Slater*.
46. Ibid., p. 187.
47. Ibid., p. 9.
48. Ibid., p. 102.
49. *Harris*.
50. See *Hagen*, who does not treat the symbolism and fantasy of McClelland's n Ach, but does indirectly affirm McClelland's view of the negative relationship between the authoritarian father and n Ach. Hagen characterizes the 'traditional' society as 'authoritarian' in its child-rearing, hence discouraging 'innovation', as in the behavior of the entrepreneur. Through the process of 'withdrawal of status-respect', the child-rearing gradually becomes less authoritarian until finally the innovative personality emerges. Based on case and comparative analysis, Hagen's study usefully supplement's McClelland's in postulating the *process* by which the psychology of modernization operates.
51. *Malinowski* (1).

6
Transition to Modernity

The Aesthetic Aspect

Max Weber has distinguished three relationships between person and object: the technological, the religious, and the aesthetic.[1] An object regarded as religious, e.g. a crucifix, is treated as sacred because it stands for a moral or theological conception. An object regarded as technological, e.g. a hammer, is used for some practical end, such as driving a nail. An object regarded as aesthetic, e.g. a painting, is appreciated neither because of its utility nor because it expresses a moral or theological idea, but because of the sensuous qualities of its physical form. Drawing on this set of distinctions (which became more useful as society became more modern since especially in traditional society the three spheres fuse), we can say that to the extent that a symbolic form is regarded purely as form —appreciated for its sensuous qualities rather than as a tool or a vehicle for an idea—it is 'art'.

Insofar as a symbol is art, or contains a strong aesthetic component, understanding of its meaning is possible only by analysis of its form. Social Science unfortunately discourages such analysis. Social scientists are taught by virtually every major school and theory to emphasize not form but content, to analyze symbols not for their form but for the ideas and values they express. Even where form is demonstrably important, social scientists ignore it and stress content.

Exemplifying this social science bias against form, I first survey studies by anthropologists of myth and sociologists of media. I suggest that they miss that aspect of modernization which logically follows from the Weberian frame of reference. I then survey several literary critics and sociologists of literature who show the kind of insight into the aesthetics of modernization which a concern with form would reveal. In a concluding discussion, I contrast the aesthetic and the religious aspects of modernization. Weberians have appreciated the latter but not the former, owing to their bias against form.

Anti-form

The social anthropological tendency to stress content rather than form is exemplified by the myth analyses of Malinowski, Leach, and Lévi-Strauss (Chapter 3). These studies are alike in that they concentrate on mythical portrayal of social relationships and social events rather than on the literary form of the myths. Malinowski and Leach analyze mythical accounts of clan origins and genealogies while Lévi-Strauss bases his study of the Oedipus myth on its description of kinship relationships. All of these studies ignore the narrative structure.[2]

Their de-emphasis of narrative form follows from their assumptions about the social function of myth. For Leach and Malinowski, myth is a charter from which social institutions or personal claims are deduced and validated. For Lévi-Strauss, myth is a logical model deducing both cosmological and social thought from the same premise, thus validating cosmology by grounding it in society. What matters is the logical homology between the myth and the pattern it validates. How the myth is told is unimportant since myth validates through deduction. Were other mythical functions (such as inspiring an audience by drawing it into empathy with a story) deemed significant, the form of the narrative would doubtless be treated with more care.[3]

Among social scientists concerned with the role of symbolic form in modernizing or modern societies, the most influential, affluent, and populous school is that of the mass media analyst. Names such as Schramm, Hovland, Lazarsfeld, Lasswell, and more recently, Klapper, Riley, Wright, de Sola Pool, and Lerner belong to the more prominent members of this group. They are sociologists or political scientists rather than anthropologists, and they rely on questionnaires and statistics rather than on the 'participant observation' that has been the forte of anthropological fieldwork since

Malinowski. They give more heed to audience response to forms than do the Malinowskians, (who were so concerned to link performance to the larger social context that they ignored their immediate aesthetic context) but they measure response by questionnaire or mechanical device rather than observing it with the eye and ear. Indeed, so stubbornly do the mass media analysts avoid looking and listening that their entire approach seems to assume that the investigator is deaf, blind, and has lost his sense of smell.

The media analysts' analysis of response has traditionally followed what Wright calls the 'hypodermic needle' model.[4] Each listener or spectator is considered to be 'stuck' by the medium's message, and his attitudes are influenced if the message is potent enough to 'take'. Hovland's Second World War studies, based on stimulus-response psychology, illustrate the method nicely.[5] Hovland's method was experimental. He would vary the stimuli to which he exposed his subjects and then measure the effects of this variation on the response. In one study, for instance, he presented to one set of radio-listeners two sides of a controversial argument, to another only one side, then he compared the different effects. One of Hovland's significant discoveries was the Sleeper Effect: a subject may reject a message immediately after exposure, but much later, when the message has had time to take, an effect can be discerned.

A major advance in the study of media was achieved when the investigators finally realized that groups mediated between stimulus and response. They then began to speak of the 'two-step-process', whereby the media influence an opinion leader who in turn influences the opinion of the face-to-face networks in which he is influential. This model was developed during Paul Lazarsfeld's study of the 1940 presidential campaign in Erie County, Ohio.[6] The investigators at Erie County were surprised to discover that people voted more in accord with the groups to which they belonged than in response to the mass media. Face-to-face influence could overide that of the media.

Interesting as such a finding may be, it was not based on direct observation of communicative behavior. The investigators do not report what actually happened during political rallies, for example, and none of them seem to have done fieldwork to observe how the opinion leaders actually operated. The conclusions are based on polls, questionnaires, and periodic interviews which are so impressive in their methodological precision as they are lacking in homely observation.

Supplementing the study of the response, the media experts have developed methods for the study of the stimulus: 'content analysis'.[7] The name itself reveals a bias; there exists no field of 'form analysis'. In spite of its one-sided concentration on the message (primarily verbal) rather than the medium, content analysis has an advantage over the impressionistic approach of the journalist or critic. The advantage of content analysis is that *all* content relevant to a given hypothesis must be taken into account. The journalist arguing that television is filled with violence may cite violent programs while ignoring the peaceful ones. The content analyst would be obliged to define certain indices of violence and non-violence, view some objectively selected sample of programs, and count how often the violent as opposed to non-violent indices appear. Such an objective method is obviously superior to axe-grinding, but its reliance on counting of precisely defined bits of information discourages apperception of the total thrust of a symbolic form.

Consider, for example, a content analysis of all television programs broadcast in New York City during a certain week.[8] The stated object of the study was simply to see what television was saying. To answer this question, eighty-six drama programs were analyzed, first in terms of settings, then in terms of the social and psychological traits of heroes, villains, and supporting characters. Statistics such as the following were recorded. Characters were usually white Americans (four times out of five), and heroes were usually younger than villains. By various rating techniques it was ascertained that heroes were usually depicted as brave, attractive, honest, kind, fair, loyal, admirable, and moderately happy or generous, while villains were typically ugly, deceitful, cruel, unfair, despicable, and moderately sad dirty, miserly, and disloyal. When characters were classified by occupation, it was found that journalists were honest, strong, tough, and quick, while teachers were clean, kind, fair, but also slow, dull, and soft. Lawyers were conniving. Suggestive findings like these reveal the obvious merit in content analysis, but also exemplify a bias. What is categorized and counted is discrete bits of information, what is ignored is the total narrative form. The study does not adequately deal with questions such as, what are the characteristic climax structures of television drama, what does the periodic intrusion of commercials do to the dramatic form, and what patterns of consciousness do these forms embody?

During the post-Second World War years, the media analysts have transferred their methods to the new nations as they have assumed responsibility for laying bare the role of media in modernization. Though uncovering much useful information, their researches have overwhelmingly emphasized the verbal messages and images carried by the media, while ignoring the total form. Consider a summary of the role of media in modernization provided by Ithiel de Sola Pool. Pool's opening statement is that telephones, radios, television, and movies are important in the developing societies because they 'bring in words that carry advice on agricultural practices or public health'.[9] His second sentence states that '... the media show what opportunities exist for using new commodities such as electricity, refrigeration, or automotive transportation'.[10] Pool considers only verbal messages and discrete particles of information while failing to take account of the total form of the medium or the total system of consciousness of which the images are a part. Pool's perspective supports Merton's criticism that the American analysts typically concentrate on 'discrete tidbits of information'.[11]

Merton goes on to propose that the media analysis approach be fertilized by the European sociological tradition; the suggestion can be applied to Weber. Weber's theory of action[12] sought to characterize and compare gross complexes of behaviour according to how these are structured toward an end. Action of the type Weber termed 'Zweckrational' is concerned with deploying means to attain the actor's rationally chosen ends. 'Wertrational' action is concerned with the ends themselves. Affectual or traditional action, what Weber deemed 'Brauch', is less a conscious orientation toward means or ends than an unconscious expression of emotion or custom. Much of Weber's empirical work consisted of exemplifying these basic types of action: his Calvinist-capitalist was concerned with *Zweckrational* whereas his Confucian-bureaucrat was governed by *Brauch*. Weber himself rarely dealt with the media, but his perspective would seem to lead toward an emphasis absent from the American school of mass media analysis: a view of the medium as defining through its total form broad types of action. Definitions of action, communicated through the shape of narratives and the organization of programs, would seem as crucial for the modernization of consciousness as are the tidbits of information, the 'scratches on the mind',[13] with which the media analysts seem preoccupied.

Literature as Symbolic Form

Though the mass media analysts have systematically ignored form, analysts of literature have taken it more into account. A survey of some of these studies is instructive for the social scientist concerned with the relations between form and change.

Lukacs

Most closely mirroring the perspective of the European sociological tradition is the work of Georg Lukacs. Though a Marxist, Lukacs was part of Weber's 'circle' at the University of Heidelberg, his seminal analysis 'Zur Soziologie des Modernen Drama', was published in a periodical of which Weber was an editor, and Lukacs acknowledges that during his early years he 'saw . . . through spectacles tinged by . . . Weber'.[14] Lukacs, a Hungarian, was Commissar of Education in the short-lived Hungarian Communist regime of 1919. After the government's fall, he lived in exile, first in Austria and Germany, then in Russia, somehow managing to write and survive during the 'years of blood'. During this period, his life was a pattern of 'theoretical deviation, vulgar abuse from party spokesmen, periods of disgrace, ritual recantation and further deviation'.[15] Finally, at the age of seventy, he declared a clear-cut deviationist position by joining the cabinet of Nagy. When the Russian troops entered Hungary, he was forced to flee, with Nagy, to the Yugoslav Embassy. He was abducted by the Russians to Romania, lived for a time under house arrest, returned to Hungary, and, until his recent death, lived quietly in Budapest at work on a theory of aesthetics.

Many of Lukacs' perspectives appear in his seminal work, *The Historical Novel*.[16] Lukacs argues that the historical novel has passed through three phases, beginning with the first real historical novel, Sir Walter Scott's *Waverly*, published in 1814. *Waverly* marked the onset of the 'classical period', which was followed by a time of bourgeois realism and decadance, an unfortunate epoch now hopefully resolving into 'democratic humanism'. Lukacs believes that Scott's masterful portrayal of such folk groups as the Scottish clans came from his own direct, feudal contact with them. Bourgeois realists such as Flaubert were alienated from the masses, an alienation resulting in distortion of literary form. Lukacs sees the decadence of bourgeois realism as beginning with the June battle of the Paris proletariat in 1848. Literature now enjoyed an orgy of the exotic, exemplified by Flaubert's exoticization of Carthage. History, too, was exoticized, treated not as dynamic process but as a quaint and ornamental setting for petty private affairs of the political leaders whose significant social actions were ignored. These deformities of form derived from the bourgeois writer's alienation from important social and political forces.

The onset of Democratic Humanism came with the 'humanist literature of protest', as in the works of Zola, Anatole France, and Wilhelm Raabe. Lukacs applauds their protest against the 'barbarism of the imperialist age', but he deplores their 'abstract' relationship to the masses, which is reflected in their schematic representation of folk heroes. Lukacs is forced to conclude that the perfect specimen of the Democratic Humanist novel has yet to be written. He contents himself with Hegel's assurance that history proceeds by 'negation of negation': there will emerge a novel that negates bourgeois decadence while recapturing, in more perfect form, the virtues of the classical period.

In the course of presenting his argument, which is developed with more ingenuity and erudition that can be reproduced in a summary, Lukacs sets forth certain general propositions concerning the relationship between literary form and society. These compare historical drama and the historical novel as types of form.

He first remarks the similarity between them:

Both. . . present the objective, *outer* world; they present the inner life of man only insofar as his feelings and thoughts manifest themselves in deeds and actions, in a visible interaction with objective, outer reality. This is the decisive dividing line between epic and drama, on the one hand, and lyric on the other.[17]

The two forms differ, however, in the extent to which their action depends on setting. In 'King Lear', for example

Shakespeare portrays in the relations of Lear and his daughters,
Gloster and his sons, the great typical, human moral movements
and trends, which spring in extremely heightened form from
the problematicalness and break-up of the feudal family.[18]

These colliding movements produce the dramatic force, and what
is not included in the play is

The entire life surroundings of parents and children ... the
material basis of the family, its growing, decline, etc.[19]

Precisely such 'background objects' are emphasized in a novel
such as Mann's *Buddenbrooks*; insofar as they are stressed in a
play, Lukacs terms the drama 'novelized'.

Turning to the drama itself, Lukacs sets forth the 'facts of life'
that inspire it: the crucial decision that is a turning point in an
individual's or a society's life, the day of reckoning when all consequences of early deeds suddenly converge and the individual
must settle his accounts, the requirements that life, to further its
own ends, simplifies and generalizes itself as the individual or
group focuses on one path chosen from among many, and the
collision of life around some particular Hegelian 'world-historical-
individual'. In drama, these attributes of real life are perfected and
distilled into aesthetic form.

With modernization, drama has undergone a decline. The essence
of drama is the public, collective function; Lukacs quotes Pushkin,
'Drama was born in a public square.'[20] Immersed in the community,
drama must work an effect which is '*immediate*, direct impact upon
a multitude'.[21] With the rise of capitalism and urbanism, life has
become so fragmented that no community can unite for a public
performance. Instead, the elite read plays in private or watch
intimate theater, while the masses seek cheap entertainment that
lacks dramatic force. As a result of this situation, drama has
become both more analytical and more realistic than in traditional
society: more analytical in that it raises questions and quests after
meaning instead of voicing assured moral judgment, more realistic
in that its props are naturalistic instead of stylized as in traditional
ritual-drama. And with the fragmentation of social life, the
dramatic action has splintered into fragments, replacing the dualism
of Shakespeare and the Greeks, where the hero confronted one

opposing force, with a multitude of forces.[22] As society has become more complex, the forces that 'collide' around the world-historical-figure have become random and accidental rather than determined, with a resultant loss of dramatic power.

In Lukacs' analysis of dramatic action as related to social action, we glimpse possibilities for the elaboration of Weber's theory of action with respect to literary form. Instead of attending merely to the discrete tidbits of information such as the slogans, images, and traits that the media people have analyzed as 'content', Lukacs formulates the total form of action staged by modern as opposed to traditional theatre. Traditional dramatic action is stylized, dualistic, moralistic, deterministic, and it collides around a central figure. Modern dramatic action is naturalistic, pluralistic, questing after meaning instead of decreeing morality, and its random forces spew in all directions rather than colliding around a center. Lukacs parallels Weber in regarding such a shift in type of action as correlated with the modernization of society. He differs from Weber in taking a more pessimistic, Marxist view. For Lukacs, the shift in action is not toward rationalization but toward chaos and confusion.

Burke

The American critic, Kenneth Burke, has spun out a sprawling theory of symbolic form which enriches Lukacs' through its greater attention to the psychological processes by which form operates. Burke's scheme for the analysis of action strikingly resembles Weber's.[23] But Burke has never systematized a literary equivalent of the *Religionssoziologie* such that the world's major types of literary action are categorized in relation to the major types of social action. Burke's forte is as a polemicist and analyst of particular forms rather than as a typologist. From his flood of articles, poems, a novel, and a dozen books, it is possible to abstract at least some major themes. A strategic place to begin is Burke's view of form.

For Burke, consciousness is always to be understood in relation to the form that expresses it. He ridicules the 'savants' who would 'catalogue for us the "thoughts of" a stylist like Milton, by stating them simply as percepts divorced from their stylistic context'.[24] Literature is never simply a projection of the artist's thoughts and feelings. Indeed, the artist may sacrifice expression of self-consciousness in order to evoke response from others: Mark Twain *wanted* to utter bitterness, instead he wrote humor 'evoking what he best could, rather than utter more and evoke less'.[25] The end of the artist is to manipulate the 'blood, brains, heart, and bowels ... '[26] of the audience, and Burke defines artistic form as precisely such manipulation: form is 'the creation of an appetite in the mind of the auditor and the adequate satisfying of that appetite'.[27]

Categorizing literary forms in these terms, Burke sets forth a scheme which is more illustrative than exhaustive but nevertheless useful. His basic distinction is between progressive and repetitive form, the first type of which is divided into two sub-types: 'syllogistic' and 'qualitative'.[28] Syllogistic form is set forth so that the audience can predict each step as in a well-conducted argument. Poe's stories are good examples, as is 'Oedipus Rex', and a less exalted illustration is the soap opera where A marries B because of event C. Qualitative form evokes a mood or atmosphere which leads naturally to another, as in 'Macbeth', where 'the grotesque seriousness of the murder scene [prepares] us for the grotesque buffoonery of the porter scene'.[29] Burke's qualitative progression is useful in reminding us that a definition of symbolic form must include aesthetic patterns that are typically ignored in social science studies of 'logico-meaningful culture'.

Progressive form is distinct from repetitive form, exemplified by lyric poetry that develops a theme instead of a plot by saying the same thing in varying ways. A final type, 'conventional' form could be either repetitive or progressive, but it draws its appeal from aesthetic convention rather than from existential content. An example:

> I'll tell you a story of Jack O'Norey
> and now my story's begun.
> I'll tell you another about his brother,
> And now my story is done.

Burke believes that the task of symbolic form, the arousal and gratification of expectations, is achieved by the use of guilt, scapegoats, and catharsis. This dialectic is intrinsic to symbolic form, which both pollutes and purifies:

If there is a cleansing, there must be persons or things that do the cleansing (agencies) and there must be off-scourings that result from the cleansing.[30]

And these must be disposed of, neutralized. If one thing becomes clean, another must get dirty—a bath yields dirty water. For Burke, the abstract categories of human action (agent, agency, scene, act, and purpose) inevitably find dramatic expression in this type of purge, which originates with guilt and culminates in the scapegoat. Burke is keen on the idea that literary characters serve merely as agents to carry forward this process. Othello, Desdemona, and Iago are not (as some might suppose) two lovers and a third party. Instead, Othello and Desdemona are agents to crank up the tension that necessarily derives from their monogamous relationship, while Iago is the scapegoat who must torture the plot forward to the point that he can provide catharsis by carrying away the audience's guilt when both he and it are disposed of at the end.[31]

Burke is particularly concerned with this catharsis as it occurs in tragedy. His numerous insights into the process can be synthesized as follows. The tragedian elevates a character through exaggerating his natural endowments, such as beauty and strength. He then incites the audience to resent the character by portraying him as proud. Next he makes the character suffer, thus evoking pity. Pity and pride have a psychoanalytical relationship. Pride is anal: does not the proud man turn his *back* to his fellows and show his *bottom* to them as they kneel below? Pity relaxes the anal-retentive rigidity of pride by a 'bath of pitiful tears, a benign orgiastic downpour', which is made more pungent by the spectator's fear that he may suffer in the place of the character; that fear evokes the teary substitutes for Coleridge's diuretic 'soft flowing daughter of fright'. The tears also symbolize ejaculation. Unable either to urinate or copulate on the spot, the audience weeps instead.[32]

Secretly pleased that the mighty have fallen, the audience mixes pity with contempt. They may break into 'derisive laughter', an outburst that lacks the cathartic power of 'sympathetic laughter', and certainly that of pity. For Burke, Tragedy is more cathartic than comedy, possibly because it steadily builds tension to a point of release. Comedy punctures the balloon rather than blowing it full before the explosion.

Burke as sociologist asserts that dramatic catharsis comes from 'civic tension', by which he means tension felt by the audience as a whole. An example is Euripides' 'Trojan Women'. The play ostensibly depicts the destruction of Troy and the resulting grief of the Trojan women. Burke believes that the play was written to depict indirectly the Athenian razing of Melos, which had occurred only months before. The decision to attack Melos was opposed by a faction of doves, but supported by the hawks, so that Athens was divided by the event. Burke believes that the civic tension was transformed by the drama into a timeless myth which, by its distance from the actual event, could evoke empathy and solidarity more powerfully than a direct portrayal:

> Euripides' illusions could both be there and discreetly revealed ... The entire audience, be they members of either the Peace party or the War party, could join in weeping together. And would not that moment, at least for the duration of the dramatic experience, be indeed a pungency of the whole discordant city?[33]

Like Weber, Burke believes that the essence of modernization is rationalization, but Burke, like Lukacs, stresses the destructive results. Rationalization destroys traditional meaning, as when a tree symbolizing father and tradition is cut down in the interests of engineering, or a lion symbolizing monarchy is classified with an alley cat for the sake of science. Such offenses against traditional cosmologies, belief systems, and complexes of feeling arouse tension and guilt which cry out for catharsis. Lacking primitive ritual, modern men must rely on literature and other artistic forms. Burke believes that any symbolic form, regardless of its content, possesses the power to transform tension and guilt into sequence, catharsis, and order:

> The symbol-using animal experiences a certain kind of "relief" in the mere act of converting any inarticulate muddle into the orderly terms of a symbol system.[34]

Frye

The literary critic, Northrop Frye, resembles Burke in castigating those who would too readily read an author's philosophy from his works:

... the poet never imitates thought except in the ... sense of imposing a literary form on his thought. The failure to understand this produces a fallacy to which we may give the general term "existential projection." Suppose a writer finds that he is most successful with tragedies. His works will inevitably be full of gloom and catastrophe, and in his final scenes there will be characters standing around making remarks about the sternness of necessity, the vicissitudes of fortune, and the ineluctability of fate. Such sentiments are a part of the *dianoia* of tragedy; but a writer who specializes in tragedy may well come to feel that they speak for the profoundest of all philosophies and begin to emit similar utterances himself when asked what his own philosophy of life is.[35]

The fallacy is to assume that consciousness came before the form, where the reality may be the reverse.

Formulating what he calls a 'theory of modes', Frye classifies the forms of literary fiction into five types distinguished according to the hero's power.[36] *Mythical* heroes have the greatest power of action, since they are gods who are superior in kind to men. Heroes of *romance* boast marvellous powers but are identified as human beings. Heroes of *high mimetic* are great men but lack supernatural power. Heroes of *low mimetic* are simply like us. The hero of *irony* is less than we who, as the audience, enjoy the sensation of looking down on him, as he is trapped in some situation of bondage, frustration, or absurdity. Elaborating his typology with respect to tragedy, Frye delineates such typical plots as the myth of the god's dying, and the high mimetic narrative of the hero's fall. The same typology is employed to classify comic plots, to delineate the 'thematic' modes of poetry, and to associate each formal type with a social context. Only a hint of the power of Frye's schema can be given here, but noteworthy is his elaboration of a theory of literature based on the total thrust of varying types of symbolic form.

Duncan

Sociologists of literature have tended to join their colleagues in the media analysis school by emphasizing the content of form rather than the form itself; an example is Leo Lowenthal's well-known and suggestive analysis of change in the imagery of production and consumption found in popular American biographies during the past half-century.[37] But one sociologist of literature, Hugh D. Duncan, has announced his allegiance to Kenneth Burke, and he has launched an all-out attack on the insensitivity of sociologists to symbolic form. According to Duncan, sociologists reduce the analysis of symbolic form to the analysis of techno-social systems conceived after the analogy of the machine. Such models (exemplified by the Weberian/Durkheimian-inspired 'theory of action' of Talcott Parsons) may claim to incorporate symbol systems, but they really spawn 'theoretical monsters' that

> almost rival the chimeras of antiquity; firebreathing monsters, with a lion's head, a goat's body, and a serpent's tail, have been matched by grotesques with mechanical heads and symbolic bodies.[38]

The difficulty with these models is that they do not treat symbolic forms as important in their own right but merely as

> epiphenomena which exist on the surface of a social system whose "gearing" and "meshing" (in modern mechanistic parlance) really determine human motivation.[39]

Among the evil consequences of this viewpoint in sociology are the dominance of content analysis, which ignores form; preoccupation with life histories, which are mediocre autobiographies; and the failure to accord symbolic forms their proper place in social process. Duncan lays the blame for these lapses on the founding fathers, Durkheim and Weber. Treating religion as the key for understanding society, they established a custom of relegating art, i.e. symbolic form, to a subordinate place in social theory. Accordingly, the classic sociologies consistently underestimate the social power of form:

> The point is not that Giotto painted on his knees, or that Bach worshipped through music, but that they give religious experience new forms and new realities which would not have been possible without such forms.[40]

As an alternative to the mechanist model, Duncan proposes a

'dramatistic' one inspired by Burke. Duncan's definition of drama-tistic action is vague, but from his potpourri of insight, harrangue, and analysis emerge two images of social process, the tragic and the comic.

Society as tragic is hierarchical, emphasizing relations between superiors and inferiors, gods and men. Oppressed and beset with guilt, men purge their troubles by blaming scapegoats who are purged from society. Balancing the negative movement toward purge is a positive movement toward sanctification. Through associ-ation with symbols of dignity and radiance, the highest principles of social order are glorified. The elite scale these heights of glory even as the lowly are shoved deep into the depths of pollu-tion.

Society as comic is egalitarian, emphasizing relations among men. The thrust is neither upward nor downward, neither toward gods nor devils, but horizontal. In comic society, 'we talk to *each other*, not to our gods, about the social ills that beset us'.[41] The comic victim is the clown, and, unlike the scapegoat, he is never totally banished from society. Instead he remains with his audience always. Conversing with them, he objectifies their doubts and frustrations. Rationality emerges through discussion by equals.

Duncan proposes that Communism and Democracy exemplify the two types of socio-symbolic action:

Communism is essentially a tragic drama of victimage in which enemies within the state are killed in solemn and awful rites called purge trials ... democracy is more a comic drama of argu-ment, bickering, disputation, insult, beseechment, and prayer.[42]

Duncan's perspective goes to the opposite extreme from the sociologist who would reduce the analysis of symbolic form to the analysis of the social system; Duncan subsumes the social system under a paradigm of symbolic action. The perspective merits at least brief discussion.

Talcott Parsons, one of Duncan's primary targets, has defined four major exigencies that any social system must meet in order to function and survive. These are adaptation (generation of re-sources), goal-attainment (mobilization of the resources toward collective goals), integration (coordination of all units and pro-cesses composing the system), and pattern-maintenance/tension-management (the formulation, legitimation, and expression of values which define the dominant pattern of the system and the release or control of personal tensions such that they do not erupt into action which destroys the system).[43] A model such as this is presumably what Duncan has in mind when he says 'mechanistic'. His dramatistic alternative would presumably see the primary exigency of society as one not listed in Parsons' scheme: the organizing of process in a pattern sufficiently dramatic so that either tragic or comic catharsis is achieved.

It is not difficult to think of societies which, at certain times, seem to mobilize their efforts toward dramatic ends. Most nations, at one time or another, have staged military attacks, sports events, and political campaigns which, while partially oriented toward the functions outlined by Parsons, seem primarily for the purpose of putting on a show. Indonesia was so flamboyant in this respect during the days of the late Sukarno that political scientists have written monographs comparing Indonesian politics to the traditional shadow drama,[44] and Sukarno characterized himself as like the *dalang*, the puppeteer.

One could even hypothesize principles governing society-as-drama parallel to those governing its other aspects, such as 'supply and demand' or 'reciprocity'. According to rules of classical theater, the society might endeavour to organize its public events in order to sustain units of time and place. Or maybe it should, as often seemed the case in Indonesia, simply 'leave 'em laughing'. In the tragic idiom, according to Burke's law of catharsis, it should produce a scapegoat who can be blamed to purge guilt.

Such a model might freshen the sociological perspective with a dash of the dramatic, but it is as reductionistic in its way as the mechanists are in theirs. It seems more accurate to recognize that human existence contains both the casual-functionally organized networks and the logico-meaningful (including aesthetic) systems of symbols. Put differently, there are both the front stage and the back stage, neither of which is reducible to the other. The actors cannot repair the lighting system by hamming it up before the audience, nor can the electrician create a drama by installing a new backstage switch.

At the beginning of this chapter, I follow Weber (and convention) in asserting that religion lays emphasis on moral and metaphysical conceptions expressed *by* symbols while art emphasizes the form *of* the symbols. The statement is obviously simplistic and careful scrutiny will elicit a flood of objections.

To begin, the anthropologist and the historian remind us that in traditional society religion and art are typically a single complex. Only in recent centuries has secular art emerged as a field relatively independent of religious art. Without arguing the point beyond noting that even in traditional society there can be distinguished forms which are *relatively* more appreciated for their form compared to others whose significance derives largely from the metaphysical/moral message they express, let us accept this observation and define more specifically the scope of discussion. I shall concentrate here solely on the respective roles of art and religion in *modernization*. Excluded from consideration are both the largely traditional and the largely modern societies. All hypotheses are intended to apply only to societies whose condition is best defined as one of transition between these two types. An illustrative case is the West during the past three centuries or so.

With this familiar case in mind, let us scrutinize our initial statement further. Obviously the distinction between art and religion is one of degree. There is no pure art or pure religion, not even among those who cry 'Art for art's sake' or 'Revelation without communication'. Can we say, then, 'to the degree emphasis is laid on moral and metaphysical conceptions expressed by symbols, the symbol is religious, and to the degree that emphasis is laid on the form of the symbol, it is art'? No, for there are limits. Form entirely bereft of moral and metaphysical meaning is merely a physical object (as Lévi-Strauss would say, nature rather than culture), and moral/metaphysical meaning is communicated only through form. What is more, both great art and great religion achieve a fusion of form and meaning. Stylistics alone never produces the novel of an age, and the historic religions are notable for their symbols as well as their doctrine.

In spite of these caveats, we can grossly distinguish forms that are more strongly religious (orientated toward the expression of metaphysical and moral conceptions) from those which are more strongly aesthetic (appreciated for their formal or sensuous qualities). These two extremes are like Weberian ideal types. To the extent that a given form is closer to one or the other extremes, it will function in a certain predictable way. To simplify discussion, I shall speak simply of 'religion doing this' and 'art doing that', but what I mean is that to the extent that a form fits the ideal type of religion it will tend to function in one way, to the extent that it fits the ideal type of art it will tend to function in the other way. Because no real-life form ever perfectly fits either of these ideal types it will never conform perfectly to the functional generalizations I set forward. (The facts may also fail to fit my generalizations because I am simply wrong, but that is another problem.)

Religion bestows meaning, identity, community, and legitimacy through cognitive, classificatory processes. A theology may thus bestow meaning by subsuming particular acts or problems under general premises of belief, while an ethical system subsumes (and therefore legitimizes) particulars through a similarly deductive process.[45]

Art also classifies, but in a different way. The first and foremost function of art is to codify experience by transforming it into sensory (visible, audible, tactile) form. An example is the narrative which transforms the directionless conflict of daily life into the climax and resolution of Burke's progressive form. Codifying experience, art resembles religion. Both subsume reality into categories. But the aesthetic categories differ from the religious ones. The religious categories refer to two realms outside the forms that express them: the moral and the metaphysical. The aesthetic categories refer to the forms themselves. A sermon in church (a symbolic form) is primarily designed to tell about God and Christ and to remind the congregation of what is good and what is bad. Both the metaphysical and the ethical messages refer to realms extrinsic to the sermon; they speak of celestial realms and the afterlife as well as of daily behavior outside the church on days other than Sunday. Consider, by contrast, a secular painting appreciated primarily for its beauty. The aesthetic categories in terms of which the painting's portrayal of experience is perceived refer simply to the form of the painting. These categories define rules of style, definitions of genre, and clichés of fashion in terms of which the form is evaluated as tasteful or tasteless, beautiful or ugly, exciting or dull. Insofar as these categories are purely aesthetic and not moral or metaphysical, they do not refer to any social or celestial realm independent of the form itself.

As art becomes more purely art, which is to say, more abstract and less representational, its function perhaps becomes more fully that of succintly elucidating the rules that define its form. Burke's poem about Jack O'Norey tells nothing except that a poem should have a beginning and an end, and non-representational paintings, according to Lévi-Strauss, serve only to 'represent the pattern in which [the painter] would execute his pictures if by chance he were to paint any'.[46] Such conventions or rules of form may derive from experience, but they do not obviously tell of the good life or the afterlife. To the extent that Lévi-Strauss is right, the primary function of abstract art is simply to formulate the rules that define itself.

This narcissism of art led Weber to regard it as in competition with religion. Both art and religion treat objects as more than means, as sacred or beautiful but not merely utilitarian. Accordingly, both offer salvation from the utilitarian world of everyday. But in return for its gift of salvation from the world, religion obligates the believer to commitment to a set of moral values which prescribe his behaviour as a member of the brotherhood of men. Art, by contrast, offers salvation without obligation. Art is idolatry, a kind of fetishism which gives the pleasure of beauty as an end in itself. Art, from the religious standpoint, is a 'deceptive bedazzlement' that leads to a 'secret lovelessness'.[47]

Weber's disciple, Talcott Parsons, makes a similar point when he writes that appreciative standards which artist and audience share are

> ... institutionalized only in "acceptance" terms. As we ordinarily put it, we are "pleased" or "moved" by a work of art or its performance. But this attitude does not have specifically binding implications for our actions beyond this specific context.[48]

Put operationally, attendance at a performance or an exhibition is usually voluntary in the first place, and rules of the theater or gallery apply only in those places rather than ramifying into spectators' lives in the wider society. Parsons would not claim that the artistic event fails entirely to affect daily life, but he would assert that such influence is not primarily through explicit prescription and organizational sanction, the way a church can govern its members' lives. When art does have effects, it is more likely through psychological than through institutional processes. As Parsons has put it: religion, embodied in evaluative and cognitive symbols, is institutionalized in the social system, while

F

expressive symbols such as art are internalized by the personality.[49]

Art can, of course, become a religion, as when coteries or schools of art set aesthetic standards to which their members must conform in widely ramified spheres of their lives. Parsons believes that such schools could never become the model for an entire society. They require that beauty be the sole end in life, and the majority of a society's members will, perhaps must, devote their primary energies to other objectives. Parsons does note that in some societies, such as the Communist ones, aesthetic standards become crucial *parts* of the morality controlling the entire society. Thus, certain Communist ideologies prohibit literary portrayal of any private emotions which do not directly serve collective aims.[50] While considering the possibility of these wider social and moral ramifications of art, Parsons takes as his paradigmatic case pure or fine art, and he concludes: 'The "fine" artist... we may say, is not orientated to the influencing of the attitudes of his public in other than expressive terms, but only to giving "form" to their expressed interests.'[51]

At this point, we seem to have excluded art (insofar as it is 'pure') from a moral or metaphysical role equal to that of religion. Aesthetic rules have been defined as referring solely to the artistic form, and both Parsons and Weber regard such rules as carrying no normative obligation which governs daily behavior and organizes society. Must we conclude, then, that art has no social function? The conclusion is difficult to avoid if we follow current social science models of society. Consider Parsons' own image of society which expresses the assumptions of most social scientists, including anthropologists.

Parsons' recent view is that society is like a cybernetic system, analogous to the system linking a thermostat and a furnace. The furnace supplies fuel for producing heat (equivalent to physical, human, and organizational resources) while the thermostat provides direction, telling the furnace when to come on and when to cut off. Such direction is analogous to that provided by the norms of society. In Parsons' conception, the most specific normative prescription is the role, which prescribes particular acts of the individual; roles are legitimized by norms; norms are legitimized by values; and values are grounded in a cognitive and ethical system of metaphysical belief. The stable social system, like a house whose room temperature is kept at a constant level, balances the normative and the informational inputs with the input of resources; the changing social system responds to an overdose of one type of input with some modification of the other type.[52]

This model is extremely useful in avoiding either a naive idealism (which awards too much prominence to the informational inputs) or a naive materialism (which awards too much to resource inputs). It does, however, bias the analyst against serious attention to art. Parsons' conception is that informational processes are normative: beliefs prescribe values, values prescribe norms, norms prescribe roles, and roles prescribe proper behaviour. This prescriptive function is precisely where conventional religion has been potent, through supernaturally sanctioned sermons, decrees, and moral codes, and where art has been weakest. Where art becomes prescriptive, it is propaganda. Viewing social change from the Parsonian (or main-line social science) perspective, we may do fairly well at recognizing the normative contribution of religion, but we are likely to ignore the role of art. There has been a Weber to set forth the massive religious aspect of modernization, but no analysis of equivalent power to treat the aesthetic. How, then, does art operate? I would hazard that it works its influence through subtle psychological processes as yet ill understood. The following speculations are tentative.

Especially in the modernizing, individualistic society of the Western type, art tends to be organized according to certain principles of childhood experience: magical thinking, aesthetic fit, and convention rather than rationality, utility, and efficiency. These latter are the norms of the wider society, particularly business, science, and practical affairs. Art is like play in its possession of these qualities as well as in its narcissistic self-containment. The zealous worshipper feels obligated to apply his faith in all of life, but play is play only when it is 'for fun', which is to say, independent of any wider function. Some regard art similarly: art is art only when it is art for art's sake.

If art parallels in certain ways childhood fantasy and play (which is not to deny that in other ways art is as distant from childhood as one could get), then childhood Oedipal and sexual impulses are doubtless associated with the artistic urge. George Devereux argues that art is rooted in pre-genital sexuality, and Kenneth Burke arrived independently at a similar view illustrated by his somewhat far-fetched claim that Keats' line 'Truth is beauty...' was a veiled expression of the unconscious image 'Turd is body . . .'[53] If pre-genital sexuality is important, childhood experiences with the mother must be also, a connection that can be argued on sociological as well as psychological grounds.

'Particularism' is a concern with an object for its own qualities rather than because of its use for some exterior purpose. Probably the most significant experience with particularism for most people involves the mother. She loves her child particularistically—for its own qualities and because it is her child rather than because of its use or merit according to some exterior purpose or criterion. The employer, on the other hand, may not love his employee at all, but pay him because of his utility. Now our distinction between religion, art, and technology, introduced at the beginning of this chapter, emphasizes the fact that of the three types of orientations art is the most particularistic. The *objet d'art* is appreciated for its own qualities rather than of its use as a tool or a medium for expressing belief. Owing to this commonality between the aesthetic and the maternal attitude—both are particularistic—one would predict that art naturally tends to evoke memories of the mother. For different reasons, if Erikson is correct, the morality and punishment of reformist religion will evoke memories of the father. The connections are not quite so simple, of course, and it is erroneous to entirely equate art and mother. As is suggested by the phrase, 'a face only a mother can love', the mother appreciates her child regardless of how well it fits society-wide standards of beauty. Art is judged by precisely these standards unless it is 'folk' art in the pejorative and particularistic sense of 'fit only for your folks'.

If art and childhood share attributes, involvement in art will tend to evoke, at some level, memories of childhood. These 'remembrances of things past' are discrepant from the real world, and the discrepancy is perceived either consciously or unconsciously. This perception evokes a different response from that of the reformer who compares the Kingdom of God to reality. The reformer is goaded into angry and energetic action: reform. The participant in art, such as the reader who has just finished a novel or the viewer who leaves the cinema, is more likely to feel nostalgia, sadness, and reluctance to lose the world of fantasy which emotionally re-enacts loss of childhood. The participant in art experiences emotions more narcissistic and less oriented toward systematic action than the reformer acting out the prescriptions of his calling.

I suspect that this holds true even when the art form is of the revolutionary type deliberately designed, as Brecht put it, to elicit decision.

If this analysis is correct, and the dominant social science framework is accepted, then the view that art is less significant than religion in modernization would seem justified. The dominant framework, we recall, assumes that change comes about through input of environmental resources or normative prescription. But many people resent normative prescription. Hating sermons, they reject their supernatural and political base as well, and they seek motives for action within the self. Insofar as processes of this type (which formerly were important in the Renaissance and Romanticism and today are exemplified by the radicals and hippies) become important for social change, the processes of art become important as well. Modernization becomes less a result of prescription and more a result of movement within the self prompted by fantasy evoked through art.

Notes to Chapter 6

1. See *Parsons* (3), pp. 1128–9 and *Weber* (4), pp. 223–45.
2. In subsequent studies both Leach and Lévi-Strauss have taken fuller account of narrative form. For powerful reinterpretation of the Oedipus myth taking account of narrative, see *Terrence Turner*. *Crites* makes an interesting argument that narrative rather than structure is the fundamental category of thought.
3. See, for example, *Lord* and *Dundes*.
4. *Wright*.
5. *Hovland, et al.*
6. *Lazarsfeld*.
7. See *Holsti, et al.* and *Berelson*.
8. See *Wright*.
9. *de Sola Pool*, p. 99.
10. Ibid., p. 99.
11. *Merton*, p. 439.
12. *Parsons* (1), p. 115, and *Weber* (1).
13. *Isaacs*. This critique of the mass media school is elaborated in *Peacock* (3), and an alternative approach (which also has its difficulties) is given in *Peacock* (1). To take one example from this source (pp. 209–10; also see Chapter 8 in the present work): in the proletarian Indonesian drama known as *ludruk*, lyrics of songs would be adjudged by typical methods of content analysis to express activistic nationalism. Yet if the context and form of the songs are observed, the conclusion is different. The activist lyrics are chanted in a slow voice by transvestite singers dressed in feudal costumes in a melody normally used in recalling poignant experience, and

the only audience response to the songs is that mothers sing them to their children as lullabies. Granted, the scope of the media analysts' projects force them to reduce communicative events to discrete categories suitable for precise measurement. My polemic has de-emphasized the impressive achievements of this school using such methods. Nevertheless, as this *ludruk* example suggests, it would seem that observation of form and context are essential to correctly interpret the results of content analysis.

14. *Lukacs* (4), p. ix.
15. *Howe*, p. 8.
16. *Lukacs* (3).
17. Ibid., p. 90.
18. Ibid., p. 93.
19. Ibid., p. 94.
20. Ibid., p. 130.
21. *Lukacs* (3), p. 130.
22. *Lukacs* (1).
23. Compare *Burke* (6) and *Parsons* (4). Burke expounds 'action' and Parsons 'social action'. In both, the key elements are the scene (or situation) in which the action occurs, its purpose (or end), the agency (means), the act (or action) itself, the actor, and in Parsons' scheme, the norms governing the entire complex. All that is present in Parsons' (Weber's) paradigm and lacking in Burke's is the norms governing the action.
24. *Burke* (2), pp. 168–9.
25. Ibid., p. 53.
26. Ibid., p. 36.
27. Ibid., p. 31.
28. *Burke* (2), p. 125.
29. Ibid., p. 126.
30. *Burke* (5), p. 123.
31. *Rueckert*, p. 166.
32. *Burke* (5).
33. *Burke* (4), p. 351.
34. Ibid., p. 364.
35. *Frye*, pp. 63–4.
36. Ibid.
37. *Lowenthal* (1); also *Grana* and *Wilson*.
38. *Duncan* (3), p. 17.
39. Ibid., p. 6.
40. *Duncan* (2), p. 375.
41. *Duncan* (3), p. 24.
42. Ibid., p. 25.
43. See *Parsons* (3), Introduction to Part II.
44. See the interpretation in *Anderson*.
45. See *Parsons* (3), Introduction to Part IV.
46. *Lévi-Strauss* (3), p. 30.
47. See *Parsons* (3), pp. 1128–9. An interesting example of this is transvestitism, to be discussed in chapter eight with reference to Java. In Java and also in America (see *Newton*) the transvestite performer places great emphasis on his role as an artist. The medium is his own body, which he lovingly decorates to produce an illusion of feminine beauty. Yet by various devices the audience is made aware that the illusion is just that, that the

figure is no real woman. By denying the extra-symbolic ramifications of the symbolic illusion (such as sexual and reproductive capacities that are normally implied by the image of the woman), transvestitism would seem to state the premises that underly art in general.

48. *Parsons* (2), p. 411.

49. See Parsons' paper, 'Expressive Symbolism', in *Parsons* (3). Analysis and criticism of Parsons' conception of 'expressive symbols' can be found in *Peacock* (6).

50. *Parsons* (2), p. 412.

51. Ibid., p. 412.

52. The thermostat analogy derives from lectures by Parsons at Harvard University, 1963, but the scheme is expounded in *Parsons* (3).

53. See *Devereux*, p. 375, and *Burke* (6), p. 728.

7
Modern Society and Consciousness

The Protean Perspective

The great quartet, Durkheim, Weber, Marx, and Freud, have provided the basis for most analyses of traditional and modernizing society, the present one included. Relevant as they remain, radical change has occurred since they died. Since the Second World War, the highly modernized societies have experienced the end of colonialism, ecological disaster, and a counterculture profoundly disillusioned with the modernization that has brought it into existence. We should avoid making too much of the new movement. Many of its values hark back to such early groups as the Romantics, Agrarians, and Taoists. And few would claim that the economic problems of industrialization are sufficiently desperate to prompt ideological revolution equal to that in old Russia or China. Nevertheless, a host of commentators sense a new day dawning. Whether embodied in the image of 'Protean Man', the 'Greening of America', or 'the medium is the message', essentially the same pattern is glimpsed by all these prophets.

Protean Man and Young Man Luther

Among the numerous commentaries on emerging modern consciousness, the most succinct is probably Robert Jay Lifton's characterization of 'Protean Man'.[1] Lifton's portrait has the advantage of generalizing about trends both inside and outside the West; Lifton, a psychiatrist who has done research in the Orient, draws on his impressions of patients and informants in China and Japan as well as America. Acknowledging the inspiration of Erikson, Lifton intends his portrayal to apply to the patterns of consciousness that have emerged since the early modern period from which Erikson draws so much of his material. The distinctive qualities of Protean Man can be highlighted by a comparison with those represented by Erikson's description of Young Man Luther.

Protean Man, writes Lifton, is alienated from 'vital and nourishing symbols of [his] cultural tradition—symbols revolving around the family, idea systems, religions, and the life cycle in general.'[2] In place of these root symbols, he is flooded with images produced by an 'extraordinary flow' of media.[3] Crossing all boundaries, these images permit Protean Man to contact everything, but only superficially: the messages are incoherent and undigested. The contrast with Luther is obvious. He rebelled and reformed within well-defined boundaries of family, religion, life cycle, and regional identity. Luther's father was certainly present, his religious framework highly ordered, and Luther, whom Erikson terms a 'provincial on a grand scale',[4] was deeply rooted in the regional tradition of medieval Germany. Sheltered from the bombardment of images transmitted by the modern media, Luther worked (as Erikson emphasizes) within the bounds of a single central text, the Holy Scripture; through painstaking analysis of this one system of symbols Luther derived the notion that shook the West, justification by faith.

Lifton suggests that Protean Man lacks a superego, at least in the traditional sense of the term. He describes one of his patients, a 'gifted young teacher', who mentions that in literature there is a representation of 'every kind of crime, every kind of sin', then adds, 'For me, there's not a single act I cannot imagine myself committing.'[5] Conceiving of the total spectrum of wrong actions, Protean Man is unable to commit himself to a fixed conception of the right. From him can come no heroic Lutheran 'Here I stand. I can do no other.' Protean Man is an oscillating, vacillating relativist who perceives the good and the bad in every possibility.

Eliminating, or stretching shapeless his superego, Protean Man seems to have dispensed with his father as well, indeed with every authority figure who could instill a conscience. Lifton quotes from Sartre, whom he takes as a prototype of Protean Man:

There is no good father, that's the rule. Don't lay the blame on men but on the bond of paternity, which is rotten ... Had my father lived, he would have laid on me at full length and would have crushed me ... I'left behind me a young man who did not have time to be my father, and who could now be my son. Was it a good thing or bad? I don't know. But I readily subscribe to the verdict of an eminent psychoanalyst: I have no Superego.[6]

The crux of Erikson's analysis is that Luther had both superego and super-father. Hans Lueder personifies in the grossest possible way the jealous, punitive authority figure whose imprint in everything from toilet training to sexuality left Luther with a corrosive guilt and punitive conscience that drove him, finally, to create a doctrine of ethical justification.

Lifton warns against seeing Protean Man as free of superego and guilt altogether; he has simply lost his 'classic' superego, those rigidly defined criteria of right and wrong that were, traditionally, transmitted with a sense of certainty from parents to child. 'Freud's original description of the Superego, in other words, referred to stable moral and psychological structures much more characteristic of traditional cultures than of our own.'[7] Instead of guilt in the classical sense of offence against a clearcut and total ethical prescription, Protean Man feels a vague unworth owing to his failure to attain any clearcut good—a failure which is inevitable as long as he has no notion of what such a good might be.

Protean Man's identity is diffused. Lacking any clear definition of the good self, he cannot identify his real self; in fact, he wonders if he has one. As Lifton's patient put it, 'Is it a futile gesture for the actor to try to find his real face?' The contrast with Erikson's characterization of Luther as 'meaning it' is strong. Possessed of a thundering certainty that he was something, Luther heroically struggled to break through the mask of ceremonialism and say directly what he was.

Lacking a fixed and certain identity, Protean Man changes ideological commitments as easily as he changes clothes (and perhaps more frequently). Writes Lifton:

Until relatively recently, no more than one major ideological shift was likely to occur in a lifetime, and that one would be long remembered as a very significant inner individual turning point accompanied by profound soul-searching and conflict. But today, it is not unusual to encounter several such shifts accomplished relatively painlessly within a year, or even a month, whether in politics, aesthetic values, or style of living. Among many groups the rarity is the man who has gone through life holding firmly to a single ideological vision.[8]

Lifton gives examples of Chinese and Japanese who have shifted rapidly through a series of widely conflicting ideologies: an American equivalent would be the child of an upper-middle-class organization man who, in the course of a decade, shifts from 'straight' to 'freak', and, for all we know, will eventually go back into a role like that of the parent. Martin Luther exemplifies the traditional mode of change. During his entire life, he underwent only two crucial shifts: into the monastery and out. The entry was of such personal gravity as to be signalled by a thunderbolt. The exit shook the world, was permitted only after years of tortured visions and painstaking scholarship, and was accomplished against brutal opposition.

Protean Man is allergic to what strikes him as 'inauthentic', and virtually any conventional piety does. His defense is mockery and absurdity: Pop Art, Camp, *Catch-22*, and *The Tin Drum*—this latter, an embodiment of modern German counterculture, stars as its anti-hero a dwarf. Luther strove to be a giant, a genuine hero, and his stolid piety would have struck Protean Man as unbelievably stuffy and rigid. Less absurd than obscene, Luther's humor was essentially a loud belch. Other pious reformers share this heaviness of wit.

Luther drove toward a reformation, which in certain respects was in the direction of modernization and rationalization—a soulful and sincere but eventually relentless purge of the overtly ritualized, the sensuous ornamentation of medieval ceremony, language, and life style. Protean Man craves to regain the richness that Luther lost. He craves not reformation but, Lifton writes, 'rebirth whether in ideas, techniques, religions and political systems, mass movements, drugs, or prophets. He wants experience, ecstasy. And instead of driving relentlessly toward some single object or consequence, the direction of Protean man's prophecy lies in new, fluid, threatening, liberating, confusing, and revitalizing personal boundaries.'[9]

The Greening of America

> There is a revolution coming. It will not be like revolutions of the
> past. It will originate with the individual and with culture, and
> it will change the political structure only as its final act.[10]

Charles Reich's now somewhat soured forecast of the *Greening
of America* suggests a revitalization movement. The 'revolution' is
the creation of what Reich terms 'Consciousness III', a new system
of beliefs, values, and symbols that induce a shift in lifestyle no
less drastic or sudden than that brought about by the Vailala Mad-
ness or the Ghost Dance. While sceptics may protest that no
major revolution has ever occurred in a society as highly modernized and affluent as the United States (and this would seem to be
true), Reich believes that it is precisely the oppressive modernization
of the United States that is producing a mental disorientation leading to the 'Greening'. In spite of the naively romantic tone of
Reich's argument, he probably does reveal tendencies of thought
that significantly vary from orthodox Americanism.

Reich argues that American consciousness has evolved through
three stages, Consciousness I, Consciousness II, and Consciousness
III. Consciousness I is the rugged individualism of the frontier ethic,
a system of values and symbols still important to such persons as
the small businessman who glorifies free enterprise. But Consciousness I is out of touch with the reality of bureaucratized
contemporary America. During the early part of this century,
reformers endeavoured to protect the freedom of enterprise by imposing controls on various abuses, but in the end they merely increased the machinery of government control. Their efforts gave
rise to the Corporate State, which is the techno-social basis of
Consciousness II.

Exemplified by America's hundreds of air bases around the
world that permit an overkill of many thousands, the Corporate
State is a vast expanse of private as well as governmental bureaucracy which is ultimately dehumanizing. The consciousness and
lifestyle of the individual is dictated by this bureaucratized social
system, which forces conformity of taste in music, sport, dress,
and cuisine, as well as imposing the more obvious controls. The
executive is isolated from the reality of life and harried by abstract

demands, the hireling stops thinking and starts obeying bureaucratic commands. In return for loss of selfhood, the person receives only status, and 'artificial inner warmth' derived from his occupancy of a particular position in the hierarchy. Lost is sensuality, ceremony, the sense of total oblivion to measured time; manufactured adventure, as in television, is substituted. In a typical romanticization of the spontaneity of 'natural man', Reich sees the media as depriving the person of an essential characteristic:

> One of the natural urges of man is to perform for his friends by playing a musical instrument, singing, dancing, acting, or cooking. It is a mode of communicating and relating that is very different from conversation and, to judge from primitive societies, at least as important as conversation.[11]

Evil as it is, Reich argues, the Corporate State carries its own seeds of destruction. The system will not be destroyed by orthodox, direct attack through force. A century of political and physical struggle by liberals and radicals has resulted merely in the expansion of the powers of government and the police. Instead, 'The revolution must be cultural. For culture controls the economic and political machine, not vice versa.'[12] For example, if the consumer changes his lifestyle, he changes what he buys, which in turn forces the producer to change what he sells.

The lifestyle of Consciousness III includes long hair, beards, drugs, rock, and clothes contoured to the body rather than tailored. The underlying values are like those of Protean Man. The self, rather than external standards, is the basic point of reference. Thought ceases to be linear and directed toward a single goal. There is no fixed moral standard, no rigid judgment of others. Relationships cease to be impersonal, they depend solely on feeling, and after the feeling is gone there is no point in sustaining the relationship. And finally Consciousness III seeks a 'childlike, breathless sense of wonder'; to this feeling is given the 'ultimate sign of reverence, vulnerability, and innocence: "Oh Wow!"'[13]

The Medium is the Message

A medium is 'any extension of ourselves',[14] states Marshall McLuhan. McLuhan's definition would seem to include virtually everything, but by listing his examples we gain an idea of the kinds of extensions he has in mind: paper, clothing, housing, money, clocks, comics, print, wheels, bicycles, airplanes, photographs, newspapers, motorcars, telegraphs, typewriters, telephones, phonographs, radios, television, weapons, games, speech, and computers. Except for games and speech, which are activities, all of these extensions are materials and machines: technology. McLuhan's originality derives from his view of the uses of such elements. The usage is not 'technical', which is the orthodox view of the function of technology: a plow is used to plow, a hammer to drive a nail. Instead, for McLuhan, technology is an extension of ourselves, a medium for the expression of consciousness. In short, McLuhan is talking about symbols. If he were to analyze the plow, he would not ask whether by making more furrows than a digging stick it permits a denser concentration of population, but what thoughts, feelings, and perceptions the plow evokes. McLuhan has been termed a 'technological determinist', but he is more accurately labelled a symbolic determinist: his argument is that technology and its products serve as symbolic forms that express and elicit a distinctive pattern of consciousness.

McLuhan's major methodological premise is that only by examining the distinctive *form* of the medium, and not by attending merely to its content, may we understand the consciousness it expresses and evokes. Hitler and Kennedy had their respective impact McLuhan argues, because of their respective media, radio and television, and not because of what they said.[15] The typical mass media analyst who attends only to the content of media, the verbal messages, is derided by McLuhan as entirely missing the point in spite of his elaborate research designs. 'Professor Lazarsfeld's helpless unawareness of the nature and effects of radio is not a personal defect,' he consoles, 'but a universally shared ineptitude.'[16] The media analyst's view is simply the 'numb stance' of everyone who permits himself to be hypnotized by the media into attending only to their content. The content of a medium is like the juicy piece of meat carried by the burglar to distract the 'watchdog of the mind' from the medium's true message, which is carried by its form—its shape, sound, configuration of imagary, and the particular sensory channels that it utilizes.

The most basic medium is the spoken word. Involving, instantaneous, and communal, it is also configurational rather than linear.

The spoken word is at the basis of tribal society with its 'oral tradition'. But, since Gutenberg, speech has been increasingly replaced by print, which, owing to its straight-line visual form, has fostered a linear consciousness that finds expression in every realm of life:

> For the West, literacy has long been pipes and taps and streets and assembly lines and inventories. Permeation of colloquial language with literate uniform qualities has flattened out educated speech until it is a very reasonable acoustic facsimile of uniform and continuous visual effects of typography ... print taught men to say, "Damn the torpedoes, full steam ahead!"[17]

McLuhan claims that literacy has fostered values such as privacy. He cites the example of a tribesman, the only literate member of his community, who served as a reader for the others when they received letters. In order not to violate the privacy of their messages, he would put his fingers to his ears as he read aloud.

Elaborating his argument through surveying other media, McLuhan suggests that writing itself is linear in impact, the Roman roads being an example. Instead of conforming to local contours, the roads were linear, and they were held together with writing and paper, which fueled the bureaucracy. When paper supplies were cut off by the Muslims, the Roman empire collapsed. Movies encourage linearity in that they present a film sequence. McLuhan supplies another 'primitive' example, claiming that when a certain tribe watched a film depicting someone disappearing off the side of the screen, they wanted to know what had happened to him. And when the camera shifted, the tribesmen thought they saw trees moving and buildings growing or shrinking. McLuhan claims that the literate audience has learned assumptions about space which permits it to interpret the images of the screen. The TV generation, however, is losing the linear perspective induced by literacy. The television image is not as lucid as film or print. TV is a configuration of rough dots which call for the viewer to close the lacunae in the grid by a 'convulsive sensuous participation' that is profoundly kinetic and tactile. This tactile, primitive participationality is akin to the attitude induced by the entirely oral and communal society of primitive man. With TV, shouts McLuhan, gone are the stag line, the party line, the receiving line, and the pencil line from the back of nylon stockings. Gone too is a linear orientation toward the future, a loss which McLuhan chooses to announce with a head*line*: 'Why the TV child cannot see ahead.'

With the television era has come the hirsute pattern, the covering of the self with hair, and a craving for burying oneself in contoured clothes, wrap-around small cars, beads, babies, food, and art. America is 'back in touch' with the European emphasis on partici-pationality, involvement, and sculptural values. Gone are the thrills of the strip-tease: 'Nudity could be naughty excitement for a visual culture that had divorced itself from audio-tactile values ... Peasants don't relish nudity and Kruschev didn't enjoy the Holy-wood can-can. Naturally not.'[18] With the new participationality, McLuhan predicted the return of round houses (now exemplified by the Holiday Inn) on the pattern of the wigwam, tent, and cave which replace the square building that does not contour to the body but is instead a set of properties abstracted from vectors of tension. Ads become more important than editorials, for the news-paper is a mosaic successor to the book. Telephones are properly oral and involving; were we to teach our physics or maths via tele-phone, even a highly literate and abstract modern could eventually comprehend the non-spatial assumptions of physics.

The electronic era, which permits instantaneous, non-visual, world-wide communication, bids to resurrect the primitive village on a global scale: 'Up to the point just short of electrification, in-crease of speed produces division of function, and of social classes, and of knowledge', but with electronics, 'implosion and contraction replace mechanical explosion and expansion'.[19] The world shrinks to a village, as people in their round houses, small cars, and nests of hair are drawn together by electronic communications to a state of 'total simultaneity of consciousness.'[20]

Runaway World

In Reith lectures delivered over the BBC, the British anthropologist Edmund Leach[21] has made some comments about the future which supplement the views presented thus far by focusing on England rather than America, and (in the portion to be summarized here) on the family instead of the society as a whole. The general theme of his lectures is that the world is ready for a major psycho-social upheaval, and those who decry the breakdown of law and order may be denouncing a creative ferment.

Why, asks Leach, do men kill each other? He argues that the reason is not instinct but language. Because humans have language, they verbally categorize people as though they were different species, then they attack them. Through history, varying types of abnormality have been seen as indicative of radical difference. Thus

> in the 18th century, when reason first became exalted, madness became terrifying, and the crazy were herded into dungeons and caged like wild beasts.[22]

Later it was the poor, today it is the young who are treated as the alien species: 'wild beasts with whom we cannot communicate'. Leach suggests that parents consider not 'why are the young so disorderly' but 'why do the old imagine that the young are so disorderly'.[23]

The cause is definitely not, he protests, the breakdown of family life, as has been claimed by just about everybody. Nearly all the large scale social changes that have taken place over the past century should have brought the child closer to his parents: shortening of the work hours, improvements in the standards of housing, paid holidays, prohibition of child labor, extension of formal day-school education, and the disappearance of domestic servants. Instead, Leach argues, the young today are rebelling against too much familism. The old system favored the docile conformist to parental ideals, exemplified by the English public (in American terms, private) school boy who was, to put it in bucolic American language, a good boy instead of a 'good ol' boy', a blue-blood instead of a red-blood. The schoolboy took for granted the values of an ossified, class-stratified society, and he was quite happy to continue the tradition by quietly moving into his appointed station, displaying the appropriate symbolism in manners and dress. The opposite is the 'teenager', the disgusting hoodlum type, who rejects both the values and the symbols of the class hierarchy, which is rooted in the family. Youth vandalism in the churches, which has shocked respectable family men, is a rebellion against the hierarchy of class and kinship.

The anti-familism derives, Leach suggests, from the isolation of the nuclear family, which has come about, in England as everywhere, through residential mobility: the 'go-ahead young man moves to the place where he thinks he can earn the most, quickest...'[24] and he brings his family with him, isolating it from its network of kin and neighbours. Isolated, the family

> looks inward upon itself; there is an intensification of emotional stress between husband and wife, parents and children. The strain is greater than most of them can bear. Far from being the basis of the good society, the family, with its narrow privacy and tawdry secrets, is the source of all our discontents.[25]

Huddled together in their isolated household, parents and children demand too much of each other, and the children react by rebellion.

In a capitalist society, the isolation would seem essential to the mobility which permits the individual to sell his labor to the highest bidder, but Leach believes that the children need to grow up in larger, more relaxed domestic groups 'centered on the community rather than on the mother's kitchen'. The Israeli kibbutz, the Chinese communes, and other communal experiments suggest models. As an anthropologist who has spent much time in extended kin groups, Leach admits that it is difficult to adjust to the lack of privacy, but he proposes that the modern psyche change in order to do so. Privacy is the source of fear and violence, for it encourages the setting of boundaries: 'I am isolated, lonely, and afraid because my neighbor is my enemy.'[26]

Comment

These several authors broadly agree on the dominant trend in modern consciousness: away from linearity, specialization, superego, guilt, the Protestant Ethic, print, vision, and future-orientation; toward configuration, oneness, multiple identities, anxiety, the Protean Ethic, television, orality, and immersion in the 'now'. The techno-social basis of this 'Consciousness III' would seem to be the breakdown of the Corporate State and, following Leach, the emergence of communal arrangements in place of the isolated nuclear family; McLuhan extends this idea to envisage a world commune, a 'global village'. Considering that these arguments imply a return to the primitive, or a gargantuan equivalent thereof such as the global village, the anthropologist is probably more qualified than most to comment.

As for McLuhan's global village, a major question is whether the tangle of wiring and machinery underlying it would not require considerable specialization and centralization. Three possibilities can be envisioned. (1) The specialized, centralized pattern of social organization undercuts the experience of simultaneous, communal participationality, so that the village becomes a bureaucracy. (2) The breakdown of specialization and centralization destroys the experience by turning the 'village' into anarchy as the circuits go on the blink. (3) A compromise is reached, which could be of several combinations: specialists run the machinery while the drugged and lobotomized masses enjoy the orgy of global participationality; specialists and participants exchange roles such that whoever is on duty runs the machinery, and those off-duty enjoy the orgy; computers take over so that everyone can enjoy the orgy. Even in the latter case, the complex technological basis of the global participationality would render it quite different, phenomenologically, from the experience of the villager.

The most concrete modern manifestation of the 'village' is the commune. Essentially two types of communes have emerged in modern times: those with a reformist religious basis, such as the Amish, Hutterite, and Israeli, and those populated by Protean Man, such as the so-called 'hippie' communities. The protean communes are permissive but generally insolvent and unstable. The religious communes are generally solvent and stable but authoritarian. Neither of these would seem to satisfy the Protean Man's desire to at once 'belong' and 'do his own thing'.

What about a return, then, to the tribal or peasant village? These traditional communities derive their stability from hard facts of physical survival. Their rigid proscriptions such as incest taboo and customs of avoidance are, in their way, as authoritarian as the religious group. Probably the most fulfilling group which anthropology could suggest to Protean Man is Turner's 'communitas', discussed in Chapter 2. Communitas offers brotherly warmth, mystical efficacy, and social freedom of a sort. It is liminal, marginal, and temporary. In fact, it is like the protean communes that already exist except for its social backdrop: stable traditionalism in the classical case.

Consciousness III is certainly not 'straight', as its 'freak' adherents emphasize. The basis of Protean Consciousness is configurational and participational rather than linear. This participationality can be illustrated by comparing one of the major media of Consciousness III, the rock band, with the big band of Consciousness II. Carefully organized into specialized 'sections', such as brasses, woodwinds, and percussions, the big band was also centralized under a clear-cut leader who directed with a baton. The rock players are 'in it together'. They huddle and weave about the stage absorbing their nominal leader. The big band would 'feature' a soloist, who stepped to the front into a spotlight. The singer in the rock group is barely audible as his voice is absorbed into the mosaic or the din. In the big band, each instrumental specialist would take his turn in improvising ('taking a [linear] ride') on the melody *line*; this sequential pattern is submerged into the multiplex harmonies and polyrhythmic beat of rock configuration. The big bandsman was as well groomed as the big businessman, but the rock man is hairy, sweaty, and prone to mix categories by adopting the dress of the opposite sex or oppressed minority. The big band crooner sang in a flawless and smooth middle-class accent, duplicating the contours of the written word. Rejecting such McLuhanesque literacy, the rock singer adopts the speech of blacks and whites from the provincial South and the vocal inflections of blues and jazz.

Does the lapse from linearity in rock music signal a return to the primitive? Relevant here is a wide-ranging study by Alan Lomax.[27] Analyzing some 4000 song performances from some 400 cultures, Lomax is able to correlate certain features of song style with techno-socio evolution, which he divides into ten phases ranging from the African and Australian food-gatherers to the 'Old High Culture' associated with the spread of cities, irrigation, and craft specialization in Asia, the Middle East, and Central Africa. Lomax explicitly considers rock music in terms of his scheme: 'Certain forms of rock combine and integrate more independent musical levels than any other form of music analyzed by Cantometrics.' A cursory survey of Lomax's typology lends strong support to his statement; elements of the rock music complex can be found at virtually every phase of evolution, whereas the big band is identifiable only with those musical features prominent in the agrarian and industrial cultures of Europe and America. What is said about rock could be said also about other elements of the protean consciousness: that it is protean, rather than purely primitive. It is sufficiently multi-faceted to embrace (though not always with great profundity) myriad lifestyles and phases of socio-symbolic evolution.[28]

The various perspectives for viewing modern consciousness converge on a common core. But no Durkheim or Weber has yet formulated a systematic theory and methodology for treating this emerging pattern. Certainly the efforts of main-line anthropology have been feeble in this regard. Nor does the present work elaborate such a frame, though I hope to have suggested the need for it.

We turn now to case studies in order to explore concretely perspectives thus far expounded by theory.

Notes to Chapter 7

1. See *Lifton*, pp. 37ff.
2. Ibid., p. 43.
3. Ibid., p. 43.
4. *Erikson* (1), p. 87.
5. *Lifton*, p. 43.
6. Ibid., p. 47.
7. Ibid., p. 49. Lifton's statement is misleading since traditional cultures (such as the Australian aborigine) do not possess the type of superego described by Freud, nor do the 'archaic' cultures such as ancient Egypt. The classical Freudian superego is found in historic and modernizing societies nourished by the great Semitic religions, Islam, Christianity, and Judaism; Freud's Vienna and Luther's Germany are of this type.
8. Lifton, p. 53.
9. Ibid., p. 63.
10. *Reich*, p. 2.
11. Ibid., p. 195.
12. Ibid., p. 329.
13. Ibid., p. 285.
14. See *McLuhan*, p. 23.
15. Ibid., pp. 260–1.
16. Ibid., p. 260.
17. Ibid., pp. 89, 162.
18. Ibid., p. 116.
19. Ibid., p. 102.
20. While I have not indulged in criticism of McLuhan's ideas, I enjoyed the following assessment by a student writing an examination. Mr. Christopher Darrouzet wrote (I quote with his permission) that McLuhan's thesis is 'ideas which come packaged as books *are booky*; those which come in films *are filmy*; those which appear on TV are intrinsically TVish. But the human mind soon learns that *Hamlet* on stage, on screen, on phonograph, on TV, in a book or however you want to serve him up still comes up good ole Prince "to be or not to be"—Is the Play the thing, or is the Tube the thing or could possibly the thing be the thing?' In short, the message simply

is not reducible to the medium. The other observation that should be made regarding McLuhan is that his ideas are more soundly developed by, and were perhaps partially taken from, *Ong*.

21. See *Leach* (3).
22. Ibid., p. 35.
23. Ibid., p. 37.
24. Ibid., p. 43.
25. Ibid., p. 44.
26. Ibid., p. 46.
27. See *Lomax*.
28. The very fact that we construct an evolutionary scheme and empathize to some extent with all levels reveals a protean capacity similar to that underlying the rock music. This type of evolutionary empathy is being taught at Scituate High School, Massachusetts, by Mrs. Carol Ryan and Mr. Jed Fitzgerald in a course entitled 'The Family of Man' and sponsored by the National Humanities Faculty. As the course has proceeded, the class has endeavored to evolve ritually. Thus, they have staged the Ndembu healing rite, with students taking the role of Kamahasanyi, Maria, Ihembi, Ndono, and Jackson; they have performed a human version of the archaic Javanese shadow play, and so forth through the various types of sociocultural patterning elucidated in this book (see Conclusion). They expect that the experience of evolving together during their two-year course will multiplexify their relationships enough to permit a Gluckmanian ritual of social relations at the end. Whether or not this proves to be so, the attempt at vicarious evolution is itself protean.

8
Traditional Society and Consciousness in Java

The Durkheimian Perspective

After elaborating a theoretical point of view by summary and illustration, useful discipline is imposed by working through a single case. The choice of Java, the most populous island of Indonesia, as the case is based on two considerations: first, that I have done fieldwork there, second, that the history and culture of Java are complex enough to express virtually all of the Durkheimian and Weberian concepts. A fascinating civilization, Java is rich in nuance that illustrates universal history.[1]

I propose to begin by considering that aspect of Javanese existence which most powerfully illuminates the Durkheimian perspective: the relationship between ritual, classification, and the social order. Though my analysis is guided by the fundamental Durkheimian premise that symbols gain meaning from social roots, the social structure we encounter in Java is different from that primitive type normally within the Durkheimian ken. The Javanese society is multiplex but hierarchical, based on kingship instead of kinship. Java provides an opportunity to extend the Durkheimian logic into a wider realm.

Were information available, we could begin our analysis with Java Man (Homo Erectus) some 400,000 to 600,000 years ago, or with his descendant Wadjak Man, who was evolving into a Homo Sapiens type by 40,000 BC. Like some of Durkheim's Australian aborigines, Java Man probably hunted and gathered in small bands, and Wadjak probably developed a kind of jungle gardening, cultivating starchy root and fruit crops in the sunless tropical forests. One anthropologist has ingeniously speculated that the ancient Javanese tribe was divided into two major groups (moieties) which intertwined with cosmic divisions such as left and right, male and female, a pattern still dominant in the remoter hills and islands of Southeast Asia.[2] Long before Lévi-Strauss, Dutch anthropologists of the so-called Leiden school were arguing on the basis of Indonesian data that the 'savage mind' has this dualistic structure, and they appreciated the implications of Durkheim and Mauss' *Primitive Classification* decades before it gained attention in England and America.[3]

Unfortunately, we know little about Java prior to the influence of Hindu civilization, the emergence of Hinduized kingdoms, and the existence of peasant counterparts to the courts. This hierarchical Hindu-Javanese civilization, which revolved around kingship, has existed at least since the eighth century AD. In order to highlight the basic structure, emphasis will be placed on the constancies rather than changes that have characterized these kingdoms during the last millennium.

The gross features of these kingdoms could be described as a combination of those which Weber emphasized in his study of archaic China and India. As in China, the emperor was a priest, ritually mediating between celestial and mundane spheres. He was also a god, reflecting the Hindu motion that a ruler is incarnated as Siva. Both aspects insured an intimate relationship between kingship and religion, which renders Durkheim's insights particularly relevant. As in China, the king was surrounded by a bureaucracy. The Javanese bureaucracy lacked the impartiality and rationalization of the Chinese, but it had a similar notion of the gentleman as a microcosm of heavenly order through his own politesse and self-control. The kingship was conceived as a microcosm of the cosmic order, and the duty of king as well as bureaucrats was to maintain this order.

The Hindu notion of caste worked some influence on Javanese civilization. Although the concept of a rigid hierarchy based on purity and pollution was not as much elaborated in Java as in India, there is enormous stress on social stratification. Expressed in Javanese dramatizations of the Hindu myths, there is a strong belief that each stratum should follow its own 'dharma', but this is not connected to any clear conception of a cycle of rebirths. Nevertheless, Java, like India, has developed a strong stream of individualistic mysticism, with the associated bond between pupil and teacher: murid and guru. The aim of such mysticism is not to escape the wheel of karma, but simply to gain inner peace and order in self and society. Probably, as Weber concludes in the case of India, both the 'dharma' and the mysticism of Java served to reinforce rather than to reform the social order.

While it is interesting to see in Javanese civilization this Weberian combination of the Chinese and the Indian, the Javanese society and consciousness have formed a unique configuration while flourishing on this tropical island for the past thousand years.[4] The political history of the Javanese kingship divides into three epochs: first, the series of Hindu-Buddhist kingdoms in several locales of Java culminating in Madjapahit during the period spanning the eighth to thirteenth centuries AD; second, the resurgence of traditional patterns in the nominally Islamized but essentially Hindu sultanate of Mataram that knew its zenith during the regime of Sultan Agung from 1613 to 1645; third, the period beginning after the Dutch defeat of Mataram and extending to the present time. During this period, Mataram has lacked political hegemony but has remained a repository for the cultivation of symbolism derived from the ancient hierarchy.

The basic concept underlying these kingdoms is that the terrestial order mirrored and embodied the celestial. In the Hindu-Java period, the king was a god, incarnated as Shiva or Vishnu, his birth celebrated by volcanic eruptions, his person illuminated by the shining light of royal charisma (wahju). Possessed of such supernatural power, the king could call down from on high the forces that calm the raging chaos of Kalijuga, the ominous period in Hindu history that preceded the world's complete destruction and which always seemed to be in session during the rarely peaceful existence of each of the Hinduized kingdoms.

The kingdom as well as the king was designed to replicate and order the cosmos. The capital was oriented to the four points on the compass, conceived as a reflection of the Hindu-Buddhist cosmos. Temple and palace symbolized the cosmic center, representing Mount Meru or some other holy pivot. Four queens or four princesses, each representing a cardinal direction, further personified the cosmic design, as did rituals such as the king's systematically paying homage to each of the four corners of the kingdom.

In Java, the god-king was always at the apex of the cosmic-social hierarchy, unlike in India where the priestly caste, the brahmins, outranked the princely caste, the ksatriya. The difference is probably due to the lack of emphasis in Java on purity and pollution, which permits the priest, through his purity, to outrank the prince. Nevertheless, the two highest ranks in India, the royal and priestly, were also the highest in Hinduized Java, and the bureaucratic as well as the ecclesiastical orders were carefully graded into ranks. To order relations between high and lowly, elaborate and refined systems of etiquette were developed, reflected in the ordering of persons in processional marches, dance, and in other symbolism. Javanese during the time of Madjapahit, like Javanese today, may have entertained a view that ordering the social hierarchy through manners orders other realms as well—from the inner depths of the soul to the expanse of the cosmos. Gluckman's notion of the ritualization of social relations to insure the harmony of the unseen is quite relevant here, with the proviso that the relations that are being ordered are hierarchical rather than egalitarian, based on kingship rather than kinship.

Gluckman's theory is further applicable to the ritual-dramas emerging during the advent of the Hinduized kingdoms and extraordinarily popular even today. Whether in puppet or dance form, these *wajang* plays stage legends of royalty in counterpoint to comedies of manners. The characters are of three major types: the royalty, their clown-servants, and their monster-enemies. Represented by the shadow puppets, the refined (*alus*) princely heroes, epitomized by Ardjuna, have narrow, almond-shaped eyes, a downturning nose, a slightly bowed head, no chin whiskers, and a delicate, almost effeminate physique. The crude (*kasar*) monsters are fat, with bristling eyebrows, round eyes, bulbous noses, and red faces (after the onset of Holland's colonization, Javanese found it appropriate to represent these monsters as the corpulent Dutch). During battle scenes, the alus prince stands quietly as he parries with one delicate outstretched finger the vigorous thrusts of the demons who turn somersaults in confusion until eventually they are dispatched with a piercing royal arrow.

The clowns, said to be of pre-Hindu origin (ca. 600 AD) and to represent the earthy, the authentic, the indigenous Javanese, mock the elite, make hilarious slapstick, and converse in local dialect about current events. Symbolizing the common man, some of the clowns nevertheless have power which exceeds that of the princes. Semar, the clown-servant to Ardjuna, is a fallen Javanese god, brother of Shiva. Boasting immense wisdom and power, Semar is the figure who appears on the screen at midnight, the time when the elements rage, to restore order. Much of the joking of the clowns is mockery of the alus princes, who move serenely in their predetermined ksatriya path, sustaining the Bhagavagita ideal of inner tranquility during outer struggle.

Without elaborating yet the relevance of Gluckman's notions to these wajang plays, we might simply note that they possess the essential qualities of the ritual of social relationships. They are stylized in form (as in the case of the schematicized puppets); their performance is believed to mystically order the social and cosmic order (certain of the wajang plays are believed to possess so much power that performance is prohibited except in time of great crisis); and the relationships depicted are those which are fundamental to the structure of the society believed to be mystically affected. In this last respect, the case of the plays requires a broadening of Gluckman's conception. The actors do not simply play their daily roles. In fact, they may reverse them as when princes play the clowns in a dance form of the wajang. What is essential is that the relationship which is ordered in the plays is that which is the major axis of the society: the relation between patrician and plebian, which is the basis of kingship and aristocracy of Hinduized Java.

After Madjapahit's collapse with the coming of Islam, the Hindu-Javanese notions of kinship were reinstituted through the new Mataram, the nominally Muslim, essentially Hindu-Javanese empire that rose to power under the rule of Agung beginning in 1613. Though Islam permitted no man to be a god, the king was *kalipatullah*, God's representative on earth, a sacral figure from whom shone the holy light (wahju) in the form of seven moons, and who bore the titles 'He who holds the world on his lap' and 'nail of the world' (the latter is still borne by the current sultan of Jogjakarta who, as the Indonesian minister of finance, is one of the three most powerful men in the nation). Like the Hindu-Javanese *kraton* (palace), that of Mataram was oriented toward the four cardinal directions. The empire was conceived as extending out from the palace in a series of circles eventually encompassing the distant countries of Southeast Asia where the divine light of the king gradually dimmed until it was absorbed into the jungles. Administrative offices were divided into right and left sides, the palace into male and female divisions, and in other ways too, the kingdom embodied conceptions of the cosmos that were of indigenous Javanese as well as Hindu origin.

The initial influence of Westernization enriched rather than destroyed the archaic consciousness of the Mataram hierarchy. The court, rendered militarily and politically impotent by the Dutch, turned inward to elaborate the sheerly symbolic aspects of their once-powerful empire. The eighteenth century is regarded as the period of the greatest florescence of the Javanese arts. During this time, unbelievably rarified and graceful dances such as a *bedojo katawang* and the *serimpi* were introduced in the court, the structure of the *gamelan* (percussion orchestra) was elaborated, the design of *batik* (wax-dyed fabric) became more splendid and intricate, and the sultan himself created the human version of the puppet plays, the *wajang wong* dance drama, which has now built the myths of Ardjuna and Semar into vast cycles of great popularity. Most striking of all, during this period of Mataram involution, the Javanese language evolved into an incredibly subtle and precise system of status-markers. Speaking the various levels of high language (*krama*) to various grades of superiors, the earthy language (*ngoko*) to inferiors, the Javanese developed the hierarchical ideal into perhaps its most precise linguistic symbolization, a language that is now spoken by the fifty million members of the Javanese society.

Primitive Classifications: Clowns and Transvestites of the Ludruk

The logical place to seek understanding of a symbolic-social complex such as that centering around the hierarchical consciousness of Java is in the Great Tradition: the classic court forms of the dramas, dances, and theosophies. Possessed by a rebelliousness and perversity, the social anthropologist is naturally attracted to the parochial and sleazy places where the Great Tradition has worn thin. Such is the case with the only field experience that I can bring to bear on the Hindu-Java pattern. The setting, distant from the court cities of Mataram nestled among the rice lands of inner Java, is Surabaja, a port city on Java's northeast coast. A scene in Joseph Conrad's novels, *Surabaja* is a sailor's town, a place of commerce, whores, thieves, raucous marketplaces of multiple ethnicity, and wild traffic of bicycles, pedicabs, and careening ram-shackle busses. Arriving there in 1963, my wife and I settled with a family in a small house within a *kampung* (ghetto) beside the rail-road track and prepared to witness the event for which I had come: a performance of a drama both enacted and viewed by the working class, the *ludruk*.[5]

The theater was at the THR, the People's Amusement Park. Running a gauntlet of whining beggars, a deafening rock band, and assorted urban types, the spectator finally reaches, in a corner beside the toilet, a bamboo-post, tin-roofed, open-side theater guarded by a barefoot ticket-taker. 'Kasar' (crude) is the Javanese term for ludruk, and the category applies to the context as well as the show. Pickpockets and prostitutes are wriggling amongst the spectators, children are alternately urinating on the ground and suckling their mother's breasts, and the true fans are munching kwatji nuts and loudly screaming insults at the actors. The actors are all males, the most effeminate of whom play females and frequently live as women, occasionally seducing members of the audience. The generally tawdry and illicit aura of ludruk is combined with its wild hilarity (the typical response of a Javanese to the mere mention of the word 'ludruk' is coarse laughter) and, in 1963, affiliation with the Indonesian Communist Party. The troupe periodically takes to the road, travelling as a standing mass on the backs of trucks to villages and towns of East Java. Most of the actors earn their rice by some kind of laboring occupation.

After enduring more than eighty of the ludruk performances, including some that lasted all night and none less than five hours, I managed to perceive certain common patterns, which may be briefly summarized under three categories: the preliminary skit, the main story, and the interlude characters who form a symbolic opposition: the transvestite and clown.

The preliminary skit begins with a song by a single figure, who then joins one or two additional figures who do evil to some victim. This victim is always older and more traditionalistic than the victimizers, who are urbanized reprobates of the street and slum. The best interpretation that I could draw of the skit was that it denigrated the traditional in favor of the modern, thus setting the stage for a 'modernizing' thrust of the main story.

These main stories were of a wide variety, not all of which I have succeeded in drawing into any coherent scheme. But the largest single type was known as the 'domestic story' (*tjerita rumahtangga*), and most of the twenty-odd examples of the type fell into two sub-types, the first of which is exemplified by a story entitled 'River of Solo' (Solo is one of the Mataram court-cities of central Java):

After enticing a servant girl with promises of marriage, an aristocrat impregnates her. When the girl gives birth, he rejects her, and she, in her despair, jumps into the River of Solo and drowns, abandoning her baby plus another child previously born to her. As the girl leaps into the river, it happens that two childless couples hear her screams and arrive on the scene. They are too late to save her but soon enough to discover her abandoned children. One couple is aristocratic, the other proletarian. The aristocratic couple adopts the child fathered by the aristocrat, the proletarian couple adopts the other child. Twenty-five years pass. The aristocratic man of the first scene is now arranging a marriage between his son (by his aristocratic wife) and an aristocratic girl. Unbeknownst to this man, the aristocratic girl is the child spawned by himself and the servant girl twenty-five years ago. She has been raised by her aristocratic foster-family. At the wedding the long-lost brother of the girl (who was reared by the proletarian family in the scene at the river) suddenly appears, declaring that the bride and groom cannot marry since they have the same father. The groom and his parents all smile chummily at the girl and say they accept her into their household as a kinswoman instead of a bride.

An example of the second type of 'domestic story' is 'The Final Duty'. A pretty village girl is romanced by an aristocratic army officer who is fighting in the hills during the revolution. After the war, the officer returns to Surabaja and opens a profitable business. While selling fried bananas on a Surabaja street, the village girl accosts the officer, flirts with him, and entices him into marrying her. After a violent scene resulting in the arrest of one of the officer's old comrades-at-arms, the story ends in happy domesticity as the officer stands in his office (which is attached to his house), flanked by his pretty wife and their new child.

The first thing to be said about the two types of plots is that the second type is increasingly popular, the first decreasingly so. Stories of the second type were, in 1963, spreading fast. Troupe A would 'invent' a story of the second type, perform it, troupe B would pick it up, then C, D, and E, and it would become the rage, while not a single story of the first type was ever performed by more than a single troupe.

It happens that stories of the type growing increasingly popular share a common structure which can, according to several criteria, be deemed more modern (hence I shall call these 'M') while those of the other type display a structure and world view that is more traditional (and I shall call these 'T'). In T-stories, the main proletarian character (usually a heroine, played by a male transvestite) fails at climbing socially (the servant girl dies in the river). In M-stories, she succeeds (the peasant-girl successfully marries an elite male and moves into an elite house). T-stories are dominated by comic twists of chance, such as the Fielding-like discovery that lovers are siblings, which block characters' plans to marry. M-characters achieve their objects by sexual alliance. The T-story climaxes with a solidification of family ties, as a blood-relationship is re-established; M-stories climax with violent punishment of a scapegoat resulting in smashed family or friendship ties (the old comrade-at-arms is taken away to prison), thus freeing the lovers to enjoy their new domestic life. The T-story takes an average of two decades to unfold, the M-story only a few weeks or months.

In sum, among the 'modern' notions depicted by the M-stories is the conception that persons of lowly status can achieve high status through their own means (sexual), and that they can do so quickly. The T-stories express the idea that a person cannot move out of his status by his own designs, though the lowly can imagine that their children may, through a trick of fate, be incorporated as kinsmen into the circles of elite whose family solidarity is symbolized by the final scene.

The form of the stories, as well as their content, varies. Empathy is more fragmented in T-stories than in M-stories, one reason being that in T-stories, clowns (stereotyped figures in white coats) interrupt the narrative more than in M-stories. In the T and M stories viewed, approximately 70 percent of the T-stories were interrupted by clowning, as opposed to only 23 percent of the M-story scenes. T-stories are periodically punctuated by comic relief, while M-stories wait until the end to unleash tension, as spectators scream at a scapegoat. The ludruk, then, is evolving toward a rationalized, sustained thrust of action that culminates in a social climb and emotional climax. This is the type of change in form as well as content of symbolic action which was suggested in Chapter 6 to be more profoundly indicative of modernization of consciousness than change in content alone.

In addition to the social content and symbolic form of the plays, a third aspect must be distinguished: the cosmological framework which lends meaning and legitimacy to the other aspects. Here is where the clown, the transvestite, the Great Tradition of Javanese civilization, and Durkheim and Mauss become relevant. In the wajang complex, the shadow plays and dance dramas, the relations between clown and cosmology are made quite explicit; they are the subject of scholarly and speculative works, theosophies, and meditation, and they can be expounded conversationally by anyone. The ludruk, on the other hand, is considered an obscenely lowly form, not worthy of cosmological elaboration, and few care to discuss ludruk's philosophy. Nevertheless, analysis of the structure of the plays themselves does reveal, I think, an unconscious pattern which links certain cosmological meanings to the complementary actions of the clown and the transvestite.

The clowns, as one Javanese put it, are the 'intellectuals of ludruk'. They are wiser than the other characters and they stand aloof, contemplating and satirizing the values that guide the others' lives during the story. It seemed that the clown's jokes could be divided grossly into two types which define values that underly both the fictional world of the ludruk and the real world of Java. The first set of values turns around the distinction between *alus* and *kasar*, refined and crude; the opposition, it will be recalled, pervades the *wajang* in which it distinguishes the princes from the monsters. I have heard ludruk participants use the terms *alus* and *kasar* to contrast castles with villages; gods, kings, and aristocrats with peasants and workers; humans with animals; *krama* (high) Javanese language with *ngoko* (low) language; *batik* cloth with cheap cotton; fine-grained substance with coarse-grained substance; central Javanese peoples and cultures with those of east Java; restraint with coarse outbursts; wajang with ludruk. By classifying acts, emotions, objects, substances, peoples, cultures, statuses, qualities, and art forms into this alus-kasar opposition, the Javanese formulate what Durkheim and Mauss term a 'primitive classification system'.

A clown's joke that turns around the alus-kasar distinction: mocking the way his master would offer guests coffee, a clown servant simply invites them to 'slurp it up'. The joke mocks the alus. The ritual of offering and drinking coffee is ordinarily designed to display alus restraint since guests ascetically suppress their burning thirst on a hot tropical day to wait with the drink in front of them until, after a delay of a number of minutes, the host croons, in high alus Javanese language, 'Please drink'. The servant exposes the kasar animal desire by barking in kasar Javanese language, 'Slurp it up'.

The other major opposition is between 'madju' and 'kuna'—'progressive' and 'traditional'. The terms have been used by ludruk participants to oppose visible female underarms kept out of sight; women's hair hanging free with hair in a bun; national culture with provincial culture; volley ball with pigeon races; Indonesian language with Javanese language; feminists with idyllic submissive wives; romantic love with parent-arranged marriage; electric guitars with the gamelan; efficiency with tranquility. Like the alus-kasar distinction, the opposition may be said to form the core of a 'primitive classification'. A simple and well-worn joke that works on this contrast is the clown's accusing a woman of being 'wanita madju'—a feminist-type who is progressive to the point of being ridiculous.

After classifying all clowns' jokes recorded in my field notes into these two types, I counted the number of each that were associated with each type of story. It turns out that most madju-kuna jokes are made during the M-stories, most alus-kasar jokes during the T-stories. The correlation makes sense. M-stories deal with the conflict between the traditional and modern, depicting a modernizing movement in the form of upward mobility of the lower class. T-stories remain within the traditional framework, where the relevant conflict is between the dominant ideal of alusness exemplified by the aristocratic establishment and the counter-force of kasarness expressed by the clown. Though none of the ludruk participants had been aware of this pattern before I brought it to their attention, several of them agreed that it jibed with their way of looking at things. The clown can be regarded as expressing a Durkheimian system of classification, unconscious but nonetheless coherent.

The strangest ludruk creature, in the eyes of both native and observer, is the transvestite. He performs the opening dance, sings seductive songs between scenes of the story, and plays all female roles within the story. My first inclination was to follow the

G

viewpoint of Western-educated Indonesian psychiatrists and assess merely the psychosexual motives of these individuals.[6] In life as on stage, many of them go about as women, and their life histories characteristically show a pattern of strong identification with women, in accord with hypotheses of the psychiatrists who discover in their backgrounds domineering mothers and too many sisters. But a more relevant question for the discussion here is whether, in the framework of the plays, the transvestites have an important symbolic function.

The distinction between male and female is basic to the cosmologies of Indonesian societies, where it distinguishes between types of deities, types of rulers, levels of the universe, and other fundamental entities.[7] In some of these societies, transvestites have served as priests and shamans, mediating between the cosmic oppositions. In Java, this situation may have held once, but it does no longer; society and cosmology have grown so complex that the male-female distinction is no longer the primary one in terms of which major institutions are conceptualized, and the transvestite no longer plays a sacral role. Yet even in a play as tawdry as the ludruk, the transvestite retains some imagery of the sacred. He is the only player to sing of ancient legends, he preserves dance-forms identical to those of shaman and priestly transvestites on the more traditional islands, he is secluded (by the dropping of a curtain) from the mundane scenes of the plays, he is believed to possess magical powers, and he is generally regarded as a disturbing, fascinating, and mystifying figure.

The transvestite can be seen as symbolically similar to the clowns, even though, at first sight, the two are perfectly in opposition. The clown is garbed in proletarian jacket, the transvestite in a refined gown; the clown speaks *ngoko* (low) Javanese, the transvestite sings in *krama* (high); the clown appears in worldly settings, the transvestite in otherworldly ones. The two are complementary, but they are also alike in their symbolic function.

Javanese of the Hinduized abangan persuasion, which is to say, those of the ludruk audience and troupe, gain pleasure and security from conceiving existence as structured around such cosmic axes as the alus-kasar and the male-female. Given their concern with cosmic order, Javanese thrill at abnormal combinations of these categories which demonstrate both disorder and, paradoxically, a deeper order than is apparent on the surface. Thus, Javanese ludruk goers get excited at seeing a male projecting the illusion of a female. They constantly repeat that 'It is a man dressed as a woman' as though to remind themselves of this juxtaposition of the illusion and reality which combines the two sexes into one body. The clowns, for their part, collapse the normal opposition between alus and kasar; they reduce the one to the other, mock the one by the other, and generally mix the two categories in a way not permitted in normal life. In sum, clown and transvestite serve the common symbolic function of mixing cosmic oppositions, male-female and alus-kasar, in order to project an image, for the duration of the play, of a fundamental unity of the Javanese cosmos.

The association between the clown and transvestite and the archaic cosmology of the Hinduized Javanese world view is shown by the fact that the decline in one correlates with a decline in the other; the decrease in clowning associated with the increase in M-stories has been mentioned, and a similar trend is true of transvestitism. Indeed, the modernizers would, on occasion, seem to deliberately diminish the role of these two primordial figures. Sjamsuddin, formerly a co-director of the ludruk Marhaen, launched a campaign to strip the transvestites of their effeminacy, except insofar as it was necessary on-stage for the staging of the revolutionary propaganda that he composed. He forced them to cut their long tresses, control their mincing gait, and, in some instances, to marry and procreate. Sjamsuddin's opposition to the clowns was less deliberate, but he was necessarily in competition with the lead clown and co-director of the troupe, Bawa. Sjamsuddin, who played serious parts and wrote serious dramas, strove to integrate the plots and reduce the role of the clown whose jokes undercut suspense and climax. Sjamsuddin's rivalry with Bawa ended in 1964 when the clown was run over by the troupe bus.

Why this opposition between revolution and modernization on the one hand, transvestites and clowns on the other? Particular explanations can be cited for particular instances, e.g., Sjamsuddin's rivalry with Bawa. A more general view is that the world view of traditionalism is more compatible with these figures than the world view of modernization. Transvestite and clown derive their meaning from a 'primitive classification', an image of a statically conceived cosmos whose categories they serve to connect at any moment to sustain an illusion of eternal, balanced unity. The revolutionaries, like Sjamsuddin, prefer to imagine reality as a linear history, composed not of static divisions but a series of means harnessed to future ends in a process of struggle and dynamism (*perdjuangan dan dinamisme*). The classificatory world view, which emphasizes the subsuming of symbols within a frame, nourishes and is nourished by such symbols of reversal as transvestite and clown; the modernizing world view, which emphasizes the sequential harnessing of means to an end, threatens and is threatened by such symbols. The modernizing world view would ultimately reduce all forms to mere means toward ultimate ends, but symbols of reversal call forth enchantment with the form and veneration of the cosmic categories they embody, a fixation dangerous to the forward movement, the struggle, the *perdjuangan*.

I had the opportunity, in 1970, to revisit the ludruk players with whom I had spent so many hours in 1963. During the intervening years there had occurred the disastrous Gestapu massacre of so-called Communists which had resulted in the death of at least a hundred thousand Indonesians. Among these were a few ludruk players: the head of a certain hare-lipped clown would grimace no more, since it had been severed from his body. Yet in 1970 ludruk was prospering even more than in 1963, at least in number of customers. But the context had changed. Sukarno had fallen, Suharto had become president, and the army had taken control of much, including all the ludruk troupes. The strange result was that the plays were becoming retraditionalized. Sjamsuddin was in prison, his innovative plots would not be staged again, and the trend from T to M-stories had apparently been neatly reversed. With that reversal, imagery of magic (now bolstered by the advanced technology of skeleton-suits that shine in the dark) had regained its old dominance in the stories. Clowns were popular as ever, but had been shorn of political satire. Many of the old transvestites were still around, chattering and mincing as before. I had entitled my original study 'Rites of Modernization,' to argue that the plays distilled a trend in thought from the traditional to the modern. It now seemed as though, for the ludruk, history was running backwards.

What, then, has Durkheim to say to Java and Java to Durkheim? In their archaic, as opposed to primitive pattern, the Javanese exemplify the Durkheim postulates but with a multiplex order that is hierarchical instead of horizontal. Rituals become

dramas as they involve stock characters instead of direct participants, yet they still possess mystical efficacy. Society derives meaning from a cosmology resembling the primitive classification of
Durkheim and Mauss, but the system is dualistic and unity is given
only by such ambiguous and ironic figures as the transvestite and
clown. And, finally, the Durkheimian anti-evolutionist can smile in
grim pleasure upon observing the reversal of modernization following the massacre of 1965.

Notes to Chapter 8

1. For background on Indonesian prehistory and Indonesian society in
general, see *Peacock* (5).
2. See *Rassers*.
3. See *Needham* (3).
4. The following account is drawn from the more detailed summary in
Peacock (5), Chapters 3 to 5.
5. A detailed analysis of the *ludruk* is in *Peacock* (1).
6. See *Amir* and *Ling*.
7. See *Schärer, Hoek, Needham* (1), *Matthes, Cunningham, de Josselin de
Jong*, and *Pigeaud*.

9
Society and Consciousness in Java

The Weberian Perspective

Durkheim may best illuminate the archaic patterning of Hinduized Java, but Weber is most revealing of the transition that began with the coming of Islam. This trend in modernization can be divided into two phases: first, the general shift from Hindu to Muslim values that began around 1500 AD, second, the reformation of Islam that began around 1900. While Javanese Muslim reformism is enough like Protestantism to make Weber's Calvinist-capitalist analysis suggestive, the interests of both Javanists and Weberians are best served by considering the differences as well as the similarities between the two movements.

By the end of the thirteenth century, Islam had begun to spread into Indonesia through networks of trade manned by Muslim merchants from the Near East, and throughout the islands a pattern could be seen of small rulers converting to Islam, followed by their subjects. The motives were often political and economic (Muslim rulers could more easily attract the taxable Muslim merchants into their ports than could Hindu rulers), but religious factors were important too.

Clambering on board the ships to accompany the Muslim traders to the East, the fourteenth-century Sufis brought with them a missionary impulse and a passionate religion. They rejected both the over-simple Islam of the desert Arab and the over-legalistic Islam of the canonical scholar, in their search for emotional and philosophical meaning. Their speculative theosophies illuminated the opposition between creator and creation, a union of which was achieved, they believed, through chanting and trance. Their magic and personal charisma did not fail to impress the animistic, pan-theistic Hinduized Javanese civilization that was already disposed to the mystical, theosophical, and cosmological.

By 1600 the Sufis had established throughout Java small schools known as *pesantrèn*. In these, Sufi teachers taught an ascetic indi-vidualism alien to the feudal Hinduistic kingdoms. The student in the school, known as a *santri*, rose at dawn, cooked his own simple breakfast, worked in the fields and chanted by day, and engaged in meditation, mysticism, and training in Javanese karate (*pentjak*) at night. Contemplation of the self, together with ascetic exercises, chants, and isolation induced trance among the pesantrèn youth and doubtless worked important effects on their psyches. But together with these more emotional aspects of Islam, the santri learned the orthodox pillars. Upon re-entry to village life, he faithfully carried out the pious practices now associated with the wider meaning of the term 'santri': regular attendance at the mosque on Friday, prayer five times daily, payment of the religious tax, fasting during the month of Ramadan, abstention from eating pork and drinking alcohol, and the pilgrimage to Mecca if health and finances permitted. Affecting quasi-Arabic modes of dress, the santri had also learned to enjoy Arab music, chant in Arabic, utter Arabic incantations ('If God wills . . .' or 'God, God, God . . .') at the slightest excuse, to fight pentjak style, and, most important, to rely on the Muslim doctrine and text as his ultimate guide to proper conduct.

Standing in contrast to the santri was the Javanese who had come to be known as 'abangan'. Cosmologically and animistically orien-ted, the Hinduistic abangan was nominally Muslim but practiced few if any of the pillars. He did not pray regularly, fast during Ramadan, or pay the tax. Happily eating pork and drinking rice-wine, he felt no desire to make the pilgrimage to Mecca. His central ritual was the *slametan*, the feast of neighbors, and he pro-fessed a more communal ethos than the santri, who were typically individualistic merchants. It was the abangan who created and enjoyed the clowns and transvestites, both of whom were and are bitterly condemned by the puritanical santri.[1]

From a Weberian perspective, the santri ethos encouraged a certain modernization. The Indonesian merchant who had con-verted to Islam was emancipated from his local community and made part of an international one, the *ummat*. Islam preached an ethical universalism, a belief that all believers must deal honestly with one another, irrespective of ethnic, kin, or caste affiliation. By extending the range of honesty, this ethic extended the range of transactions into which a trader could enter, and he could escape the kind of particularism that pervaded trade in Confucianist China.[2]

Transcendentalizing the ultimate, Islam removed it from the shoulders of the god-king and his kingdom, placing it unambiguously in a celestial sphere. Released from bondage to any particular figure or territory, the peddler felt assured that he would go to heaven no matter where he might be when he died. Nor was he burdened with the Hindu-Javanese attachment to a particular complex of localized ceremonies; Muslim ritual was simple, requiring only God, who is everywhere. Nor were the elaborate Hinduized rites of status important in Islam, since the believer was judged not by his status but his piety; the distinction between castes was cross-cut by that between faithful and infidel.

Islam, unlike Javanese Hinduism, idealized the vocation of trade. Trade was, after all, the vocation of the prophet during his early manhood, whereas it had been a necessity (but hardly a virtue) under Javanese-Hinduism. The most glorious life style for the Javanese Hindu was that of the god-king who expressed his greatness by ostentatious display and haughty indolence, and bureaucrat or courtier imitated him as closely as he could.

The languid politesse of the Hindu-Javanese aristocrat was doubtless encouraged, somewhere in the back of his mind, by a faith that he could be reborn repeatedly. The Muslim knew he had but one life within which to earn salvation or be doomed to damnation, and he felt a drive to prove that he deserved heaven. While the correlation between after-wordly salvation and this-worldly success was never so explicit in Islam as Weber believes it was in Calvinism, the general thrust of Islam would seem more likely than the static Hindu-Javanism to encourage activism and striving. Whether for this reason or for others, an indisputable fact is that of all the Javanese, the santri, the pious Muslims, have been the most outstanding in commerce. All of this points toward a parallel between Weber's Calvinism-capitalism in the West and Islam-commercialism in the East. But the parallel is spurious in both its religious and economic aspects.

Javanese commerce was not 'capitalistic' in Weber's sense.

Workers were not free wage earners employed in factories, but peasants, artisans, and servants. Businessmen were not rising industrialists of the Calvinist-capitalist prototype, but patrician princes of itinerant merchants. Production was not in mechanized factories but in the peasant fields or cottages. Business was not the methodological, rationalized life way of Weber's ascetic capitalists, but an adventurous, get-rich-quick variety, often depending on piracy—a type of power profiteering precisely excluded from true 'modern capitalism' by Weber's definition.

Nor was Indonesian Islam 'Protestant' in Weber's sense, though it was certainly more so than Javanese Hinduism. Early Indonesian Islam was strongly Sufistic and syncretic. Its attraction lay partly in mystical ecstasy, magical charms, and theosophic schemes. It relied on the authority of the teacher rather than the scripture. While encouraging egalitarianism more than did Hinduism, it resulted in the rise of sultanates.

Closer than the parallel to the Protestants is that to such movements as the Gottesfreunde that preceded them (see Chapter 5). Both Sufism and Gottesfreunde were associated with the rise of commerce, both rebelled against feudalism, canon law, and the scholastics while retaining patrician loyalties. Both taught stages of meditation leading toward union with the ultimate. Freeing the inner life, neither directly attacked the objective hierarchy of society.

From Weber's viewpoint, the mystics and merchants soon gave way to the Protestants and capitalists. From the Indonesian side, Western capitalistic expansion resulted in the Indonesian-Malayan commercial-mystical phase dissolving under colonialism. The Dutch arrived in Java at the turn of the seventeenth century, and the modernizing initiative was seized by the West. The Muslim reformation was postponed until the twentieth.

The three hundred-odd intervening years can be summarized briefly as a time of accelerating social change and eventual cultural response. Penetrated first by a private Dutch company (VOC), then by a succession of Dutch regimes, Java experienced the transformation of its peasantry into wage laborers on plantations and its Hinduized courtiers into alienated intelligentsia employed in the colonial bureaucracy. The peasantry reacted by sporadic wars throughout the nineteenth century, but the intelligentsia did not harness its forces until the twentieth when significant movements arose simultaneously in two central spheres, the Hinduized nationalist revolutionary and the Islamized commercial reformist.

The earliest example of the first was the Budi Utomo (High Endeavor), founded in 1908 by three students from the Javanese medical school, one of whom was also a nobleman. Basing its philosophy, or theosophy, on the Hindu-Buddhist culture of Java, Budi Utomo looked to India's Tagore and Ghandi for inspiration in its endeavor to revive an appreciation of the aristocratic cosmology of indigenous Java as an alternative to the bourgeois Western pattern. The interesting fact that the founders were from a medical school and most of the followers were undergoing veterinary and engineering training suggests that it was the sheerly technical Western education of the colonial regime that was found wanting in meaning; a nativism was needed to provide the symbolic frame under which to subsume technique.

Flourishing simultaneously with Budi Utomo, a santri reform movement was spreading throughout the Malayo-Indonesian region, inspired by the ideas of Muhammad Abduh of Cairo. These reformists, known as the Kaum Muda, preached a return to the fundamental truths of the text and tradition, the Qur'an and Hadith, that were believed to record verbatim the word of Allah. Other authorities, such as the previously venerated teachers and scholars of Islam, were dismissed as merely human, and believers were, like Protestants, exhorted to strive to discover their own truth through rational analysis of the texts. Return to the scripture implied a certain modernization since the texts did not mention the rites and spirits of the abangan; accordingly, these must be purged from the believer's life as he rationalized it into a somewhat Calvinist-like plan for achieving his salvation. It was believed, too, that the scripture contained the germ of modern science, economics, and politics, thus justifying a modernization of Islamic activity in these spheres. In Java, the most significant reformist organization was the Muhammadijah, founded in 1912 in the court city of Jogjakarta by an industrious, merchant-teacher known as K. H. A. Dahlan.

Muhammadijah

If the ludruk is a bizarre and tawdry slice from the history of the abangan, Muhammadijah is a widely recognized and respected santri force. On New Year's Day, 1970, after the excitement and chaos of arrival in Djakarta the previous eve, I began making arrangements for a study of this movement as a way of concretizing the gross trends within what is known as the Indonesian Muslim Reformation (*Reformasi*). I may have arrived sixty years too late, since the true radicalism of the movement was most apparent before the First World War, but the Muhammadijah remains a dynamic, expanding organization which still has qualities illuminating the Weberian viewpoint.

As analyzed by Weber, the Calvinist must rationalize his life cycle into an ever more methodical and single-minded movement toward glorifying God and assuring himself a place in Heaven. Life was a calling to continuous and methodical striving. Wasting time was the deadliest of sins, since it distracted men from their God-assigned task. Hard, continuous physical and mental labor glorified God and purified the soul, while 'idleness is the Devil's workshop'.

Rationalizing his life, the Calvinist must amputate his ritual. Ritual was dangerous for it deflected the reformer from his ascetic drive to reform the world, seducing him into enchantment with wordly form and sensuous surface. Reformation movements typically recognize this danger in ritual, and reformers typically purge their lives of traditional rituals; the Muhammadijans were no exception. Even today, sixty years after their reformation began, they strive vigorously to purify at least their own lives of virtually all of the major ritual complexes around which, in archaic and Durkheimian fashion, the existence of the Javanese has been organized for a millennium.

These ritual complexes can be subsumed under three terms: *slametan*, *wajang*, and *hormat*. Slametan, the ritual feast shared by neighbors, serves many functions, but one is gradually to usher in life and death. Slametans are held at set points before and after the birth of a child and at 3, 7, 44, 100, 355, and 1000 days after the death of a parent. This is the practice among the traditional abangan Javanese, and the graduated funeral is a pattern throughout Indonesia—a fact subjected to a Durkheimian interpretation by his disciple Hertz.[3] In spite of the deep roots of slametan in Javanese life, a survey of Muhammadijans in Jogjakarta, Java shows that only some 20 per cent of them continue to practice these rituals, compared to some 80 per cent of the abangan.

The wajang complex includes puppet and human plays, which

are true rituals in that they are believed to work cosmic effects. The role of drama in Java is grossly suggested by the statistic that Java harbors approximately forty times as many dramatic troupes per capita as does the United States of America.[4] The imagery of the wajang has been incorporated into every major abangan ideological movement, including that of the late President Sukarno. Yet despite the central role of wajang in Java, Muhammadijans strip themselves of this ritual complex, almost never sponsoring or performing such plays and rarely attending them.

The hormat complex subsumes the various rituals for venerating rank: the elevation of language and the lowering of the body, two modes of behavior elaborated in Java to a level of remarkable refinement; pomp and pageantry in clothing, titles, and etiquette that venerated or imitate royalty; and modes of breeding (such as training in dance) wherein the child imitates the bodily postures and speech of parent or mentor so as to develop the requisite refinement of manner. Hormat has traditionally been sacralized into ritual with power to harmonize social and cosmic relations, and it has a central place in Javanese civilization. But again it is de-emphasized by Muhammadijah. Muhammadijans tend to be less infatuated with the stratified Javanese language, to cut pageantry from their weddings, downgrade the importance of titles (which, of course, few of them possess), and they cease to train their children in the courtly dance and other patterns that encourage a passive imitation of superiors.

Though elucidating the psychology of reformism, Weber lacked a psychology—at least a depth psychology of the psychoanalytical type that would encourage him to carry his insights into the analysis of life histories and unconscious motives. While I cannot, with confidence, delve into these aspects of Muhammadijan personality, certain data do suggest psychological implications in their purge of ritual.

Ceasing to practice the birth and death slametan cycles, the Muhammadijan is encouraged to conceptualize and organize his life cycle in a new way. Birth and death slametans are regarded by the syncretists as cosmicly structuring the individual's entry into life, the course of his life, and his entry into the next life. To cease the slametan shifts responsibility from cosmos to individual; individual choice, in relationship to God's will, determines whether a Muhammadijan will be successful in this life and saved in the next.

Two modes of relation to God present themselves—the episodic and the methodic. The episodic approach is that of Sufism, where life is splintered into episodes of ecstatic experience. The methodic approach, preferred by Muhammadijans, calls for the believer to assure his salvation by methodically, systematically, and continuously conforming to the law of Allah.

In a short story, 'Before Long Perhaps...' published by the magazine *Suara Muhammadijah* ('Voice of Muhammadijah'), a young man habitually fishes with an old man who lives a life of pleasure 'from inn to inn'. The young man abandons his fishing and begins to organize his life so that he works at an accounting office in the morning, studies book-keeping in the afternoon, and reads religious books in his spare time. He exclaims:

With my programmes I was no longer lonely. How delightful it is to have a regular life with clear plans and aims. I no longer wished to have a wild friend, the old man included.

But one midnight comes a knock at the door. It is the old man, frightened of death. The young man convinces him to accept Allah, join a religious body, and leave his savings to it three days before he dies. The young man concludes:

Who can be sure when and where death will come to us? The old man, the humorous fatalist, could not escape it. Before long, dear reader, it will come to you.

The story reveals a concern with methodically organizing the life in its devotional and occupational aspects, rather than living episodically from inn to inn. Like the Calvinist, the pious Muslim thereby demonstrates his continuous accord with the commands of God and his destiny for salvation. A similar methodicism, at least by comparison with the abangan, is apparent in other aspects of Muhammadijah life: in commerce, education, and the organization of the movement itself.

Turning now to the wajang: these dramas teach certain patterns for organizing the life cycle. The teaching ranges from the explicit to the deeply symbolic, as in the division of the all-night wajang performance into the different ages of man: childhood, youth, adulthood, and old age so that the spectator vicariously passes through the life cycle, presumably emerging from it at dawn with an empathetic comprehension of the right way of life. The Muhammadijans replace this dramatic and empathetic mode of instruction with the scriptural and legal: they teach the good life through laws abstracted from the holy book. If the dramatic mode encourages a view of life as a series of episodes, the Qur'anic would seem to encourage a view of life as systematically conforming to a set of fixed laws.

While it is difficult to trace this relationship, various types of information suggest that the Muhammadijan view of his life cycle is more legalistic, that of the abangan more dramatistic. The contrast can be illustrated by the difference in the way ludruk players and Muhammadijans narrate their life histories. Every ludruk player but one who told me his life story moved spontaneously into a nostalgic remembrance of a premarital romantic affair that was more delightful than his current marriage. Not a single Muhammadijan narration took this turn, but instead moved, after a few minutes, into a sermon on how the narrator's past, present, and future life conformed to the law of Islam.

Brief persual of the autobiographies of Muhammadijan leaders (such as K. H. A. Dahlan, the founder) and abangan leaders (such as Sukarno) suggests a methodic life pattern for the Muhammadijans, an episodic one for the abangan. And the Muhammadijan accounts frequently allude to the Qur'anic law, the abangan ones to wajang.[5]

The shrinkage of hormat would seem to encourage the general rationalization of life style that Weber postulates whenever convention is replaced by a relentless search for more efficient means to ends, but rather than develop this implication, I would like to explore a psychological aspect as tentative as it is intriguing. The decline of hormat may be one factor in shifting the Muhammadijan's disposition to mental disease. Admittedly skimpy data suggest that the syncretist abangan are more likely than Muhammadijans to suffer from the disease known as latah. Latah sufferers compulsively imitate sounds and actions that occur in contexts emphasizing manners and status. Possibly the Muhammadijan's de-emphasis of manners and status, coupled with his de-emphasis of child rearing rooted in the mimicry of sounds and actions of a superior, has diminished his vulnerability to latah.

Slight evidence suggests, however, that the Muhammadijans

replace latah with a tendency to depressive disorder, reportedly rare in prewar Java. The cases I have seen involved a sense of sin in the eyes of God, which would of course flow from Muhammadijan ideology.[6]

All of this may give an impression that Muhammadijans directly parallel Weber's Calvinist-capitalists, demonstrating the validity of his thesis by resurrecting both the Protestant Ethic and the Spirit of Capitalism in a tropical land. Indeed, given the exotic milieu of the movement, the extent to which the Weberian correlations hold is striking. But if Muhammadijah is seen as a new Protestantism, three hundred years late, its significance is missed. In the first place, the Muslim reformation could not assume a role in modernization as central as the Protestant reformation, simply because it occurred simultaneously with other powerful modernizing movements that stemmed from a preceding Westernization. Nationalism and Communism were both initiated in Indonesia simultaneously with the founding of Muhammadijah, and they diverted energy and manpower from that movement. In the second place, Islam is not Christianity, and certain of the elements of the Protestant Ethic (e.g. belief in original sin) have not emerged with Muslim reformism. Owing to both of these reasons, the Muhammadijan movement has not had the total social or economic impact that Protestantism did in England and America, but, on the other hand, Muhammadijans have avoided some of the destructiveness of the Puritanical impulse.

Muhammadijan rationalization of life has not been so relentless as that of Calvinism in one respect. While purging themselves of traditional ritual, they have escaped the uncertainty that derives from the premise that *no* form is sacred, that a form is acceptable only so long as it achieves the most with the least the quickest. The Muhammadijans stubbornly hold *one* worldly form sacred, namely the holy book, the Qur'an. The book and the law are considered immutable.

Christ said, '*I* am the law,' and Christians have placed more emphasis on Christ's life, his birth, death, and resurrection, as a drama of mystical significance, than on any law prescribing rites and taboos. The Muhammadijans view Muhammad less as a liver of life than a giver of law, as was revealed by their responses to a poll conducted in Jogjakarta. Each respondent was asked if he could recall any episode (*peristiwa*) in Muhammad's life that had made a strong impression on him when he was young. Striking is the extent to which Muhammadijans chose to recall not an episode in Muhammad's life but a law that Muhammad taught—even though respondents were pressed to recall an episode. Striking also, by contrast to Christians, is the small number of Muhammadijans (only 1 per cent) who recalled Muhammad's birth or death as carrying any meaning for them.

One might argue that the Christian emphasis on the drama of Christ's life would lead the Christian, including the Calvinist, to think dramatistically, to strive to rationalize the episodes of his life ever more tightly into a system of climaxes, means, goals, and resolutions, and to suffer the psychological instabilities inherent in such striving.

The Muslims are more disposed to think of the law, and to orient their efforts at rationalization toward ever more systematization of the religious law. Less worry is wasted on rationalizing the sequence of episodes composing one's life. Once the law is set, one need merely follow it. Life, de-ritualized in one respect, is re-ritualized in another, but now with a written and explicit statement of the rules.

Muhammadijans are strongly conscious of the tranquility flowing from their stubborn adherence to this semi-ritualized life cycle. They sense the guilt, tension, and insecurity that flows from the totally rationalized life, what Weber termed *Zweckrational* and they call *akal*, where every choice is made according to its efficiency in achieving some tentatively defined pragmatic end. In a fashion that is really quite Javanese, they emphasize that dynamism and action should flow from inner peace rather than from guilt, anxiety, or impatience, and they derive peace from their trust in the law and the book.

Certainly the case of Java has not 'tested' or 'confirmed' the theories of Durkheim and Weber. Hopefully we have heightened our awareness of the resources of these two perspectives by mixing them with data. And some insight into Java may have been gained as well. Without some awareness of Durkheim, few Javanists have pursued very far the interconnections between ritual, drama, symbolic reversal, and social hierarchy. Nor have any raised certain of our Weberian-derived questions about the psychology of the Muslim reformation. The classical sociologies are not always easily reducible to testable hypotheses, but no one who has kept them in mind when confronting fact will fail to appreciate their enduring power to suggest relationships.

Notes to Chapter 9

1. The distinction between 'abangan' and 'santri' is most fully elaborated in *Geertz* (2).
2. Some may wonder why, contrary to Weber's analysis of anti-capitalist culture in China, the Chinese are the capitalists of Southeast Asia. The discrepancy with Weber's argument is more apparent than real, but an explanation is beyond the scope of this essay.
3. *Hertz.*
4. *Brandon,* p. 173 (Table 3).
5. Thus we can compare the biography of K. H. A. Dahlan (see *Anis*) with that of Sukarno (see *Dahm*).
6. Instances of Muslim patients with depression and feelings of sinfulness are described in *Pfeiffer.* In the twenty or so cases of latah patients that I have discovered where the religious persuasion of the patient is indicated, none is 'santri', all are abangan or syncretist.

10
Society and Consciousness in the American South

But Jewel's mother is a horse. My mother is a fish. Darl says that when we come to the water again I might see her and Dewey Dell said, 'She's in the box; how could she have got out?'
William Faulkner, *As I Lay Dying*[1]

The garbageman of the social sciences, the anthropologist scavenges for the scraps and crumbs which his colleagues shun or throw away. Traditionally, he has investigated obscure primitives who hide in jungle, mountain, or remote island, isolated from the mainstream which makes the world go 'round. More recently, he has trained his lens on the complex societies, but even so he heads for the out-of-the-way. Weber sketches the world panorama of India, China, and the European Reformation; it remains for the anthropologist to explore the expression of these Great Traditions in the provincial regions. So doing, he hopes to enrich the gross vision, to search by fieldwork as well as theory, to get his hands as well as his mind dirty. Java and the American South are provincial societies, variants of the Great Tradition, Asian and the European. Both are capable of illuminating important aspects of the classical sociological perspective. What will be said about the South is based on unfortunately little systematic fieldwork but primarily on reading and impressions drawn from birth, maturation, and a few years of adulthood there.

'The South' is that region of the United States of America which is most inclusively defined as comprising those states south of the

Potomac and east of the Rio Grande. Like regions in many nations—Bavaria in Germany, Scotland in Britain, Friesland in the Netherlands, and Java in Indonesia—the South is distinguished from the common norm by its own speech, manner, economics, and politics. In 1860 the South seceded from the union, established its own government, and provoked an incredibly violent five years civil war which ended in the region's defeat, colonization, and bitter hatred of much that is represented by America.

Within the boundaries of the United States, it is the South whose experiences come closest to those of an archaic but modernizing society such as Java. Both Javanese and Southern society are essentially agrarian, deriving their values from an hierarchical ideal rooted in a minority of highly idealized aristocrats and a majority of small farmers. Both shoulder a burden of history. They have lost to a more highly modernized conquering force and succumbed to colonization, and each has evolved, in its fertile, warm, sweaty milieu, a fatalistic, pessimistic, and ironic world view expressed through rich and grotesque symbolism.

The Southern Protestant Ethic[2]

The classical Protestant ethic, exemplified by Calvinism and Puritanism, postulated a terrifyingly great distance between man and God. So distant was God that His will was unknowable to man in any determinate way. God had willed that some men be among the saved, others among the damned, but no man could learn definitely into which group he fell. None of the techniques or media of the medieval church, no rite and no sacrament, could signal or assure a man's salvation. Seeking desperately to discover some sign or assurance that he was saved, the believer concluded that incessantly, methodically, and piously believing *as if* he were called by God was the surest sign and assurance that he was, in fact, destined to serve Him as one of the Elect, who were blessed with eternal life.

The search for salvation drove the Calvinist, Puritan Protestant to systematize his entire life in an incessant, methodical, pious straight and narrow movement of service to God's glory and kingdom. The arts, conversation, sex, adornment, or elaborate ritual and ceremony were sensuous indulgences that distracted from the ascetic and disciplined life of service. One should, like St. Paul, be in the world but not of it. Sacredness had been removed from the earth, and this valley of sin must be manipulated, exploited, and reformed in the image of God's Kingdom.

Massachusetts was settled by, and drew its dominant values from, the Puritans who had crossed the Atlantic on an 'errand into the wilderness': to extend the reformation by conquering the New World and establishing there a Kingdom of God. Virginia was settled by, and drew its dominant values from, adventurers, capitalists who came to the American colony not so much to establish a new order as to duplicate, under advantageous circumstances, the pattern of the old. Contrary to legend, few of these Virginians were actually Cavaliers, but they were English Anglicans, and they patterned their life style after that of the English country gentleman, building great families on spacious lands. Their religious and social ethic placed more emphasis on public ritual and mannered gregariousness than did that of the New Englander, who was driven to lonely introspection in search of his plan for personal salvation. Possessing relatively little sense of being called by God to subdue a harsh land, the settler of the South came to feel that his environment (which, after all, was warmer and more fertile than rocky Maine or chilly Massachusetts) was hospitable and good, as was the social order planted in it, and he began to feel lazily comfortable with it. James McBride Dabbs writes that 'Of all the Americans, the Southerner is the most at home in the world. Or at least in the South, which, because of its very at-homeness, he is apt to confuse with the world.'³ Dabbs cites Weber in drawing a comparison between the New Englander and the Southerner, and he proposes that the New Englander's great sense of tension between the godly ideal and the world is mirrored in the dichotomous stereotype of 'Yankee' and 'Puritan'. The first is nakedly materialistic, the second, transcendentally idealistic. Dabbs suggests, and I believe he is correct, that no such extreme dichotomy is found in the South.

The Anglican religion had begun to lose ground in the South by the nineteenth century, and only a minority (one estimate has it that one out of seven hundred families) were gentlemen planters. Only the fortunate few lived in white-columned, ante-bellum mansions surrounded by cotton fields worked by happy and devoted darkies. The majority of whites lived in cabins, worked the land themselves, and delighted in frontier brawls consumated by the gouging out of eyes and the biting off of ears. But the myth of the landed gentry was strong, bolstered even by the masses who could at least aspire to that status. Standing astride the expanding frontier populated by nomadic farmers in search of new land, the gentry enacted an archaic social vision. The gentleman would ride, hunt, and shoot when he was not overseeing his plantation, he might have received a classical education abroad, and he was chivalrous and courtly toward the idealized Southern Lady. (The planter stereotyped her as virginal, say some, to excuse his lust for the black woman who was not. In any event, courtly manners are not necessarily bereft of lust; what psychoanalyst could fail to perceive the phallus in the gentleman's standing erect to greet a lady?) Slaves were oppressed (though legend has it that the hardest overseers, such as the notorious Simon Legree, were Yankees) and mistreated (in patterns strikingly similar to Dutch treatment of Indonesians on their tea, coffee, tobacco, and rubber plantations). But, in an apparent attempt to bestow the dignity of antiquity on an institution based on hard economic fact, owners gave slaves Roman names, and the stability of the archaic order is suggested by the absence of any significant slave revolt.

In the eighteenth century, the so-called Scotch-Irish migrated to America to escape religious oppression in Northern Ireland. They enriched but did not destroy the old ethic. Settling in regions such as North Carolina where the planters did not dominate, the Scotch-Irish brought a certain Puritanism, and they encouraged the movement of the Westward bound populace away from Anglicanism and toward the Methodist, Baptist, and Presbyterian denominations that found their most dramatic expression in the great revivals and camp meetings of the nineteenth century. To the Southern Protestants, the horrors of damnation loomed as vividly as to New Englanders, epitomized by the revivalist preacher's graphic account of sulphurous fumes and eternal burning. But the Southern solution was different. Instead of idealizing a total life of relentless, systematized, and cumulative service and reform, the Southerner pinned his hopes on a single instant of emotional, climatic, conversion experience that need bear no integral relation to his total life plan. The drinking, gambling, whoring Southerner of the frontier was herded to the camp meeting (which did not fail, on occasion, to offer additional whoring) where he would experience an ecstatic surrender of self to Jesus. No matter how rowdy his life had been, he could be reborn if he felt the proper emotional jolt, a viewpoint still shared by many Southerners: a Southern Sunday school teacher who was asked if Adolf Hitler was in heaven, replied that it depended entirely on whether or not he had undergone the necessary conversion experience. What counted was not how Hitler had spent his life but whether he converted before it was too late. The example is extreme, but it illustrates the Southern Protestant emphasis on the instant of conversion rather than the entire life cycle harnessed to God's plan.

Purifying himself through conversion, the Southern Protestant evolved toward a certain puritanism, a rigid discipline of body and senses. But the discipline had a different significance from that of the classical Protestant Ethic. For the Weberian Calvinist, asceticism is instrumental, a rational means for streamlining his life in order to more efficiently achieve sacred objectives. Lacking this instrumental emphasis, the Southern Protestant treated ascetic prohibitions less as means than as unquestioned and absolute givens. Taboos against hard drink, loose sex, and gambling became deeply imbedded in the Southern character. Even today, drink for invited guests is confined to iced tea (or the Southern-created coca-cola and other non-alcoholic beverages) in the majority of middle-class Southern homes. Many Southern counties are dry (forbid the sale of hard liquor) and churches feature temperance unions. The counterpart to these institutions are moonshine stills, bootlegging, juke-joints at the county line, and drunken sprees with brawling and shooting. The identity between the Anglican minority and the consumption of alcohol in public settings such as weddings is expressed in the derogatory term, 'Whiskey-palians'.

Though the Anglican tradition and the Baptist-Methodist-Presbyterian (supplemented nowadays by such sects as the Holy Rollers, Snake Handlers, and highly organized pentecostal groups) may differ on the matter of drink, each in its own way has supported the traditional Southern social order. None has pushed strongly either the capitalist spirit or the social gospel that would undercut the agrarian society.

Max Weber himself once visited relatives in North Carolina, and he reports observing a local citizen baptized by immersion in a river on a chilly day. Weber's irreligious cousin spat in contempt of such irrationality, and Weber asked why the man submitted to the ordeal. The cousin replied that the man planned to open a bank and wished to demonstrate his honesty by his piety in order to attract customers.[4] The example may demonstrate the association between piety and honesty, but it is difficult to see how the Southern Protestant Ethic could equal the classical one in inspiring the relentless capitalism of which Weber wrote. In the first place, Southern Protestantism has permitted salvation through instant ecstasy rather than the life-long rationalization of action that Weber felt crucial for the spirit of capitalism. In the second place, the Puritanism of the South has become an end in itself rather than a means of streamlining action in order to achieve such ends as the capitalistic. This point suggests a flaw in the argument of Weber's most strident recent critic, Kurt Samuelsson, who claims that the presence of Puritanism in the South along with the absence of capitalistic florescence refutes Weber's theory that the two are necessarily correlated.[5] Samuelsson misses the mark. Southern Puritanism is different from classical Puritanism, and the latter is what Weber had in mind.

Personal conversion and personal discipline are much more important than social reform in Southern Protestantism. Reform became prominent in Northern Protestantism first with the Social Gospel movement, more recently in campaigns such as Freedom Rides, sit-ins, and other endeavors aimed at correcting racial oppression. These invasions of the South by the North were reformist. Invasions of the North by Southern Protestants have been evangelistic rather than reformist: aimed at saving souls by conversion rather than changing society through action. Billy Graham is the most famous contemporary Southern evangelist, but many others are influential. An entire congregation of Alabama fundamentalists has reportedly moved to Long Island, New York, where the members have procured jobs and proceeded to go about converting heathen. Emphasizing the twin themes of conversion of the soul and morality of the self, Southern Protestantism has hesitated to challenge a deeply felt value, drawn from both frontier individualism and aristocratic feudalism, that one individual should not interfere in the affairs of another, and that radical change based on abstract ethics is dangerous. The Southerner has become prickly about 'outside interference', and he typically retorts to his self-appointed social physicians, 'Heal thyself'. Increasingly, however, native reformers are coping with the undeniable abuses.

Lacking a strong emphasis on social reform, the South has placed relatively little emphasis on social science, in fact, has regarded it with scorn and suspicion. The exception is the field of history, in which the South has excelled. The other field of academic distinction is literary criticism. Such distinguished critics as Cleanthe Brooks and John Crowe Ransome have drawn at least some of their inspiration from Southern writers such as William Faulkner, Eudora Welty, Tom Wolfe, Flannery O'Connor, Walker Percy, Allen Tate, Robert Penn Warren, and themselves. The relative pre-eminence in these fields, compared to the lack of distinction in social science, lends support to Dabbs' generalization that the Southerner is inclined to cite images instead of analyze relationships. The images are either literary, which derive from the sensuous reality of particular places, or historical, subsuming Southern institutions under archaic models drawn from England, Greece, Rome, Sir Walter Scott, the Old Testament, and the ante-bellum plantations, civil war valor, and family genealogies of the region itself.

Given the dramatic emphasis of a religion orientated toward emotional conversion, one might expect a dramatic pattern in life. The obvious is not true; though spawning such a playwright as Tennessee Williams, the South is not a center for legitimate theater, but this is explainable by the region's general lack of urbanization. Popular culture in the South has a decidedly dramatic flair. Religious oratory can be remarkably powerful, indeed it must be to sway sinners to convert, and political campaigns are notable for their flamboyant characters ranging from Huey Long to George Wallace and Lester Maddox. Ku Klux Klan rallies with their robed figures and cross burning lend a lurid drama to Southern life. The most popular Southern sport is American-style football, to which the South has contributed more than its share of outstanding players, teams, and coaches. The game, as one of my students has vividly demonstrated,[6] can be viewed in the dramatic and climactic imagery of the sexual act. The object is to thrust the body of a player across a goal line, followed by kicking an elongated ball (as phallic as a sphere could be) between two posts after which the referee makes the sign of a female vagina and the crowd experiences an orgasm of joy.

This interpretation may be subject to debate, but the sexual imagery of a faith healing service which I witnessed should seem manifest. The preacher was white and male, the audience primarily female and black. The preacher's public name was a pun on the word 'erection'. He played up his masculine style of so-called 'hard preaching' by contrasting himself with his effeminate black organist who bore a girl's name and exploiting a shapely female assistant. At the end, he asked the sick to come forward. His first client was a young woman:

> *Preacher:* 'What's your trouble, honey?'
> (Woman whispers something to him.)
> *Preacher:* 'She has trouble in the lower part of her anatomy.'
> (Pause) 'Be healed!' (As he shouts, he thrusts his hand directly at her abdomen, after which she falls on the floor and twitches violently. After a moment she rises.)
> *Preacher:* 'How do you feel now, honey?'
> *Woman:* 'Real good.'[7]

Methodical, systematic, rationalized cures such as psychoanalysis may be suited to those endowed with the classical Protestant Ethic, but the episodic, emotional drama of the faith healing would seem to better fill the needs of the fundamentalist Southern Protesant who, according to Samuel Hill, is accustomed to feel himself 'stricken, then released, remorseful then joyful, doomed then pronounced free of condemnation'.[8] For him, the tent meeting has the power of the tooth for the Ndembu.

Dramatic salvation is matched by dramatic fall; Virginian Edgar Allen Poe's 'Fall of the House of Usher' has been seen as a metaphor for the Southern experience. The South is notorious for its violence, and statistics show an amount of homicide inexplicable by such factors as class, race, or economics. The negative side of classical Protestantism, one would expect, is methodical and rationalized decline coupled with systematized delusion as the other face of the plan (I recall interviewing a Northern mental patient who literally conceived of life as a baseball field and himself as having gradually shrunk in effectiveness until now he was unable to reach first base). The Southern Protestant should, logically, go down suddenly, by drunken spree, wild brawl, or shoot-out; suddenly and publicly, handling snakes and speaking in tongues instead of committing hara kiri and withdrawing into yoga meditation.

The Durkheimian Perspective

The South is no tribal village. It is a sprawling region of a highly industrialized nation. Yet, perhaps partly because of the relative weakness of the socially corrosive classical Protestant Ethic, the South still places considerable emphasis on hierarchical and communal ties, resulting in the expected elaboration of Durkheimian ritual. What are the sources of social solidarity?

Lacking the abstract social plans and organizations glorified by the classical Protestant Ethic, the Southerner tends to locate his social norms in concrete groups and statuses. He has a weakness for hero worship and he seeks righteous and admirable individuals to emulate and respect. These have varied from Thomas Jefferson to Robert E. Lee, and, locally, the Judge, the Senator, and, nowadays, the Doctor, typically a pompous and venal physician who enjoys strikingly high status. In each instance, what is sought is a status rather than a role-model; it is not the fixer-of-bones or developer-of-suburbs who embodies the good and the true, but the status of leader which embraces and unites a multiplicity of roles or specialities.

As with the status, so with the group. One should be a 'good ol' boy' or a 'nice lady' to get along with peers and the citizenry of the town. With his more abstract, reformist designs, the classical Protestant could, if need be, justify being mean and nasty to achieve the sacred end.

The most immediate source of communal feeling for the Southerner is the kinship system. In structure and possibly in strength the family is no different in the South than elsewhere in America, but there is a discernible difference in conception. I have an impression that the Southerner places more emphasis on the distinction between bonds of blood and marriage. He would, I think, rarely address his mother-in-law and father-in-law as 'mother' and 'father' (or 'mom' and 'dad') as is done by many Americans, for this blurs the distinction between relatives by blood and relatives by marriage. I have heard of Southern family reunions restricted to blood kin with spouses excluded. And at least one Southern mother-in-law has constructed a gallery of photographs carefully restricted to her blood descendants, excluding affines except where they appear with blood kin in group pictures which would be defaced by their excision.

The writings of William Faulkner are set within the extended family, either aristocratic (as with the Compsons) or dirt-poor (as with the Bundens). Faulkner seems to sense the cultural implications of a heavy stress on kinship, for he involves his characters

n precisely the patterns that anthropologists discover in the symbo-
ism of primitive societies. *The Sound and the Fury* focuses
around incestuous attraction between brother and sister, and *As I
Lay Dying* evolves a totemic metaphor. Living in nature and in an
extended family whose members one critic has deemed 'primitive
or worse', the Bundens are represented by Faulkner as identifying
their dead mother as a fish, a horse, or other creatures in their
environment.

For the Southerner, the region itself is his most distinctively
Durkheimian 'moral community'. This is not to say that the
region is a tight social network. It has never had its own government except for the Confederacy which was so rife with schism
that representatives brought bowie knives to parliament, and
co-operation is notably lacking in such areas as telephone communications. Nevertheless, Southerners are united emotionally.
They share a sense of being different. Outside the South, one
Southerner spots another by his mode of speech or other clues, and
eventually he brings that into the conversation. At first, the other
may feel a bit embarrassed at being 'discovered', since the Southern
accent and manner remain the subject of satire. But eventually
the true fellow feeling comes out, and even a cosmopolitan type
may confide to his co-regionalist something like the following,
which I report verbatim: 'I'm not much for sacrificing my body
for a cause, and I don't know why I have this feeling, but I have
to admit if the war [the war being, of course, the North/South
Civil War of 1860–65] broke out again, damned if I wouldn't join.
And you know which side I mean!'

The crucial source of Southern solidarity, then, is Douglas'
group rather than her grid (see Chapter 2). The so-called 'solid
South' is held together not so much by a network of interchanges
among its members as by the insider opposition to the outsider.
Social boundaries are heavily guarded (against carpet-baggers,
yankees, the federal government, and George Wallace's pointy-
headed 'pseudo-intellectuals') and, as Douglas would predict, body
boundaries are carefully guarded, too, against polluting substances
such as alcohol (though Southerners have been notoriously hospitable to certain worms, insects, and indigestible foods). Douglas'
prediction that the inside/outside emphasis will encourage witchcraft does not hold, since witches were more popular in New
England. But the old South lynching of the black man fits Douglas'

theory even more precisely. The New England witch was an insider who had been tempted by the devil and could recant. The black man was unambiguously an outsider, and he threatened that most inside of institutions, the Southern Lady, who guarded the hearth and bed.

Staying home during the war, the lady's domicile was invaded by the rapacious yankees. Yet today she is 'Southern hospitality', clad as the flirtatious belle beckoning enticingly to the yankee tourist from the open porch of the restored mansion. To defend her from entry, the male Southerner must rely on his symbols (not on economics, since his business interests reflect the Bureau of Tourism and Chamber of Commerce). Symbolically, he is still the 'Johnny Reb' defending the homeland by the spine-chilling rebel yell, the Confederate song, 'Dixie', the Confederate flag, and Confederate Memorial Day, which is still celebrated in place of National Memorial Day.

But the South's most recent powerful symbolic effort at neutralizing econo-erotic invasion is the bowl game, the series of football contests held between Christmas and New Year. Except for one, all major bowl games are held in the South. These include the Sugar Bowl, Cotton Bowl, Orange Bowl, Peach Bowl, and Gator Bowl. Except for the last bowl listed, each is named for a local plant, which represents the balmy climates and fertile lands of the region. This hospitable and fecund *nature* is given a feminine imagery by the bowl shape and queen who, together with her court of voluptuous princesses, rides a float bedecked with the relevant vegetation. The femininity is elaborated by majorettes and cheer leaders, as scantily clad as the climate invites. *Culture*, to attend to the other side of the Lévi-Straussian opposition, is national rather than regional, represented by the northern-based national broadcasting systems that transplant to the local scene their smooth speech and glossy technology. The visiting team is usually Northern, too, while local pride is defended by a Southern team which often bears the name of a hostile animal, such as 'gator (alligator), bulldog, tiger, wolfpack, or yellowjacket (the most powerful of the Southern teams, Alabama, would seem at first sight an exception since it is known as the 'Crimson Tide', but its famous coach is Paul 'Bear' Bryant). The Northern team may also have the name of hostile creatures, such as the Nitanny Lions or the Fighting Irish. In the announcer's words, the visiting team endeavours to 'penetrate' the 'home territory' of the locals, an effort which, as we have discussed, mobilizes imagery of the phallic thrust and culminates in the crowd's erupting into orgasms; even more excitement is shown when the locals are able to do the same to the visitors.

Without claiming that this symbolism alone accounts for the million or so couples who attend the bowls each year and the additional millions of males who view them on television, it does not seem implausible that this ritual has emerged as a symbolic effort at playing the Civil War, as the heroic rebels once again defend the feminine land—Virgin-ia, Louis-iana, Carolin-a, and, collectively, Dixie—and its womenfolk from the tourists and carpet-baggers who once again threaten rape and exploitation in a modern Sherman's 'march to the sea'.

Male/female relations in the South are still slightly archaic. Ideally and traditionally, the Southern Lady has managed to project an image of light-headed feminine charm in addition to managing the traditionally large household. Her husband was more separated from her than in bourgeois society. He would traditionally join his male cronies for hunting (instead of camping with the family) and drinking (instead of hosting a cocktail party with his wife), and nowadays he favors football, baseball, or basketball (instead of mixed doubles in tennis). Despite the division of sexes in private life, or because of it, the ladies and gentlemen were encouraged to strut before each other in public. Scarlet O'Hara could flirt with the gentlemen who were supposed to respond with chivalry, a gesture which, as has been noted earlier, was not necessarily lacking in lust.

The archaic ethos of the South conflicts with the historic one of the church, which has identified itself to some extent with the region, as in its designation as Southern Baptist or Southern Presbyterian, but never fully.

The pagan, archaic masculine ethos of the region favors the killing of animals, combatative sports, racial prejudice, a grumpy conservatism, inarticulateness and silence save for periodic curses and obscenities, and the male/female relations already described. Due to Christian universalism, and in spite of regionalist propensities, the church is forced to favor love, kindness, fellowship among the sexes, at least some degree of inter-racial brotherhood, and lots of talk by long-winded preachers.[9] Despite the clash of values, the church tries diligently to domesticate the males, forcing them into 'Sunday suits' and such jobs as passing the collection plate. Indeed, the damatic conversion experience so dominant in Southern Protestantism is associated with the passing of a man from the pagan, archaic, and masculine ethos to one that is Christian, historic, and domestic. Evangelist preachers tell of the 'bad man' who is happily brewing whiskey in a still in the woods, 'coon hunting with his dog, stirring up trouble in town, and failing to support his little girl. Finally he falls on his knees, accepts Jesus, and becomes devoted to his family and faithful in attending church. But doubts linger. In an evangelical film produced by the fundamentalist college. Bob Jones University, a rough-and-ready, hell-for-leather Confederate general finally gets religion, but only after losing his leg and being confined to his bed under the care of a sweet Southern Christian lady; psychoanalytically speaking, his piety is purchased at the cost of castration.

Archaic Southern society is hierarchical. The model is historically the plantation, organized like a feudal manor with a multiplex relationship between master and slave. Since the freeing of the slaves after the Civil War, something of the model has been preserved in the relation between farm owner and tenant, mill owner and worker. Just as there were no important slave rebellions, so there have been few labor strikes, and unions are weak. Even outside the context of work, relations between high and low tend still to be personalistic and paternalistic (or maternalistic, as when a wealthy woman establishes a fund from which she awards scholarships not anonymously but personally to children of local workers so that their indebtedness to her is increased). The positive side of these relations is that the elite continue to feel a sense of obligation to their servants, employees, and even to the community which surrounds their 'big house'.

In association with the tradition of hierarchy, rituals of respect are emphasized more in the South than in most areas of the United States. The high and the elderly are still customarily addressed as 'Sir' and 'Ma'am', or 'Mr. Joe' and 'Miss Mary', but never by the first name without the title. Straight talk between old and young or high and low is difficult, and one can observe the young assume a stereotyped 'humoring' tone to address the old as they fail to listen to what they say, while the old enjoy the prerogative of rasping reactionary jokes that express what passes for earthy wisdom.

Between blacks and whites, additional rituals avoid contact and commensality. Racially segregated drinking fountains, toilets, and seats in public vehicles have been abolished, but the black servants still tend to enter a house through the back door, rarely eat with master or mistress, and sit in the back seat of an automobile while the mistress sits in the front (the two reverse positions when the black is a chauffeur).

In spite of its archaic mythology, the South is strongly Christianized. This universalistic religion of humility may explain the absence of true rites of kingship. Instead of great public ceremonies in which subjects are permitted to mock their rulers, mass Southern rituals have turned against the suffering servant, as in the lynching. Though long stereotyped as a grinning clown, the Southern black has not become Semar; Uncle Remus came close, but his tales were written by a white author. The Southern minstrel show has some of the expected archaic themes. Originating after the Civil War, the minstrel features a clown and a transvestite. The clown is a white man in blackface. The transvestite is a large man in bridal gown who marries a small man in a womanless wedding which evokes much hilarity. One exceedingly clever analyst suggests that the minstrel expresses in transmogrified fashion (transmogrified because it could not be expressed directly) the theme which is most threatening to Southern society: unity of the black male and the white female. In the minstrel, the two are brought together. All axes intersect: the top and bottom, the male and female, and the inside and outside, symbolizing the rape of Dixie.[10]

Modernity

Military bases, industrialization, tourists in droves, credit cards, and space centers have transformed the South since the Second World War. Again visionaries speak of the 'New South', the bourgeois industrialized society conceived by Henry Grady during the dreary years of Reconstruction. But along with the developers, salesmen, airports, golf courses, motels and Colonel Sanders Fried Chicken, there is emerging a new Southern-style soul. Uniting the hicks, hippies, and blacks, this Protean culture centers around music ranging from blues to blue grass, from rock to folk. Participational and multiplex, the sound challenges the crooner of the industrialized big band, replacing his smooth city accent with the rough and gutsy one of the black and white South. Southern exports have not been limited to preachers, soldiers, and football players after all. Bob Dylan in Hibbing, Minnesota, would lie listening to Gatemouth Page, disc jockey of Little Rock, Arkansas, as he played Leadbelly and Muddy Waters. And he idolized Woody Guthrie of Oklahoma. The music represents the South's major contribution to modern civilization: soul.[11]

The classical experimental design requires perfectly contrasting cases: the experimental group, where the variable in question is present, and the control group, where it is not. The real world is less suited to this design than the laboratory, as was demonstrated by Weber's efforts at a comparative sociology of religion. Nevertheless, Weber's comparisons were illuminating. Without claiming more, we might briefly compare Java and the South. In their hierarchical structure and male/female dichotomy, the two societies would seem broadly similar: both fit the archaic mold. But the two bases of solidarity and ritual are different. Hinduized Java has elaborated a rich schema of classification grounded in hierarchy and expressed in rites of kingship and caste. Southern symbolism would seem to be less strongly based on hierarchy and more on regionalism, which in turn emphasizes the theme of insider opposing outsider and male defending female.

Turning to the Weberian perspective, the two societies exemplify the two major responses to traditionalism delineated by Weber: the worldly ascetic and the otherworldly mystical. Muhammadijah of Java is of the first type. A legalistic movement whose members join not by mystical conversion but by signing an oath, Muhammadijah militantly strives toward reform of society. Southern Protestantism is of the second type. Less legalistic and reformist than Muhammadijah, its major objective is a mystical conversion experience in which the man accepts God. The difference between those two cultures may stem partly from the dramatism of Christianity and the legalism of Islam. But a second difference may be the male/female dichotomy in traditional Southern society, such that an intensive experience is required to attract the male from his category into the mixed sex, bourgeois society of the church. Because the sex dichotomy is perhaps less strong in the bourgeois society of the Muhammadijan, the conversion experience is less necessary for him.

Whatever the merit of these comparisons, they do serve to illustrate some of the variations and linkages which derive from the Durkheimian and Weberian approaches, and they suggest patterns in the South that complement those explored in Java.

Notes to Chapter 10

1. *Faulkner*, p. 82.

2. In addition to observation, this section draws heavily on two rather Weberian analyses of Southern religion; *Hill* and *Dabbs*. See also *Peacock* (4), *Hudson*, the extensive bibliography in *Billington*, and the excellent survey analyses by *Reed*.

3. *Dabbs*, p. 3. Although Dabbs' portrait, like Weber's, is over-drawn—an ideal type—it is supported in fundamentals by standard histories of the South.

4. *Gerth and Mills*, p. 304.

5. *Samuelsson*, p. 113–15.

6. Mr. Terry Rushin, who has made a film displaying the symbolism.

7. See *Keber*, for detailed description of such faith-healing.

8. *Hill*, p. 85.

9. Even fundamentalist Southern Christianity has universalism. In place of the regionalist, 'Get your heart in Dixie or your ass out', stickers on automobiles of some fundamentalists read, 'If you love Jesus, honk!' Anyone from anywhere could presumably gain acceptance to this Christian brotherhood by honking.

10. I am indebted for this analysis to Mr. Peter Stone.

11. In *Time* (2), p. 66, appeared a list of personages who were considered to have 'soul' contrasted with those who did not. *Time* gives no analysis of the principle underlying the contrast, but in the majority of instances the figure with soul is more traditional, the figure without, more modern, for example, Pocahontas versus John Smith and Tonto versus The Lone Ranger. Interestingly, in every case where a Southerner is pitted against a Northerner, the Southerner is the one given 'soul', as in William Faulkner versus Ernest Hemingway and Robert E. Lee versus Ulysses Grant. Note that the Southerners listed are white, even though the concept of 'soul' is essentially black.

H

11
Conclusion

There is probably no problem in the analysis of action systems which would not be greatly clarified by a better understanding of symbolism.
Talcott Parsons[1]

The materials surveyed suggest two questions: first, what statements can be made about the relations between symbolic and techno-social systems; second, what general statements can be made about the direction of change in the total pattern of human action. We tackle these inquiries with mixed weaponry, on the one hand, a consideration (by no means exhaustive) of a certain tradition of theorizing; on the other, an exposure (skimpy) to a range of cases relevant to this theoretical perspective. While various types of synthesis could be attempted, I shall employ a tentative and preliminary typology that plots variation in symbolic form and the structure of consciousness as an aspect of social evolution.[2]

Should the reader reject the evolutionary approach, he can treat the typology as simply that: a scheme like the grid/group classification of Mary Douglas (see Chapter 2) which endeavours to reveal order in the world by grouping types of social organization with types of symbolic pattern. I go further, however, and assert that each of my types has starred in a particular phase of world history; there was a time when the primitive type was dominant, a time when the archaic had its heyday, and so on. Accordingly, even though all of these types exist today, they plot an evolutionary trend in world history: from primitive to archaic to historic to modernizing to modern.[3]

Primitive Type

Exemplified by the Durkheimian treatment of the Australian aborigines, by Turner on the Ndembu, Malinowski on the Trobrianders, and Lévi-Strauss on the savage mind, primitive consciousness is expressed in such symbolic forms as myths, rites, and totemic cosmologies. Primitive social relationships are multiplex and egalitarian, strongly based on kinship bonds. The association between symbolic forms and social relationships is one of homology and emotional identity. Ritual, as analyzed by Gluckman, draws mystical power from the ordering of social relations, Myth, as analyzed by Malinowski, validates them: the rights of clans and local groups, historical events, and socially significant mountains, rocks, and trees are explained by reference to the 'greater, more primeval reality' expounded by the myth. The totemic system, as elucidated by Lévi-Strauss, shares with the social order a common structure. In sum, as society approaches the 'primitive' type, the relationship between the symbolic and the social is one of homology, intimacy, and fusion.

To the extent that the symbolic and the social are identical, primitive man is hardly driven to change the social to fit the symbolic. Certainly it is romantic and inaccurate to view primitive society as an inert and timeless mass, yet its symbolic/social pattern would seem to limit evolutionary change. This is not to deny that a primitive society is in constant flux owing to birth, death, power struggle, and nomadic movement, but this flux is not necessarily toward a more modern social type. And if Lévi-Strauss notion of the 'cold' society has truth, the primitive society tends to perceive itself as stable, even when it is in flux, by identifying with a mythical, ritual, totemic, symbolic structure that is imagined to be eternally the same.

No real society is perfectly primitive. As Weber realized, the moment the 'primitive' begins to differentiate his reflective (e.g. totemic) order from his active (e.g. ritual) practice, he sets in motion rationalization and change. Differentiating the reflective from the active, primitive man strives to explain the active. Explanation comes only through systematizing and rationalizing the reflective. But the more the reflective scheme is rationalized, the more it differs from the hodge-podge of practice. Accordingly there emerges an urge to reform the practice in order to render it consistent with the scheme. Coupled with the inevitable social conflicts and ecological instabilities of primitive life, this dialectic deprives the primitive of any Eden-like contentment and may incite change. Nevertheless, relative to the other types the primitive society is markedly stable, solidary, and imbedded securely in symbolic forms.

Archaic Type

Treated by Weber as counter-point or predecessor to the modernizing West, such civilizations as India and China are what may be termed the archaic type, as were Hinduized Java, Mesopotamia, Ancient Egypt, and the Incas and Aztecs. Aspects of the old South are archaic, as are numerous societies sometimes termed 'tribal' or 'primitive', such as Polynesian and African kingdoms. The distinction between 'archaic' and 'primitive' has been elaborated elsewhere,[4] but suffice it to say that the archaic society is hierarchical, organized around kingship or caste, whereas primitive society is more egalitarian. To support its elite, archaic society must have surplus, normally obtained through highly organized food-production, whereas primitive society can support itself through food-finding.

With kingship and caste major axes of the social order, archaic social relations are hierarchical yet multiplex. Master-servant, lord-serf, and ruler-subject relations, conceived after the analogy of father-child, are multiplex in that each party depends on the other for a wide range of services; total livelihood for the underling, economic, political, military, and social support for the superior. Owing to the diffuseness of the relationship, disturbance of it would ramify deeply and widely into the lives of those party to it and throughout the society. Accordingly, elaborate codes of etiquette are developed to maintain harmony. The underling shuffles, kneels, speaks high Javanese to his master whom he addresses by title, while the superior speaks ngoko to his underling or calls him 'boy'.

In archaic society, the cosmic or sacred is somewhat removed from local kinship groups and villages, and awarded either to gods, who, though inhabiting the earth, are outside the social order, or to the king, the nobility, the aristocracy, the Brahmin. In Hinduized Java and ancient Egypt, the king was a god, and in ancient China and Mesopotamia, he was a priest with special access to the divine. In both types, divine charisma flows on to the princes, nobles, and other elite who are regarded as occupying a cosmic-social category totally separate from that of the unwashed (and, therefore, untouchable) masses. The commoner finds it impossible to identify with these exalted figures in the way the primitive could identify with his totem.

Two major types of ritual that are prominent in archaic society are the rite of sacrifice and the rite of kingship. Through sacrifice, a priest endeavours to bridge the gap that has developed between man and god. As Lévi-Strauss has observed, sacrifice differs from totemism in numerous respects. Sacrifice is open to manipulation (one can choose one's sacrificial object but not one's totem), it is an operation designed to achieve an objective (whereas totemism is a symbolic structure designed to confer meaning), and the operation's outcome is uncertain (whereas the totemic system is a timeless structure which does not raise the issue of outcome). As Bellah has noted, sacrifice introduces contingency, uncertainty, and anxiety into the relation between the secular and the sacred.

The ritual of kingship bridges the hiatus between superior and inferior while affirming the essential strength of the socio-cosmic order that underlies their hierarchical relationship. Rituals of kingship permit mockery of the superior by the inferior, reversal of their roles, or transcendance of the normal order as when the inferior pits his wit against the superior's power. In such societies as the Swazi of Africa, where the king is in close touch with his subjects, the king may be ritually abused by his subjects in person.[5] In the more complex and bureaucratized kingdoms of Hindu Java, the ritual is a drama in which actors represent the king, the princes, and the aristocracy, while the role of the people is taken by stylized clowns. These wajang clowns cleverly trancend, mock, and reduce the status of the rulers while dancers and singers display mythic symbols to affirm the basis of their rule. Whether of the Swazi or Southeast Asian type, such ritual dramas

H*

qualify as true 'rituals of social relationships' in that they are believed to renew the cosmic-social order through mystical channels.

Compared to modern dramas, these ritual-dramas have a distinctive form. Because jokes, dance, costume, the shape of puppet-figures, and other symbolic elements count more than plot-line, unwavering concentration on the narrative is not necessary. Accordingly, the performance can last for hours, even all night, with the audience recessing to eat, sleep, socialize and excrete. The participants have been taught from birth not to identify with their superiors but to imitate their manners. Accordingly, the plays delve little into the psychology of the princely heroes but instead concentrate on their manners, as imitated by clowns, mockingly, or by dancers, admiringly.

In archaic society, the concept of statuses segregated socially but associated ritually is carried over into relations between the sexes, giving rise to codes of chivalry. Highly placed women are secluded. Viewing them from afar, men ornamentalize, romanticize, and honor them by gentlemanliness or Minnesinger poems of Platonic love. This pattern may help explain the transvestitism of Javanese drama. Because 'nice girls' were secluded from the public stage, men must take female parts. And if women are idealized, a fantasy female, a masquerading male, has great appeal. When the male/female division is elaborated into a cosmic opposition, the transvestite's uniting of the two gives a special thrill.

In the classic archaic societies, myth is replaced by cosmology which is systematized by a specialized priesthood in order to explain and venerate the gods and the godking. In the merely provincial society, such as the old South, archaic structure is sustained by isolation rather than religious elaboration. Myth is replaced by literature which is lengthy, heroic, and vivid in portrayal of both the aristocracy and the folk. Lukacs favorably contrasts Sir Walter Scott with the bourgeois novelists in this respect, and the same could be said of the grotesquely colorful epics of the South's William Faulkner.

Historic Type

The historic religions, Christianity, Buddhism, Islam (and the more metaphysical aspects of Hinduism) conceive of another world that is radically separate from this world: a heaven and hell or a Nirvana. In archaic religion, the god or god-king exists in the world, on the mountain top or in a palace. The gap between social and symbolic is thus widened with the transition from archaic to historic. What is more, the historic otherworld or afterworld is imagined to be infinitely more delightful (in the case of heaven or Nirvana) or infinitely more horrible (in the case of hell) than life on this world. Salvation, for historic man, is important.

Historic religions, rooted as they are in feudal or caste hierarchies, retain a hierarchical relationship between superior and inferior, but the relationship becomes less multiplex for several reasons. First, the superior loses some of his sacral quality since the sacral is now located outside society, in the other world. Second, the importance of obtaining salvation has encouraged the emergence of full-time specialists in that quest—monks, saints, and ascetics; these live apart from the political order, draining from it sacral functions performed in archaic society by the priest-king or god-king. The historic elite loses some of the total control —religious, political, and economic—which they enjoyed in archaic society.

Archaic man could atone for particular errors such as sacrifice, but historic man's entire self can be corrupted by sin. As a Christian, he is born evil; as a Buddhist, his very nature is greedy; as a Muslim, he is in danger of becoming the ungrateful infidel who refuses to surrender his total being to God. All of these concepts imply a notion of the total self which transcends the discrete acts of daily life: the total self, rather than merely particular acts, can err, and the total self can be saved or condemned to eternal suffering. Owing to the overwhelming importance of salvation, it becomes an end in itself to be achieved independent of worldly affairs. In all the historic religions there is less emphasis on worldly reform than on other-worldly salvation. The South is an interesting case in this regard, since in spite of a Protestant tradition, it reverts to this historic pattern of emphasizing worldly reform less than spiritual salvation, through intense emotional experience, as in Pentecostalism.

Historic ritual is oriented toward the other-world, as in prayer services in church or mosque directed at God or Allah. These rituals fail to conform to Gluckman's definition of 'ritualization of social relationships', in that they are oriented around the other-worldly sphere rather than the network of relationships among members of the congregation. Yet the prayers do fit Gluckman's definition in that they are believed to affect the natural, super-natural, and social orders through suprasensory channels. How is this possible, given the absence of ritualization of social relation-ships? Gluckman's theory could be salvaged by broadening it to include the historic rituals that are considered to order the relationships that compose such expansive communities as the Christian church or Muslim ummat. Some Indonesian Muslims feel that through perfectly carrying out the rituals of the faith, they automatically create, through mystical channels, the perfect ummat. And Christian congregations have felt that through their own perfect piety they mystically improve the larger Christian brotherhood. These wider 'rituals of social relations' could be con-sidered a communal base for the historic trust in mystical efficacy.

The third feature of Gluckman's definition, stylization, is highly developed in these rituals. They employ special, sacred languages such as Latin, Arabic, and Pali which are incomprehensible to the laity, signifying the separation between other-worldly rites and worldly life. Esoteric languages, ornamental ceremonialism, and exotic mysticism affirm the special sanctity of the differentiated religious bureaucracy, the Church, the Sangha, the Brahmin and the Muslim *ulama*.[6]

Modernizing Society and Consciousness

The Weberian notion of the Protestant Ethic can be generalized to define a cross-culturally relevant pattern of religion and ideology as a force in social transformation. Such a religion or ideology combines a transcendental framework and worldly concern. Not entirely other-worldly, as classical Buddhism or Catholic mysticism, neither is it entirely worldly, as Confucianism. Instead, the moder-nizing religion is moved by a compulsion to change the world in the image of some transcendental conception, which may be either conventional or political religion, the Protestant Ethic or the Marxist Manifesto. Even though the unit to be transformed is social, the agent on whose shoulders falls ultimate responsibility for action is the individual. In association with this pattern, the role of bureaucracy is short-circuited in two ways. First, the individual depends on himself for action. Second, he communicates directly with a deity (as in Protestantism) or with the charismatic leader (as in such revolutionary movements as Sukarnoism) for inspiration. Though the movement is rather independent of the established government, it must be oriented toward the wider society even if it is a minority sect. Where it is too exclusively concerned with its internal affairs, as in the case of the Amish or the Hutterites, its social impact is limited. Where it is too bound to the established government, as in South African Calvinism, it tends toward conservatism. The Puritans were a persecuted minority oriented toward totalistic reform of society; in a different way, so were the Nazis.[7]

What Oedipal theme is common to modernizing symbol systems is not certain, but the studies surveyed suggest that some type of parent-child conflict will be present. A vivid insight and a decisive conversion, possibly mediated through an hallucinatory vision in which the prophet, reformer, or revolutionary submits to a supernatural parental surrogate is a common, though not universal, element in the radical movement.

Modernizing movements, whether Protestant, Muslim, or Buddhist reformations, Melanesian cargo cults, or Communist revolutions all endeavor to purge traditional ritual. The obvious reason is that ritual which has supported the established order must be destroyed. A more basic reason is that ritual action by its very repetitive rigidity celebrates the eternal, the socio-cosmic structure that was, is, and ever shall be. The modernizing activity that relentlessly thrusts toward harnessing new means to valued ends unavoidably opposes a symbol of the unchanging.

Modernization is associated with a florescence of art forms independent of religion. In the extreme, secular art becomes commrcial entertainment, the qualities of which precisely negate those of Gluckman's ritual of social relations which unite form with the social and cosmic. An American 'Broadway play' is more naturalistic than the stylized rite in that, even if it is a musical, it tells a tale about 'real life'. The play is relatively powerless to order its cast's daily relations since the actors are playing fictional roles instead of themselves. Finally, though the play may have psychological impact, through making people laugh and cry, only the fanatic would claim that it directly affects the cosmic, natural, and social realms through mystical and magical channels. And the

Broadway plays occurs in urban and commercial settings where relationships are uniplex: audience and actor are united only by the purchase of a ticket, and their daily lives are composed of similarly thin threads of relationship. Commercial entertainment thus confirms Gluckman's theory by exhibiting an associated reduction of both the ritual form and the social relationships Gluckman postulates as co-existing in primitive society.

In the context of collectivist modernizing movements, such as Nazism, Communism, and the mobilization movements of the new nations, drama (whether on stage, film, or in mass ceremonials) takes a direction different from either the archaic or the commercial drama. The plot frequently depicts the individual as relentlessly but enthusiastically and heroically swept along by forces of history toward a collective goal (Siegfried Kracauer saw such plots in Nazi Germany as foreshadowed by horror movies that depicted the individual being moved by dark spiritual destinies, these destinies later secularized as political movements).[8] Though heroes lack the supernatural power of archaic princes, they have superhuman charisma (note the influence of Wagner on Hitler). Enemy scapegoats are prominent targets for the collective thrust. The archaic hierarchy is replaced by egalitarian comradeship among youthful comrades-at-arms, as in the German Brüderschaft and Hitlerjunge. With the loss of mystique of the historic otherworld, there occurs a loss of popularity of such sacral figures as clown, dwarf, and transvestite as well as priest, mystic, and ascetic. With the loss of such comic and cosmic figures, which punctuate the narrative, the plot tightens (but does not thicken, owing to the absence of multiplex socio-cosmic layers), sequence becomes important, and the narrative drives toward a climax in which forces of history, in Lukacs' term, 'collide'.

The other type of modernization is more individualistic, and the dramas that flourish in this type of society are illustrated by films of Hollywood's Golden Age in America. Depicting success mixed with romance, such films show doing for the sake of doing rather than glorifying loyalty as an abstract, collective ideal. Plots are fast-moving, with hustle and pep. Heterosexual love is romanticized, instead of homosexual comradeship, for comradeship may aid the collective struggle but it can disrupt the climb to personal success. The ambitious young man is held back by the gang on the streetcorner, the buddies in the barracks, or the workers in the

Bank Wiring Room. The social climber's only fall is in love, after which he marries and creates a mobile nuclear family unit that climbs with him. Modernizing, individualistic films tend to be short, partly in order to depict as clearly and compactly the link between initial ambition and ultimate success, partly in order not to take too much time from the job, and partly in order to make money at the box office. Owing to the individualist film's amputation from organization or ideology, it is less able to inspire revolution than emotion—happy, sad, eager, nostalgic. Adopted by teenage culture, these films become silly and trivial, yet they evoke cults of hero-worshipping fan clubs, revealing a vigorous if hedonistic fantasy life among unpoliticized youth.

Modernity

The salvation religions of historic and modernizing societies postulate a duality of metaphysical worlds, a division into heaven and hell. Ethical stances are likewise split into the good and the bad, and the self is a conflict between superego and id. Protean Man dissolves these dualisms into an infinite multiplicity of metaphysical worlds, moral stances, and masks or essences of the self.

Since Kant, there has existed the idea that as many metaphysical worlds can be created as there are ways of perceiving them. The existence of a world depends on the perceiver, in contrast to the objective existence attributed to heaven or hell 'out there', 'up there', or 'down there'. Such myths are demythologized as soon as their subjective and situational origins are recognized. When each person flees the true faith to create his own, Durkheim's moral community becomes too rigid a mode of organization, and the believer must say, with Thomas Jefferson, 'I am a sect myself.'

Given the lack of external constraints on the form of fixed norms and doctrine, the self becomes the reference point for all activity. But this self is protean. It lacks that clear identity which derives from social definition. Nor does it thrust forward toward such a well-defined goal-orientation as the Calvinist-capitalist's salvation and profit. As time ceases to be a linear path toward the future, it becomes configurational: a multiplicity of sensations and situations in which one happens to be immersed. Such immersion may be sought, but casually, and it is thought best to 'just let it happen'.

In accord with the movement from linearity, the arts and the media tend toward anti-narrative. The French staged a drama where all characters read their parts simultaneously accompanied by the roar of on airplane motor, and they published a novel in the form of unbound pages sold in a paper sack. The suspense, climax, and resolution of the novel, thriller, and tragedy, are replaced by the simultaneity and participationality of TV and rock, by the blinding lights and deafening blare of the psychedelic experience. With the rise of the 'freaks', there is a demise of the 'straights', but the linear is not wholly lost. Alice Cooper's rock shows are both dramatic and iconic. Alice deploys the cosmic, sexual, and social mix-ups of the Javanese clown and transvestite, but he also organizes his show within a melodramatic structure climaxing with the murder of Alice, whose head is lopped off by a guillotine.

Rejecting linear sterility and embracing configurational participationality, some desire the rediscovery of meaningful ritual. The feature essay of a popular American magazine is entitled 'Ritual: The Revolt against the Fixed Smile'.[9] Lack of authentic ritual is identified as a major problem of modernity. But the article naively supposes that powerful, primitive ritual is orgiastic spontaneity. The orgy is lost through the 'fixed smile' of ritualists who plod through an empty routine. More likely, in light of Durkheim, modern ritual is empty because the conceptions it expresses are too unstable to render the ritual rigidities meaningful. Rigid rules of primitive ritual carry meaning because of the stability of the cosmic and social structures they embody. Even historic rituals are rooted within a rigidly held belief in the existence of a supernatural world 'out there'. Once assuming that all worlds stem from the self, man is relieved of the puritan compulsion to cleanse the world of ritual in order to render it more like the shining celestial, but he is also deprived of a stable symbolic structure. Lacking deeply rooted structures which provide meaning and stability, yoga, drug trips, rock festivals, Hare Krishna dances, meditation at the feet of the fifteen-year-old guru, and the new camp meeting among the Jesus Freaks would seem hard pressed to provide authentic ritual.

As Durkheim would have predicted, quasi-primitivism in consciousness is correlated with a communal solidarity in the techno-social system. In the midst of accelerating modernization of society and technology coupled with the expected alienation and disillusionment, the young return to the soil and create quasi-villages: communes. Potentially of great significance, the communal movement is not simply a return to the primitive. The commune dweller is within sight of the skyscraper, within earshot of the media, and too much aware of alternative life styles to regain the primitive's assumption that he will spend his life in a tribe or village. Partly owing to this sense of alienation, the protean commune is unstable and it dissolves rigidities that the primitive found necessary for order, such as the distinction between old and young, male and female.

By comparison with the heavily moral emphasis of all major social types, whether primitive, historic, or modernizing, the communally-rooted 'counter-culture' is aesthetic in outlook. During the modernizing era of America, approval was signalled by the exclamation, 'Great!' Now the word is 'Beautiful!' With the decline in belief in a jealous father-God whose will is expressed in sermons, decrees, and sanctions has arisen a complex of sensuous forms: the media, rock music, youth rituals, orgies in paint, California's Kandy Kolored Tangerine Flake Streamline Baby, and like phenomena whose moral as well as metaphysical referent are best summarized by the current phrase 'out of sight'. In theology, Harvey Cox equates the ludic, ludicrous, and sensuous with the religious in his concept of Christ the Clown.[10] The amorality of an ethic that is aesthetic, a truth that is merely beauty, would seem suited to protean men whose identity is confused by such technological developments as sex change, heart transplant, and chemical transformations of the personality. The very mildness of our reaction to such drastic developments reveals how widely the protean ethos has already diffused.[11]

Assuming the enduring power of sanctions embedded in institutions, social scientists conceptualize stability and change as derived from prescription and legitimization: roles are legitimized by norms, norms by values, and values derive authority from metaphysical schemes. While the framework is obviously valid for much of history, and especially for the Protestant phase, is it adequate for today? A perspective is needed to explain the protean society in which action occurs not only through sanctions and institutions but also through a sensuous participation in symbolic forms which are only loosely institutionalized and which gain legitimacy and meaning primarily through their appeal and beauty.

General Themes

A balanced version of socio-symbolic evolution should note commonalities as well as differences. Without delving here into the jucier pan-human archetypes, I shall confine myself to a few generalizations about relations between the symbolic and techno-social system that can be hazarded to hold regardless of the stage of evolution.

Insofar as a system of symbols is regarded as sacred, it gains meaning and legitimacy by being regarded as more enduring in time than is any particular society in which it is institutionalized. The perceived constancy of the symbol system is to the believer what Sukarno called a *pegangan*—something to hang onto, a structure in terms of which to perceive order and meaning in the flux of events. When the structure itself is perceived to be flimsy and in flux, the people complain of chaos, disorder, and meaninglessness. Even the aesthetic ethic of Protean Man requires some grounding constancy, ('dogma to extend the instant', as a student put it), and when the symbols are claimed to formulate eternal verities, the symbols themselves must seem external. Indeed, the great sacred systems do endure longer than the societies in which they are instituted. The historic religions, such as Buddhism, Islam and Christianity, have survived the collapse of innumerable host societies. Emphatically secular symbols, such as those of the arts, media, and fashion, have shorter lives than the society, and they lay their claim on creativity, originality, and the avant-garde.

A system of sacred symbols is also advantaged by greater extensity in space than any particular society in which it is institutionalized. The believers bestow meaning on their localized society by seeing it as an expression of a more extensive system, the Muslim ummat, the Catholic Church. Secular symbols would seem to emphasize more the regional and ethnic, as in handicraft bazaars or the novelist's endeavor to 'find the universal in the particular' and avoid at all costs the abstractness of the sociologist, moralist, or bureaucrat.

Systems of symbols tend to be organized in logico-meaningful patterns; techno-social systems in causal-functional patterns. The satisfying quality of the totemic, theological, or ideological system as well as the art form derives from its capacity to fit parts together in a more or less logically and aesthetically pleasing way. Techno-social systems, on the other hand, satisfy when they work right. In real life, these two exigencies—the logical and the functional—necessarily conflict. The idealist is necessarily frustrated in his efforts to institute his vision as a working system, and the practical man necessarily distrusts the idealist.

Adults learn systems of symbols beginning in childhood, but they postpone learning their adult roles until adulthood. Only as adults do they become fathers, mothers, voting citizens, and full-fledged workers, though they may have played *at* such roles in childhood. But children begin to learn the rudiments of myths, beliefs, totems, theologies, world views, and aesthetic conventions as soon as they are born, if not before. Accordingly, such systems of symbols are imbedded in the experience of childhood, with all of its 'magical thinking,' fear, loneliness, and warmth. Symbol systems are not merely a residue of childish thinking, as some psycho-analytically-oriented scholars have argued. After all, the sacred symbol system extends beyond the techno-social realm in *both* directions: beyond the life cycle to treat problems of the afterlife as well as back to its beginning to recall memories of childhood. But insofar as the symbol system is associated with memories of childhood, it is reasonable to assume that the effort to subsume the techno-social under the framework of the symbolic is, among other things, a quest to recover qualities of childhood experience. If this is granted, then the disillusionment that is felt when the two systems fail to mesh would logically evoke the pathos of 'You can't go home again'.

The modernizer strives to transform this pathos into a technical optimism by incessantly striving to transform the symbolic into the social through 'practical' means such as reform, revolution, and development. The transformation cannot possibly be entirely successful, and some would rather keep the pathos; they consider the reformer fanatical, unfeeling, and exploitative, which, by definition, he must be.

Owing to the several differences between the symbolic and the techno-social, the two systems are always discrepant. To the extent that the discrepancy is lessened through traditionalization which casts them as homologous, both systems become more stable. To the extent that the discrepancy is first increased, then decreased through a modernization that distinguishes the transcendent from the actual and strives to apply the former to the latter, both become more dynamic. What the limits of the latter trend are is impossible to say, but even today one can see an increasing differentiation as the ultimate becomes more abstract and less rooted in such metaphors as father, son, and holy ghost while the social becomes ever more difficult to contain within any system of symbols. Some moderns despair of making the linkage altogether and, instead of applying the ultimate to life, seek merely to join it, through mysticism, occultism, and the alteration of perception.

Notes to Chapter 11

1. *Parsons, et al.,* p. 242.
2. This typology is drawn from *Bellah* (3). It is elaborated in *Peacock* and *Kirsch.*
3. See *Bellah* (3) and *Peacock and Kirsch* for elaboration of this argument.
4. *Peacock and Kirsch,* Chapter 4.
5. See *Kuper.*
6. This analysis treats primarily the 'Great Tradition' of the historic religions. Crucially relevant, too, are the folk traditions and their counterpoint with the Great. This dimension would rely on anthropological and folklore studies of magic, song, proverb, and the like. The omission of this level projects a somewhat bourgeois-centric picture of modernization such that little emphasis is given to the peasant and proletarian. The bias is partially due to the Weberian notion that evolution toward modernity *is* spearheaded by the bourgeoisie.
7. This summary draws on *Eisenstadt* (2).
8. See *Krakauer.*
9. *Time* (3), p. 42.
10. See *Cox.*
11. I am indebted to Dr. William Peck for a powerful argument that the 'Protean' ethic cannot long endure owing to a simple fact: the Bomb. With the bomb (whether military or ecological), a single individual can destroy the species, therefore an infinity of roles is not possible; we simply *cannot* extend tolerance to the point that we 'let him do his Bomb thing'. Whether the result will be the survival of Proteanism until anarchy results in destruction of the species or the firming up of the Protean ethos with a Protean Ethic remains to be seen.

References

ARON, RAYMOND, *German Sociology*, trans. by Mary and Thomas Bottomore. Glencoe, Illinois: Free Press, 1964.

ADORNO, T. W., FRENKEL-BRUNSWICK, ELSE, LEVINSON, D. J., and SANFORD, R. N., *The Authoritarian Personality*. New York: Harper, 1950.

AMES, MICHAEL, 'Religion, Politics, and Economic Development in Ceylon: An Interpretation of the Weber Thesis' in *Symposium on New Approaches to the Study of Religion: Proceedings of the American Ethnological Society*. Seattle: University of Washington Press, 1964.

AMIR, M., 'De Transvestieten van Batavia', *Geneeskundig Tijdschrift van Nederlandsch Indie*, Vol. 74, pp. 1081–3. 1934.

ANDERSON, BENEDICT R. O'G., 'The Idea of Power in Javanese Culture', in Claire Holt, ed., *Culture and Politics in Indonesia*. Ithaca: Cornell University Press, 1972.

ANIS, J., *Riwajat Hidup K.H.A. Dalan, Amal Dan Perdjoangannja* (Life History of K. H. A. Dalan, His Action and Struggle). Jogjakarta: Muhammadijah, n.d.

APTER, D. E., *The Politics of Modernization*. Chicago: University of Chicago Press, 1965.

BATESON, GREGORY and MEAD, MARGARET, *Balinese Character: A Photographic Analysis*. New York: New York Academy of Sciences, 1942.

BEIDELMAN, T. O., (1), 'Pig (Guluwe): an Essay on Ngulu Sexual Symbolism and Ceremony', *Southwestern Journal of Anthropology*, Vol. 20, No. 3, pp. 359–92. 1964.

— (2), 'The Ox and Nuer Sacrifice: Some Freudian Hypotheses', *Man*, I, pp. 453–67. 1966.

— (3), 'Lévi-Strauss and History', *The Journal of Interdisciplinary History*, Vol. 1, No. 3, pp. 511–25. 1971.

BELLAH, R. N. (1), *Tokugawa Religion: The Values of Pre-Industrial Japan*. New York: Free Press, 1957.

— (2), 'Reflections on the Protestant Ethic Analogy in Asia', *Journal of Social Issues*, Vol. 19, pp. 52–60. 1963.

— (3), 'Religious Evolution', *American Sociological Review*, Vol. 29, pp. 358–74. 1964.

BENDIX, REINHARD, *Max Weber: An Intellectual Portrait*. Garden City, New York: Doubleday, 1962.

BENEDICT, RUTH (1), *Patterns of Culture*. New York: Houghton Mifflin, 1934.

— (2), *The Chrysanthemum and the Sword*. Boston: Houghton Mifflin, 1946.

BENZ, ERNST, 'Ueber den Adel in der Deutschen Mystic', *Deutsche Vierteljahrsschrift für Literatur Wissenschaft and Geistesgeschichte*, Vol. IV, No. 1, pp. 509–16. 1936.

BERELSON, BERNARD, 'Content Analysis', in *Handbook of Social Psychology*, ed., G. Lindzey. Cambridge, Massachusetts: Addison Wesley, 1954, 1st ed.

BILLINGTON, M. L., *The American South: A Brief History*. New York: Scribner, 1971.

BRANDON, JAMES R., *Theatre in Southeast Asia*. Cambridge, Massachusetts: Harvard University Press, 1967.

BROWN, ROGER, *Social Psychology*. New York: Free Press, 1965.

BURKE, KENNETH (1), 'Thanatopsis for Critics: A Brief Thesaurus of Deaths and Dying', *Essays in Criticism*, Vol. II, pp. 369–75. October 1952.

— (2), *Counter-Statement*. Los Altos, California: Hermes Publications, 1953.

— (3), *The Philosophy of Literary Form: Studies in Symbolic Action*. New York: Vintage Books, 1957.

— (4), 'On Catharsis, or Resolution, with a Postscript', *The Kenyon Review*, Vol. XXI, pp. 337–75. Summer 1959.

— (5), 'Catharsis—Second View', *Centennial Review of Arts and Science*, Vol. V, pp. 107–32. Spring 1961.

— (6), *A Grammar of Motives and a Rhetoric of Motives*. New York: Meridian Books, The World Publishing Co. 1962.

BURRIDGE, K. O. L., *New Heaven, New Earth: A Study of Millenarian Activities.* Oxford: Basil Blackwell, 1967.

CASSIRER, ERNST, *An Essay on Man.* Garden City, New York: Doubleday Anchor Books, 1953.

CHANCE, N. A., 'Modernization, Value Identification and Mental Health', *Anthropologica*, Vol. 8, No. 2, pp. 197–216. 1966.

COHN, NORMAN, *The Pursuit of the Millennium: Revolutionary Millenarians and Mystical Anarchists of the Middle Ages.* New York: Oxford University Press, 1970 rev. ed.

COX, HARVEY, *Feast of Fools.* Cambridge: Harvard University Press, 1969.

CRITES, STEPHEN, 'The Narrative Quality of Experience', *Journal of the American Academy of Religion*, Vol. 29, No. 3, pp. 291–311. September 1971.

CROCKER, J. CHRISTOPHER, 'My Brother the Parrot', American Anthropological Association Symposium on 'The Social Use of Metaphor'. San Diego, California, November 1970.

CUNNINGHAM, CLARK, 'Order and Change in an Atoni Diarchy', *Southwestern Journal of Anthropology*, Vol. 21, pp. 359–82. 1965.

DABBS, J. M., *Who Speaks for the South.* New York: Funk and Wagnalls, 1964.

DAHM, BERNARD, *Sukarno and the Struggle for Indonesian Independence*, trans. by Mary F. Somers Heidhues. Ithaca, New York: Cornell University Press, 1969.

DE JOSSELIN DE JONG, P. E., *Minangkabu and Negeri Sembilan: Socio-political Structure in Indonesia.* Djakarta: Bhratara, 1960.

DE SOLA POOL, ITHIEL, 'Communications and Development', in *Modernization: Dynamics of Growth*, ed. Myron Weiner. New York: Basic Books, 1966.

DEVEREUX, GEORGE, 'Art and Mythology: A General Theory', in Bert Kaplan, ed., *Studying Personality Cross-Culturally.* Evanston, Illinois: Row, Peterson, 1961.

DOUGLAS, MARY (1), *Purity and Danger: An Analysis of Concepts of Pollution and Taboo.* New York: Frederick A. Praeger, 1966.

— (2), *Natural Symbols: Explorations in Cosmology*, New York: Random House (Pantheon), 1970.

DUNCAN, HUGH D. (1), *Language and Literature in Society.* New York: Bedminster Press, 1961, 2nd ed.

— (2), *Communication and Social Order*. New York: Bedminster Press, 1962.

— (3), *Symbols in Society*. New York: Oxford University Press, 1968.

DUNDES, ALAN, ed., *The Study of Folklore*. Englewood Cliffs, New Jersey: Prentice-Hall, 1965.

DURKHEIM, EMILE, *The Elementary Forms of the Religious Life*. New York: The Free Press, 1965 (orig. 1915).

DURKHEIM, EMILE, and MAUSS, MARCEL, *Primitive Classification*, trans. by Rodney Needham. London: Routledge and Kegan Paul Ltd., 1963 (orig. 1903).

EISENSTADT, S. N., *Modernization, Protest, and Change*. Englewood Cliffs, New Jersey: Prentice-Hall, 1966.

— (2), *The Protestant Ethic and Modernization: A Comparative View*, ed. S. N. Eisenstadt. New York: Basic Books, 1968.

ERIKSON, ERIK H. (1), *Young Man Luther: A Study in Psychoanalysis and History*. New York: W. W. Norton and Co., 1958.

— (2), *Childhood and Society*. New York: W. W. Norton and Company, 2nd. ed., 1963.

Family Weekly, October 14, 1973.

FAULKNER, WILLIAM, 'As I Lay Dying', in *Nobel Prize Library*. New York: Alexis Gregory, and Del Mar, California: CRM, 1971.

FIRTH, RAYMOND, *Symbols: Public and Private*. Ithaca, New York: Cornell University Press, 1973.

FREUD, SIGMUND, *Group Psychology and the Analysis of the Ego*, trans. by James Strachey. New York: Liveright Publishing Corporation, 1967.

FRYE, NORTHROP, *Anatomy of Criticism*. Princeton, New Jersey: Princeton University Press, 1957.

GEERTZ, CLIFFORD (1), 'Ritual and Social Change: A Javanese Example', *American Anthropologist*, Vol. 59, pp. 991–1012. February 1957.

— (2), *The Religion of Java*. New York: Free Press, 1960.

— (3), 'Deep Play: Notes on Balinese Cockfight', *Daedelus*, Vol. 101, No. 1, pp. 1–38. 1972.

GERTH, H. H., and MILLS, C. W., ed., trans., and Introduction, *From Max Weber: Essays in Sociology*. New York: Oxford University Press, 1958.

GLUCKMAN, MAX (1), 'Rituals of Rebellion in Southeast Africa', (1954) in *Order and Rebellion in Tribal Africa*, ed. Max Gluckman. New York: The Free Press, 1963.

— (2), 'Les Rites de Passage' in *Essays on the Ritual of Social Relations*, ed. Max Gluckman. Manchester: Manchester University Press, 1962.

GRAÑA, CÉSAR, *Modernity and Its Discontents: French Society and the French Man of Letters in the Nineteenth Century*. Santa Fe, New Mexico: Cannon, 1970.

GRAVES, T. D., 'Acculturation, Access, and Alcohol in a Tri-Ethnic Community', *American Anthropologist*, Vol. 69, pp. 306–21. 1967.

HAGEN, EVERETT, *The Theory of Social Change: How Economic Growth Begins*. Homewood, Illinois: The Dorsey Press, Inc., 1962.

HARRIS, MARVIN, *The Rise of Anthropological Theory*. New York: Thomas Y. Crowell Co., 1968.

HAYS, H. R., *From Ape to Angel, An Informal History of Social Anthropology*. New York: Capricorn Books, 1964.

HERTZ, ROBERT, *Death and the Right Hand*, trans. by Rodney and Claudia Needham. New York: Free Press of Glencoe, 1960.

HILL, S. S., *Southern Churches in Crisis*. New York: Holt, Rinehart, 1966.

HOEK, JAN, *Dajakpriesters: Een Brijdrage tot de Analyse van de Religie de Dajaks*, unpublished doctoral dissertation. University of Amsterdam, 1949.

HOLSTI, O. R., with the collaboration of LOOMBA, JOANNE K., and NORTH, ROBERT C., 'Content Analysis', in *Handbook of Social Psychology*, Vol. II. Reading, Massachusetts: Addison-Wesley Publishing Co., 1968, 2nd ed.

HOVLAND, CARL, LUMSDAINE, ARTHUR, and SHEFFIELD, FRED, *Experiments on Mass Communication*. Princeton: New Jersey: Princeton University Press, 1949.

HOWE, IRVING, 'Preface', in Georg Lukacs, *The Historical Novel*. Boston: Beacon Press, 1963.

HUDSON, CHARLES, 'The Structure of a Fundamentalist Christian Belief System', in Samuel S. Hill, Jr., *Religion and the Solid South*. Nashville: Abingdon Press, 1972.

ISAACS, HAROLD, *Scratches on Our Minds: American Images of China and India*. New York: J. Day Co., 1958.

JULES-ROSETTE, BENETTE, *Ritual Contexts and Social Action: A Study of the Apostolic Church of John Marangue*, unpublished doctoral dissertation. Harvard University, 1973.

KARDINER, ABRAM, and PREBLE, EDWARD, *They Studied Man*. Cleveland, New York: The World Publishing Co., 1961.

KEBER, H. P., *Raising the Spirit*, unpublished doctoral dissertation. University of North Carolina, 1973.

KEESING, FELIX, *Culture Change: An Analysis and Bibliography of Anthropological Sources to 1952*. Stanford, California: Stanford University Press, 1953.

KIRSCH, A. T., *Thai Buddhist Syncretism*, unpublished doctoral dissertation. Harvard University, 1967.

KRAKAUER, SIEGFRIED, *From Caligari to Hitler: A Psychological History of the German Film*. Princeton: Princeton University Press, 1966.

KUPER, HILDA, *An African Aristocracy: Rank among the Swazi*. London: Oxford University Press, 1947.

LABARRE, WESTON (1), *The Human Animal*. Chicago: University of Chicago Press, 1960.

— (2), *The Ghost Dance: The Origins of Religion*. New York: Doubleday and Co., 1970.

LA FONTAINE, J. S., ed., *The Interpretation of Ritual*. London: Tavistock, 1971.

LAZARSFELD, PAUL, *The People's Choice*. New York: Columbia University Press, 1948.

LEACH, EDMUND (1), 'Golden Bough or Gilded Twig?' *Daedalus*, Vol. 90, pp. 371–89, Spring 1961.

— (2), *Political Systems of Highland Burma: A Study of Kachin Social Structure*. Boston: Beacon Press, 1965 (orig. 1954).

— (3), *A Runaway World?* New York: Oxford University Press, 1968.

— (4), *Claude Lévi-Strauss*. New York: Viking Press, 1970.

LÉVI-STRAUSS, CLAUDE (1), 'Social Structure', in *Anthropology Today*, ed. A. Kroeber. Chicago: University of Chicago Press, 1953.

— (2), *Totemism*, trans. by R. Needham. Boston: Beacon Press, 1963 (orig. 1962).

— (3), *The Savage Mind*. Chicago: University of Chicago Press, 1966 (orig. 1962).

— (4), 'The Structural Study of Myth', in *Structural Anthropology*, trans. by C. Jacobson and B. Schoepf. Garden City, New York: Anchor Books, 1967 (orig. 1958).

— (5), *Tristes Tropiques*, trans. by J. Russell. New York: Atheneum, 1968 (orig, 1955).

LEVY, MARION J., JR., *Modernization and the Structure of Societies: A Setting for the Study of International Affairs*, 2 vols. Princeton: Princeton University Press, 1966.

LIFTON, R. J., *Boundaries: Psychological Man in Revolution*. New York: Random House, 1970.

LING, TAN TJIAUW, 'Beberapa *Segi Daripada Laporan Preliminar Projek* Research "Bantji" ' (Several Aspects from a Preliminary Report on Transvestite Research Project), *Djiwa*, No. 2, pp. 45–54. April 1968.

LOMAX, ALAN, with BERKOWITZ, NORMAN, 'The Evolutionary Taxonomy of Culture', *Science*, Vol. 177, pp. 2238–9. 21 July 1972.

LORD, ALBERT, *The Singer of Tales*. Cambridge, Massachusetts: Harvard University Press, 1960.

LOWENTHAL, LEO (1), *Literature, Popular Culture and Society*. Englewood Cliffs, New Jersey: Prentice-Hall, 1961.

— (2), *Literature and the Image of Man*. Boston: Beacon Press, 1963.

LOWIE, ROBERT, *Primitive Religion*. London: Peter Owen Ltd., 1960.

LUKACS, GEORG (1), 'Zur Soziologie des Modernen Dramas' Parts I and II, *Archiv für Sozialwissenschaft und Sozialpolitik*, XXXVIII, pp. 303–45, 662–706. 1914.

— (2), *Realism in our Time*. New York: Grosset and Dunlap, 1952.

— (3), *The Historical Novel*, trans. by Hannah and Stanley Mitchell. New York: Humanities Press, 1965 (orig. 1962).

— (4), *History and Class Consciousness. Studies in Marxist Dialectics*. Cambridge: Cambridge University Press, 1971.

MADGE, JOHN, *The Origins of Scientific Sociology*. New York: Free Press, 1962.

MALINOWSKI, BRONISLAW (1), *Sex and Repression in Savage Society*. London: Routledge and Kegan Paul, 1927.

— (2), *Magic, Science, and Religion, and Other Essays*. Garden City, New York: Doubleday Anchor Books, 1954.

MATTHES, B. F., 'Over de Bissoes of Heidensche Priesters en Priesteressen de Boeginezen', in *Verhandelingen der Koninlijke Akademie van Wetenschapen*, Vol. 7, pp. 1–50. 1872.

MAUSS, MARCEL, *The Gift*, trans. by I. Cunnison. New York: W. W. Norton and Co., 1967 (orig, 1924).

McCLELLAND, D. C., *The Achieving Society*. Princeton, New Jersey: Van Nostrand, 1961.

McLUHAN, MARSHALL, *Understanding Media: The Extensions of Man*. New York: New American Library, Signet Books, 1965, 2nd ed.

MEAD, MARGARET (1), *Coming of Age in Samoa*. New York: Morrow, 1928.

— (2), *New Lives for Old: Cultural Transformation—Manus, 1928–1953*. New York: Morrow, 1956.

MERTON, ROBERT, *Social Theory and Social Structure*. New York: The Free Press, 1957.

MITZMAN, ARTHUR, *The Iron Cage: An Historical Interpretation of Max Weber*. New York: Grossett and Dunlap, 1969.

NEEDHAM, RODNEY (1), 'The Left Hand of the Mugwe: An Analytical Note on the Structure of Meru Symbolism', *Africa*, Vol. 30, pp. 20–33. 1960.

— (2), *Structure and Sentiment: A Test Case in Social Anthropology*. Chicago: University of Chicago Press, 1962.

— (3), 'Introduction' in *Primitive Classification*, Durkheim, Emile, and Mauss, Marcel, trans. by Rodney Needham. London: Routledge and Kegan Paul Ltd., 1963.

— (4), *Right and Left: Essays on Dual Symbolic Classification*, Chicago: University of Chicago Press, 1973.

NEWTON, ESTHER, *Mother Camp: Female Impersonators in America*. Englewood Cliffs, New Jersey: Prentice-Hall, 1973.

NUTINI, HUGO, 'Some Considerations on the Nature of Social Structure and Model Building: A Critique of Claude Lévi-Strauss and Edmund Leach', *American Anthropologist*, Vol. 67, pp. 707–31. 1965.

ONG, WALTER J. S. J., *The Presence of the Word: Some Prolego mena for Cultural and Religious History*. New York: Simon and Schuster, 1967.

OTTO, RUDOLPH, *Mysticism East and West*, trans. by B. L. Bracey and R. C. Payne. New York: Red Ridian Books, 1957.

Oxford English Dictionary. Oxford: Clarendon Press, 1933.

PARSONS, TALCOTT (1), 'Introduction', *The Theory of Social and Economic Organization* by Weber, Max, trans. by Talcott Parsons and A. M. Henderson. New York: Oxford University Press, 1947.

— (2), *The Social System*. Glencoe, Illinois: The Free Press, 1951.

— (3), *Theories of Society: Foundations of Modern Sociological Theory*, two vols., ed. Talcott Parsons, E. Shils, K. D. Naegele and J. R. Pitts. New York: The Free Press. 1961.
(4), *The Structure of Social Action*. New York: The Free Press, 1968.

PARSONS, T., BALES, R. F., and SHILS, E., *Working Papers in the Theory of Action*. New York: The Free Press, 1953.

PEACOCK, JAMES L. (I), *Rites of Modernization: Symbolic and Social Aspects of Indonesian Proletarian Drama*. Chicago: University of Chicago Press, 1968.

— (2), 'Mystics and Merchants in Fourteenth Century Germany: A Speculative Reconstruction of Their Psychological Bond and Its Implications for Social Change', *Journal for the Scientific Study of Religion*, Vol. 8, No. 1, pp. 47–59. 1969.

— (3), 'Religion, Communications, and Modernization: A Weberian Critique of Some Recent Views', *Human Organization*, Vol. 28, No. 1, pp. 35–41, Spring, 1969 (German translation forthcoming in Walter M. Sprondel and Constans Seyfarth, eds., *Ideen und Interessen: Beitrage zur Max Webers religionssoziologischer Kritik des Marximus*. Frankfurt: Suhrkamp Verlag).

— (4), 'The Southern Protestant Ethic Disease', *Southern Anthropological Society Proceedings No. 4 (The Not So Solid South)*, ed. J. Kenneth Morland. Athens, Georgia: University of Georgia Press, 1971.

— (5), *Indonesia: An Anthropological Perspective*. Pacific Palisades, California: Goodyear Publishing Company, 1973.

— (6), 'Expressive Symbolism', in *Festschrift in Honor of Talcott Parsons*, ed. Jan Loubser, *et al*. New York: Free Press. (Forthcoming).

PEACOCK, JAMES L., and KIRSCH, A. THOMAS, *The Human Direction: An Evolutionary Approach to Social and Cultural Anthropology*. Englewood Cliffs, New Jersey: Prentice-Hall, 1973, rev. ed.

I

PEYRE, HENRI, 'Durkheim: The Man, His Time, and His Intellectual Background', in Kurt H. Wolff, ed., *Emile Durkheim, 1858–1917*. Columbus: Ohio State University Press, 1960.

PFEIFFER, WOLFGANG, *Transkulturelle Psychiatrie*. Stuttgart: Georg Thieme Verlag, 1971.

PIGEAUD, T., *Javaanse Volksvertoningen: Bijdrage tot de Beschrijving van Land en Volk*. Batavia: Volkslectuur, 1938.

PINNOW, HERMANN, *History of Germany*, trans. by M. B. Brailsford. New York: MacMillan, 1933.

RADCLIFFE-BROWN, A. R., *Structure and Function in Primitive Society*. New York: The Free Press, 1965.

RASSER, W. H., *Pandji, The Culture Hero: A Structural Study of Religion in Java*. The Hague: Martinus Nijhoff, 1959.

REED, JOHN S., *The Enduring South: Subcultural Persistence in Mass Society*. Lexington, Massachusetts: Heath, 1972.

REICH, CHARLES, *The Greening of America*. New York: Bantam Books, 1971.

RUECKERT, WILLIAM, *Kenneth Burke and the Drama of Human Relations*. Minneapolis: University of Minnesota Press, 1963.

SAMUELSSON, KURT, *Religion and Economic Action: A Critique of Max Weber*. Stockholm: Scandinavian University Books, 1961.

SCHOLTE, BOB, 'Epistemic Paradigms: Some Problems in Cross-Cultural Research on Social Anthropological History and Theory', *American Anthropologist*, Vol. 68, p. 1192. 1962.

SCHARER, HANS, *Ngaju Religion*, trans. by Rodney Needham. The Hague: Martinus Nijhoff, 1963.

SILVERMAN, M. G., *Disconcerting Issues: Meaning and Struggle in a Resettled Pacific Community*. Chicago: University of Chicago Press, 1971.

SLATER, P. E., *Microcosm: Structural, Psychological, and Religious Evolution in Groups*. New York: John Wiley and Son, Inc., 1966.

SOROKIN, P., *Social and Cultural Dynamics*. Boston: Extending Horizon Books, 1957.

SPIRO, MELFORD, *Buddhism and Society*. New York: Harper and Row, 1970.

STURTEVANT, WILLIAM, 'Studies in Ethnoscience', *Trans-cultural Studies in Cognition*, eds. A. Kimball Romney and Roy D'Andrade, *American Anthropologist*, Vol. 66, No. 3. 1964.

SWANSON GUY, (1), *The Birth of the Gods: The Origin of Primitive Beliefs*. Ann Arbor, Michigan: University of Michigan, 1966.

— (2), *Religion and Regime*. Ann Arbor: University of Michigan Press, 1967.

Symbolic Anthropology, ed. E. Schwimmer. The Hague: Mouton, 1973.

TAMBIAH, S. J., 'Animals are Good to Think and Good to Prohibit', *Ethnology*, Vol. VIII, No. 4, pp. 423–59. October 1969.

Time (1), 30 June 1967.

— (2), 28 June 1968.

— (3), 12 October 1970.

The Times Literary Supplement. No. S-96, 29 April 1965.

TURNER, TERENCE S., 'Oedipus: Time and Structure in Narrative Form', in *Forms of Symbolic Action: American Ethnological Society Proceedings*, ed. Robert F. Spencer. Seattle: University of Washington Press, 1970.

TURNER, VICTOR W. (1), 'An Ndembu Doctor in Practice', in *The Forest of Symbols*. Ithaca: Cornell University Press, 1967.

— (2), *The Ritual Process: Structure and Anti-Structure*. Chicago: Aldine Publishing Co., 1969.

— (3), 'Introduction', *Forms of Symbolic Action: American Ethnological Society Proceedings*, ed. Robert F. Spencer. Seattle: University of Washington Press, 1970.

— (4), 'The Center Out There: Pilgrim's Goal', *History of Religions*, Vol. 12, No. 3, pp. 191–230. 1973.

WALLACE, ANTHONY F. C. (1), 'Revitalization Movements', *American Anthropologist*, Vol. 58, pp. 264–81. 1956.

— (2), *The Death and Rebirth of the Seneca*, with the assistance of Sheila C. Steen. New York: Knopf, 1970.

WARNER, W. L., *American Life: Dream and Reality*. Chicago: University of Chicago Press, 1953.

WEBER, MAX (1), *The Theory of Social and Economic Organization*, trans. by T. Parsons and A. M. Henderson. New York: Oxford University Press, 1947.

— (2), *The Religion of China: Confucianism and Taoism*, trans. and ed. by H. H. Gerth. Glencoe, Illinois: The Free Press, 1951.

— (3), *The Protestant Ethic and the Spirit of Capitalism*, trans. by T. Parsons. New York: Scribners, 1958.

— (4), *The Sociology of Religion*, trans. by E. Fischer. Boston: Beacon Press, 1964.

— (5), *The Religion of India: The Sociology of Hinduism and Buddhism*, trans. by H. H. Gerth and D. Martindale. Glencoe: Illinois: The Free Press, 1967.

— (6), *Ancient Judaism*, trans. by H. H. Gerth and D. Martindale. Glencoe, Illinois: The Free Press, 1967.

WERTHEIM, W. F., *East-West Parallels: Sociological Approaches to Modern Asia*. Chicago: Quadrangle Books, 1965.

WHITE, LYNN, JR., *Medieval Technology and Social Change*. New York: Oxford University Press, 1962.

WINTROB, RONALD M., 'Acculturation, Identification, and Psycho-pathology among Cree Indian Youth', in *Conflict in Culture*, ed. Norman Chance. St. Paul: St. Paul University Press, 1968.

WILSON, ROBERT N., 'Samuel Beckett: The Social Psychology of Emptiness', *Journal of Social Issues*, Vol. 20, pp. 62–70. January 1964.

WINCKELMANN, JOHANNES, *Max Weber: Die Protestantische Ethik I*. Hamburg: Siebenstern Taschenbuch Verlag, 1972.

WOLF, ERIC R., *Peasant Wars of the Twentieth Century*. New York and London: Harper & Row, 1969.

WRIGHT, CHARLES, *Mass Communication*. New York: Random House, 1964.

Suggested Readings

The Weber Thesis

AMES, MICHAEL M., 'Religion, Politics, and Economic Development in Ceylon: An Interpretation of the Weber Thesis', *Symposium on New Approaches to The Study of Religion: Proceedings of the American Ethnological Society*. Seattle: University of Washington, 1964.

BELLAH, ROBERT, *Tokugawa Religion*. Glencoe, Illinois: The Free Press, 1957.

—, ed., *Religion and Progress in Modern Asia*. New York: The Free Press, 1965.

—, 'Reflections upon the Protestant Ethic Analogy in Asia,' *Journal of Social Issues*, Vol. 19, pp. 52–60. 1963.

BENDIX, REINHARD, *Max Weber: An Intellectual Portrait*. New York: Doubleday, 1962.

GEERTZ, CLIFFORD, *Peddlers and Princes*. Chicago: University of Chicago Press, 1963.

—, *Religion of Java*. New York: Free Press, 1964.

—, *Islam Observed*. Chicago: University of Chicago Press, 1971.

GREEN, ROBERT, ed., *Protestantism and Capitalism: The Weber Thesis and Its Critics*. Boston: D. C. Heath, 1959.

HAGEN, EVERETT, *On the Theory of Social Change*. Homewood, Illinois: Dorsey Press, 1962.

LENSKI, GERHARD, *The Religious Factor: A Sociological Study of Religion's Impact on Politics, Economics, and Family Life*. New York: Anchor Books, Doubleday, 1963.

McCLELLAND, DAVID C., *The Achieving Society*. Princeton: Van Nostrand, 1961.

MERTON, ROBERT, 'Puritanism, Pietism, and Science', in *Social Theory and Social Structure*. Glencoe, Illinois: Free Press, 1957.

PARSONS, TALCOTT, *The Structure of Social Action: A Study in Social Theory with Special Reference to a Group of Recent European Writers*. Glencoe, Illinois: Free Press, 1937. (See Part III.)

SAMUELSSON, KURT, *Religion and Economic Action: A Critique of Max Weber*, trans. by E. Geoffrey French. New York: Harper's, 1964.

SPIRO, MELFORD, 'Buddhism and Economic Action in Burma', *American Anthropologist*, Vol. 68, No. 5, pp. 1163–73. 1966. —*Buddhism and Society*. New York: Harper and Row, 1970.

TAWNEY, RICHARD, *Religion and the Rise of Capitalism: A Historical Study*. New York: Mentor Books, 1961.

TROELTSCH, ERNST, *The Social Teachings of Christian Churches*, trans. by Olive Wyon. New York: Barnes and Noble, 1963.

WEBER, MAX, *The Protestant Ethic and the Spirit of Capitalism*, trans. by Talcott Parsons. New York: Scribner's, 1958.

—, *Religion of China: Confucianism and Taoism*, trans. by Hans Gerth and Don Martindale. Glencoe: Free Press, 1967.

—, *Religion of India: The Sociology of Hinduism and Buddhism*, trans. and ed. by Hans Gerth and Don Martindale. Glencoe: Free Press, 1967.

—, *Ancient Judaism*, trans. and ed. by Hans Gerth and Don Martindale. Glencoe: Free Press, 1967.

—, *Sociology of Religion*, trans. by Ephraim Fischer. Boston: Beacon Press, 1964.

Messianic Movements and Social Change

COHN, NORMAN, *Pursuit of the Millennium: Revolutionary Millenarians and Mystical Anarchists of the Middle Ages*. New York: Oxford University Press, 1970, rev. ed.

HOBSBAWM, R. J., *Primitive Rebels: Studies in Archaic Forms of Social Movements in the 19th and 20th Centuries*, New York: Oxford University Press, 1970, rev. ed.

LANTERNARI, V., *The Religion of the Oppressed: A Study of*

Modern Messianic Cults, trans. by Lisa Sergio. New York: Alfred A. Knopf, 1963.

SCHARTZ, THEODORE, 'The Paliau Movement in the Admiralty Island, 1946–1954', *Anthropological Papers of the American Museum of Natural History*, Vol. 49, Part 2. 1962.

THRUPP, SYLVIA, ed., *Millennial Dreams in Action: Essays in Comparative Study*. The Hague: Mouton, 1962.

WALLACE, ANTHONY, 'Revitalization Movements', *American Anthropologist*, Vol. 58, No. 2, pp. 264–81. 1956.

WEBER, MAX, 'Religion of the Nonprivileged Classes', in his *The Sociology of Religion*, trans. by Ephraim Fischoff. Boston: Beacon Press, 1963.

WORSLEY, PETER, *The Trumpet Shall Sound: A Study of Cargo Cults in Melanesia*. New York: Schocken Books, 1967.

Ritual and Symbolic Action

BATESON, GREGORY, *Naven*. Stanford: Stanford University Press, 1958.

BEIDELMAN, T. O. 'Hyena and Rabbit: A Kagura Representation of Matrilineal Relations', *Africa*, Vol. 31, No. 1, pp. 61–74. 1961.

—, 'Further Adventures of Hyena and Rabbit: The Folktale as a Sociological Model', *Africa*, Vol. 33, pp. 54–69. 1963.

—, Swazi Royal Ritual', *Africa*, Vol. 36. No. 4, pp. 373–405. 1966.

CAMPBELL, J. K., *Honour, Family and Patronage*. Oxford: Clarendon, 1964.

DOUGLAS, MARY, *Purity and Danger: An Analysis of Concepts of Pollution and Taboo*. New York: Praeger, 1966.

DURKHEIM, EMILE, *The Elementary Forms of Religious Life*, trans. by Joseph Swain. New York: The Free Press of Glencoe, 1965.

ELKIN, A. P., *The Australian Aborigines*. Sydney: Angus Robertson, 1964, 4th ed.

EVANS-PRITCHARD, E. E., *Witchcraft, Oracles, and Magic Among the Azande*. Oxford: Clarendon, 1937.

—, *Nuer Religion*, Oxford: Clarendon, 1956.

GEERTZ, CLIFFORD, 'Ritual and Social Change: A Javanese Example', *American Anthropologist*, Vol. 59, pp. 32–59. 1957

GENNEP, ARNOLD VAN, *Rites of Passage*, trans. by. Monika B. Vizedom and Garielle L. Cafet. Chicago: University of Chicago Press, 1960.

GLUCKMAN, MAX, *Rituals of Rebellion in South-East Africa.* Manchester: Manchester University Press, 1962.

—, ed., *Essays on the Ritual of Social Relations.* Manchester: Manchester University Press, 1962.

—, *Politics, Law and Ritual in Tribal Society.* Oxford: Basil Blackwell, 1965.

GOODE, WILLIAM J., *Religion Among the Primitives.* Glencoe: Free Press, 1956.

HERTZ, ROBERT, *Death and the Right Hand*, trans. by Rodney and Claudia Needham. Glencoe, Illinois: Free Press, 1960.

HUBERT, HENRI and MAUSS, MARCEL, *Sacrifice: Its Nature and Function*, trans. by W. D. Walls. Chicago: University of Chicago Press, 1964.

KUPER, HILDA, 'The Drama of Kingship', in *An African Aristocracy: Rank Among the Swazi.* London: Oxford University Press, 1965.

LEACH, EDMUND, 'Two Essays Concerning the Symbolic Representation of Time', in *Rethinking Anthropology.* New York: Humanities Press, 1966.

MAUSS, MARCEL, *The Gift: Forms and Functions of Exchange in Archaic Societies*, trans. by Ian Cunnison. New York: W. W. Norton, 1967.

MIDDLETON, JOHN, *Lugbara Religion*, London: Oxford University Press, 1960.

MIDDLETON, JOHN and WINTER, EDWARD, eds., *Witchcraft and Sorcery in East Africa.* New York: Praeger, 1963.

PERISTIANY, JEAN G., ed., *Honour and Shame: The Values of Mediterranean Society.* Chicago: University of Chicago Press, 1966.

RADCLIFFE-BROWN, A. R., 'Religion and Society', and 'Taboo', in *Structure and Function in Primitive Society.* Glencoe, The Free Press, 1952.

RAPPAPORT, ROY A., *Pigs for the Ancestors: Ritual in the Ecology of a New Guinea People.* New Haven: Yale University Press, 1968.

SMITH, W. ROBERTSON, *Religion of the Semites.* New York: Meridian, 1956.

STANNER, W. E. H., *On Aboriginal Religion*. Sydney: University of Sydney Press, Oceania, Monograph II, 1964.

TURNER, VICTOR, *Ndembu Divination: Its Symbolism and Techniques*. Rhodes-Livingston Institute Paper, No. 31, 1961.

—, 'Three Symbols of Passage in Ndembu Circumcision Ritual: An Interpretation', in Max Gluckman, ed., *Essays on the Ritual of Social Relations*. Manchester: University of Manchester Press, 1962.

—, *The Ritual Process: Structure and Anti-Structure*. Chicago: Aldine Publishing Company, 1969.

WARNER, W. LLOYD, *A Black Civilization*. New York: Harper & Row, 1964.

YALMAN, NUR, 'On the Meaning of Food Offerings in Ceylon', in *Forms of Symbolic Action: American Ethnological Society Proceedings*, Robert F. Spencer, ed. Seattle: University of Washington Press, 1964.

The Savage (and Civilized) Mind

BATESON, GREGORY, *Steps to an Ecology of Mind: Collected Essays in Anthropology, Psychiatry, Evolution, and Epistemology*. San Francisco: Chandler Publishing Co., 1972.

BOON, JAMES A., *From Symbolism to Structuralism: Lévi-Strauss in a Literary Tradition*. Oxford: Basil Blackwell, 1972.

BOSS, MEDARD, *The Analysis of Dreams*. New York: Philosophical Library, 1958.

BRIGHT, WILLIAM, ed., *Sociolinguistics*. New York: Humanities Press, 1966.

BURLING, ROBINS, 'Cognition and Componential Analysis: God's Truth or Hocus-Pocus?' *American Anthropologist*, Vol. 66, No. 1, pp. 20–28, 1964.

CARPENTER, EDMUND, 'Space Concepts of the Aivilik Eskimo', *Explorations*, Vol. 5, pp. 13–45. 1955.

COLBY, BENJAMIN, and COLE, M., 'A Cross-Cultural Analysis of Memory and Narrative', in R. Horton and R. Flanagan, eds., *Modes of Thought*. London: Faber, 1972.

CONKLIN, H., 'Hanunoo Color Categories', *Southwestern Journal of Anthropology*, Vol. II, pp. 339–44, 1955.

DURKHEIM, EMILE, and MAUSS, MARCEL, *Primitive Classification*. Chicago: University of Chicago Press, 1963.

DOUGLAS, MARY, *Natural Symbols: Explorations in Cosmology*. New York: Pantheon Books, 1970.

ELIADE, MIRCEA, *The Sacred and Profane*, trans. Willard Trask. New York: Harper, 1961.

EVANS-PRITCHARD, E. E., 'Lévy-Bruhl's Theory of Primitive Mentality', *Bulletin of the Faculty of Arts*, Vol. II, Part I. Cairo: 1934.

FINGERETTE, HERBERT, *Self in Transformation*. New York: Basic Books, 1963.

FORDE, C. DARYLL, ed., *African Worlds*. London: Oxford University Press, 1954.

FOX, JAMES, 'Semantic Parallelism in Rotinese Ritual Language', *Bijdragen tot de Taal, Land en Volkenkunde*, Vol. 127, pp. 215–55. 1971.

FRAKE, CHARLES, 'The Ethnographic Study of Cognitive Systems', in *Anthropology and Human Behavior*, Thomas Gladwin and William Sturtevant, eds., Washington: Anthropological Society of Washington, 1962.

GIEDION, SIEGFRIED, *Space, Time and Architecture: The Growth of a New Tradition*. Cambridge: Harvard University Press, 1962. 4th rev. ed.

GREEN, ARNOLD, 'The Ideology of Anti-Fluoridation Leaders', *Journal of Social Issues*, Vol. 17, No. 4, pp. 13–25. 1961.

HALLOWELL, A. I., *Culture and Experience*. New York: Schocken Books, 1967.

HARRIS, MARVIN, *The Nature of Cultural Things*. New York: Random House, 1964.

HEINE-GELDERN, ROBERT VON, *Conceptions of State and Kingship in Southeast Asia*. Cornell University Asia Program, Data Paper 18. 1956.

HOCART, A. M., *The Life-Giving Myth*, London: Methuen, 1952.

—, *Kings and Councillors: An Essay in the Comparative Anatomy of Human Society*, R. Needham, ed. Chicago: University of Chicago Press, 1970.

HOIJER, HARRY, 'The Relation of Language to Culture', in *Anthropology Today*, Alfred Kroeber, ed., Chicago: University of Chicago Press, 1953.

HYMES, DELL, 'On Typology of Cognitive Styles in Language',

Anthropological Linguistics, Vol. 3, No. I, pp. 22–54. 1961.

—, ed., *Language in Culture and Society: A Reader in Linguistics and Anthropology*. New York: Harper. 1964.

JORDAN, DAVID, *Gods, Ghosts and Ancestors*. Berkeley: University of California Press, 1973.

KLUCKHOHM, CLYDE, 'Values and Value Orientations in the Theory of Action: An Exploration in Definition and Classification, in *Toward a General Theory of Action*, ed., Talcott Parsons *et al.* New York: Harper & Row, 1965.

LaBARRE, WESTON, 'Folk Medicine and Folk Science', *Journal of American Folklore*, Vol. 55, pp. 197–203. 1943.

LEACH, EDMUND, 'Anthropological Aspects of Language: Animal Categories and Verbal Abuse', in *New Directions in the Study of Language*, Eric H. Lenneberg, ed. Cambridge: M.I.T. Press, 1964.

—, 'Lévi-Strauss in the Garden of Eden', in *Reader in Comparative Religion*, William A. Lessa and Evon Z. Vogt, eds. New York: Harper and Row, 1965.

—, 'Claude Lévi-Strauss, Anthropologist and Philosopher', *New Left Review*, 34, November, 1965.

—, 'The Legitimacy of Solomon: Some Structural Aspects of Old Testament History', *European Journal of Sociology*, Vol. 7, pp. 58 – 101. 1966.

—, 'Genesis as Myth', in *Myth and Cosmos*, John Middleton, ed. Garden City, New York: The Natural History Press, 1967.

—, ed., *Dialectic in Practical Religion*. Cambridge Papers in Social Anthropology, No. 5. Cambridge: Cambridge University Press, 1968.

LEON-PORTILLA, MIGUEL, *Aztec Thought and Culture: A Study of the Ancient Nahuatl Mind*, trans. by Jack Davis. Norman, Oklahoma: University of Oklahoma Press, 1963.

LÉVI-STRAUSS, CLAUDE, 'Four Winnebago Myths: A Structural Sketch', in *Culture in History: Essays in Honor of Paul Radin*, ed. Stanley Diamond. New York: Columbia University Press, 1960.

—, *Totemism*, trans. by Rodney Needham. Boston: Beacon, 1963.

—, 'Structural Study of Myth', in *Structural Anthropology*, trans. Claire Jacobsen and Brooke Grundfest Schoepf. New York: Basic Books, 1963.

—, *The Savage Mind*. Chicago: University of Chicago Press, 1960.

—, *The Raw and the Cooked*, trans. by John and Doreen Weightman, New York: Harper & Row, 1969.

LÉVI-BRUHL, LUCIEN, *How Natives Think*, trans. by Lilian A. Claire. New York: Simon and Schuster, 1966.

LIENHARDT, GODFREY, *Divinity and Experience*. Oxford: Clarendon, 1961.

MAY, ROLLO, *et al.*, eds., *Existence*. New York: Simon and Schuster, 1967.

MIDDLETON, JOHN, ed., *Myth and Cosmos*. New York: American Museum of Natural History. 1967.

NEEDHAM, RODNEY, *Structure and Sentiment*. Chicago: University of Chicago Press, 1962.

—, 'Introduction' to Marcel Mauss and Emile Durkheim, *Primitive Classification*. Chicago: University of Chicago Press, 1963.

—, *Belief, Language and Experience*, Chicago: University of Chicago Press, 1972.

OBEYESKERE, GANANATH, 'The Impact of Ayurvedic Ideas on the Culture and the Individual in Ceylon', (forthcoming) in *Towards a Comparative Study of Asian Medical Systems*, Charles Leslie, ed.

PIAGET, JEAN, *The Child's Conception of the World*. London: Kegan-Paul, Trench, Trubner and Co., 1929.

RASSERS, W. H., *Panji, the Culture Hero: A Structural Study of Religion in Java*. The Hague: Martinus Nijhoff 1959.

REDFIELD, ROBERT, *The Primitive World and Its Transformations*. Ithaca: Cornell University Press, 1953.

SAPIR, J. DAVID, 'Kujaama: Symbolic Separation among the Diola-Fogny,' *American Anthropologist*, Vol. 72, No. 6, pp 1330–48. 1970.

SILVERMAN, MARTIN G., *Disconcerting Issues: Meaning and Struggle In a Resettled Pacific Community*. Chicago: University of Chicago Press, 1971.

STANNER, W. E. H., 'The Dreaming', in William Lessa and Evon Vogt, eds., *Reader in Comparative Religion*. New York: Harper, 1965.

STURTEVANT, WILLIAM, 'Studies in Ethnoscience', *Trans-Cultural Studies in Cognition*, eds. A. Kimball Romney and Roy D'Andrade, *American Anthropologist*, Vol. 66, No. 3. 1964.

TURNER, VICTOR W., 'Colour Classification in Ndembu Ritual: A

Problem in Primitive Classification', in *Anthropological Approaches to the Study of Religion*, Michael Banton, ed. London: Tavistock, 1966.

WHORF, BENJAMIN LEE, *Language, Thought, and Reality*, John B. Carroll, ed. Cambridge: M.I.T. Press, 1956.

YALMAN, NUR, "The Raw: The Cooked: Nature: Culture"— Observations on Le Cru et Le Cuit', in *The Structural Study of Myth and Totemism*, Edmund Leach, ed. London: Tavistock, 1967.

Psychoanalytic Analyses of Symbolism: Child-training or Psycho-dynamics as Related to Symbols

BATESON, GREGORY, and MEAD, MARGARET, *Balinese Character*. New York: New York Academy of Sciences (special publication, 2), 1942.

BROWN, NORMAN O., *Life Against Death*. New York: Vintage Books, Random House, 1959.

DEVEREUX, GEORGE, 'Art and Mythology: A General Theory', in *Studying Personality Cross-Culturally*, Bert Kaplan, ed. Evanston: Row, Peterson, 1961.

ERIKSON, ERIK H., *Young Man Luther*. New York: Norton, 1958.

—, *Childhood and Society* (rev. ed.). New York: Norton, 1964.

—, *Gandhi's Truth: On the Origins of Militant Non-violence*. New York: Norton, 1969.

FREUD, SIGMUND, *The Future of an Illusion*, trans. by W. D. Robson-Scott. New York: Liveright, 1928.

—, *Totem and Taboo*, trans. by A. A. Brill. New York: Modern Library, 1960.

—, *Character and Culture*. New York: Collier Books, 1963.

HONNIGMAN, JOHN J., *Personality in Culture*. New York: Harper, 1967.

HSU, FRANCIS K., *Psychological Anthropology: Approaches to Culture and Personality*. Homewood, Illinois: Dorsey Press, 1961.

KIEV, ARI, ed., *Magic, Faith, and Healing*. Glencoe: Free Press, 1964.

KLUCKHOHN, CLYDE, *Navaho Witchcraft*. New York: Beacon, 1962.

LaBarre, Weston, 'The Influence of Freud on Anthropology',
The American Imago, Vol. 15, No. 3, pp. 275–328. 1958.

—, *They Shall Take Up Serpents: The Psychology of the Southern
Snake-handling Cult.* Minneapolis: University of Minnesota
Press, 1961.

Levine, Robert A., *Culture, Behavior, and Personality.* Chicago:
Aldine, 1973.

Lévi-Strauss, Claude, 'The Sorcerer and His Magic,' in
Structural Anthropology, trans. by Claire Jacobsen and Brooke
Grundfest Schoepf. New York: Basic Books, 1963.

Parsons, Talcott, 'The Father Symbol: An Appraisal in the Light
of Psychoanalytic and Sociological Theory', in Bryson, Lyman,
et al., eds., *Symbols and Values: An Initial Study*, 13th
Symposium of the Conference on Science, Philosophy and
Religion. New York: Harper, 1954.

Roheim, Geza, *Animism and the Divine King.* London: K. Paul,
Trench, Trubner & Co., Ltd., 1930.

Spiro, Melford E., 'Religion: Problems of Definition and
Explanation', in *Anthropological Approaches to the Study of
Religion*, Michael Banton, ed. London: Tavistock, 1966.

Mass Media, Literary Forms, and Social Process

Bateson, Gregory, 'An Analysis of the Nazi Film Hitlerjunge
Quex', in Margaret Mead and Rhoda Metraux, eds., *The Study
of Culture at a Distance.* Chicago: University of Chicago Press,
pp. 302–16. 1953.

Berelson, Bernard, and Janowitz, Morris. *Reader in Public
Opinion and Communication.* Glencoe, Illinois: Free Press,
1950.

Bloch, Herbert A., 'Towards the Development of a Sociology of
Literary and Art Forms', *American Sociological Review*, Vol.
8, No. 3, pp. 313–20.

Burke, Kenneth, *Philosophy of Literary Form.* New York:
Vintage, 1957.

—, 'On Catharis, or Resolution, with a postscript', *Kenyon Review*,
Vol. 21, No. 3, pp. 337–75. 1959.

—, *Grammar of Motives and Rhetoric of Motives.* New York:
Meridian Books, The World Publishing Co., 1962.

DUNCAN, HUGH, *Language and Literature in Society*. New York: Bedminster Press, 1961.

—, *Communication and Social Order*. Bedminster, New Jersey: Bedminster Press, 1962.

EMPSON, WILLIAM, *Seven Types of Ambiguity*. London: Chatto and Windus, 1947.

—, *Some Versions of Pastoral*. Norfolk, Connecticut: New Directions, 1950.

FEIBLEMAN, JAMES, *In Praise of Comedy: A Study in Its Theory and Practice*. New York: Russell, 1962.

FRYE, NORTHROP, *Anatomy of Criticism*. Princeton: Princeton University Press, 1957.

GRAÑA, CÉSAR, *Modernity and its Discontents: French Society and the French Man of Letters in the Nineteenth Century*. New York: Harper, 1967.

HYMAN, HERBERT, ed., *The Critical Performance*. New York: Vintage Books, 1956.

INGLIS, RUTH A., 'An Objective Approach to the Relationship between Fiction and Society', *American Sociological Review*, Vol. 3, No. 4, pp. 526–33. 1938.

KRACAUER, SIEGFRIED, *Theory of Film*. New York: Oxford University Press, 1965.

—, *From Caligari to Hitler: A Psychological History of the German Film*. Princeton: Princeton University Press, 1966.

LERNER, DANIEL, *The Passing of Traditional Society*. Glencoe, Illinois: The Free Press, 1958.

LEWES, GEORGE HENRY, *On Actors and the Art of Acting*. New York: Grove Press, 1957.

LOFTIS, JOHN, *Comedy and Society from Congreve to Fielding*. Stanford: Stanford University Press, 1959.

LOWENTHAL, LEO, *Literature, Popular Culture, and Society*. Englewood Cliffs, New Jersey: Prentice-Hall, 1961.

—, *Literature and the Image of Man*. Boston: Beacon, 1963.

LUKACS, GEORG, *The Historical Novel*, trans. by Hannah and Stanley Mitchell. London: Marlin Press, 1962. Boston: Beacon 1963.

MANGKUNEGARA VII, K.G.P.A.A., *On the Wayang Kulit (Purum) and its Symbolic and Mystical Elements*. Ithaca: Cornell University, 1957.

McLUHAN, MARSHALL, *Understanding Media: Extension of Man.*
New York: McGraw-Hill Book Co., 1965.
—, *The Guttenberg Galaxy.* Toronto: University of Toronto Press,
1966.
—, *Counter Blast.* New York: Harcourt, Brace and World, 1969.
—, *Culture is Our Business.* New York: McGraw-Hill, 1970.
McLUHAN, M., and CARPENTER, E. S., eds., *Explorations in
Communication: An Anthology.* Boston: Beacon Press, 1960.
MOTT, FRANK LUTHER, 'The Thirty-three Themes of Modern
Imaginative Literature', *University of Iowa Extension Bulletin
512.* Iowa City: Iowa State University, 1941.
MURRAY, HENRY A., ed., *Myth and Mythmaking.* New York:
George Braziller, 1960.
PEACOCK, JAMES, *Rites of Modernization: Symbolic and Social
Aspects of Indonesian Proletarian Drama.* Chicago: University
of Chicago Press, 1968.
PIDDINGTON, R., *The Psychology of Laughter: A Study in Social
Adaptation.* New York: Gamut (Taplinger), 1964.
RUBIN, LOUIS D., JR., and JACOBS, ROBERT D., ed., *Southern
Renascence.* Baltimore: John Hopkins, 1965.
RUECKERT, WILLIAM, *Kenneth Burke and the Drama of Human
Relations.* Minneapolis: University of Minnesota Press, 1963.
SOUTHERN, RICHARD, *The Seven Ages of Theater.* New York: Hill
and Wang, 1961.
THOMSON, G., *Aeschylus and Athens: A Study in the Social Origin
of the Drama.* London: Lawrence, 1950.
TRILLING, LIONEL, 'Manners, Morals and the Novel', in *The Liberal
Imagination.* New York: Viking Press, 1950, pp. 199–216.
WILSON, ROBERT N., *The Arts in Society.* Englewood Cliffs, New
Jersey: Prentice-Hall, 1964.
WOLFENSTEIN, MARTHA, and LEITES, NATHAN, *Movies: A Psycho-
logical Analyses.* Glencoe, Illinois: The Free Press, 1950.
WRIGHT, CHARLES R., *Mass Communication.* New York: Random
House, 1964.

Symbolism, Ideology, and Political Development

APTER, DAVID, *The Politics of Modernization.* Chicago: University
of Chicago, 1965.

Cox, Harvey, *The Secular City*. New York: Macmillan, 1965.

Feith, Herbert, *The Decline of Constitutional Democracy in Indonesia*. Ithaca: Cornell University Press, 1962.

Geertz, Clifford, ed., *Old Societies and New States*. New York: Free Press, 1963.

—, 'Ideology as a Cultural System', in *Ideology and Discontent*, David Apter, ed. New York: Free Press of Glencoe, 1964.

Matossian, M., 'The Ideologies of Delayed Industrialization: Some Tensions and Ambiguities', in *Political Change in Under-developed Countries: Nationalism and Communism*. J. H. Kautsky, ed. New York: John Wiley, 1962.

Pye, Lucien W., *Politics, Personality, and Nation-Building: Burma's Search for Identity*. New Haven: Yale, 1962.

Sigmund, Paul E., Jr., *The Ideologies of the Developing Nations*. New York: Praeger, 1963.

Walzer, Michael, *The Revolution of the Saints: A Study in the Origins of Radical Politics*. Cambridge, Massachusetts: Harvard, 1965.

General Theories of Symbolic Forms and Religion

Baal, J. van, *Symbols for Communication: an introduction to the anthropological study of Religion*. Assen: Van Gorcum, 1971.

Berger, Peter L., and Luckman, T., *The Social Construction of Reality: A Treatise in the Sociology of Knowledge*. Garden City, N.Y.: Doubleday, 1967.

Cassirer, Ernst, *Essay on Man*. New Haven: Yale University Press, 1944.

—, *The Philosophy of Symbolic Forms*, 3 vols, trans. by Ralph Mannheim. New Haven: Yale University Press, 1952–7.

Dewey, John, *Art as Experience*. New York: Putman, 1959.

Duncan, Hugh, 'Short Biblography of Works on Symbolic Analysis that Relate Form to Social Content', in *Human Communication Theory*, Frank E. X. Dance, ed. New York: Holt, Rinehart, and Winston, 1967.

Eliade, Mircea, Images and Symbols, trans. by P. Mairet, New York: Sheed and Ward, 1969.

EVANS-PRICHARD, E. E., *Theories of Primitive Religion*. Oxford: Clarendon, 1965.

FIRTH, RAYMOND, *Symbols: Public and Private*. Ithaca, New York: Cornell University Press, 1973.

FRAZER, SIR JAMES GEORGE, *The Golden Bough*. New York: Macmillan, 1923.

FUSTEL DE COULANGES, NUMA DENIS, *The Ancient City*. New York: Doubleday, 1956.

GEERTZ, CLIFFORD, 'Religion as a Cultural System', in *Anthropological Approaches to the Study of Religion*, Michael Banton, ed. London: Tavistock Publications, 1966.

GOFFMAN, ERVING, *Interaction Ritual*. Garden City, New York: Doubleday, 1967.

HORTON, ROBIN, 'African Conversion', *Africa* 41, pp. 85–108. 1971.

JAMES, WILLIAM, *Varieties of Religious Experience*. New York: Collier, 1963.

JUNG, C. G., *Psyche and Symbol*, ed. Violet de Laszlo. New York: Doubleday, 1958.

LANGER, SUZANNE, *Philosophy in a New Key*. New York: New American Library, 1957.

LESSA, WILLIAM A., and VOGT, EVON Z., eds., *Reader in Comparative Religion: An Anthropological Approach*. New York: Harper and Row, 1965. 2nd ed.

MANNHEIM, KARL, *Ideology and Utopia*, trans. by Louis Wirth and Edward Shils. New York: Harcourt, 1951.

MERTON, ROBERT, 'The Sociology of Knowledge', in *Social Theory and Social Structure*. Glencoe, Illinois: Free Press, 1957.

NIEBUHR, REINHOLD, *Does Civilization need Religion? A Study in the Social Resources and Limitations of Religion in Modern Life*. New York: Macmillan, 1927.

NIEBUHR, RICHARD, *Christ and Culture*. New York: Harper, 1956.

PARSONS, TALCOTT, 'Introduction to Part Four', in *Theories of Society: Foundations of Modern Sociological Thought*, 2 vols., ed. Talcott Parsons *et al.* New York: Free Press, 1961.

PREUSS, K. T., 'Der Ursprung der Religion und Kunst', *Globus*, Vol. 86, pp. 388–92. 1904–5.

SAPIR, EDWARD, 'The Psychological Reality of Phonemes', and 'Symbolism' in David Mandelbaum, ed., *Selected Writings of Edward Sapir*. Los Angeles and Berkeley: University of California Press, 1949.

SCHNEIDER, DAVID M., *American Kinship: A Cultural Account.*
Englewood Cliffs, New Jersey: Prentice-Hall, 1968.
SLATER, PHILIP, *Microcosm: Structural, Psychological, and
Religious Evolution in Groups.* New York: John Wiley, 1966.
SWANSON, GUY, *The Birth of the Gods: The Origin of Primitive
Beliefs.* Ann Arbor, Michigan: University of Michigan, 1960.
TILLICH, PAUL, 'The Religious Symbol', *Daedalus*, Vol. 87, No. 3,
pp. 3–21. 1958.
WALLACE, ANTHONY F. C., *Religion: An Anthropological View.*
New York: Random House, 1966.

Games, Play, Music, Dance, Fashions, Art, and Society

ADAMS, M. J., *System and Meaning in East Sumba Textile Design:
A Study in Traditional Indonesian Art.* New Haven: Southeast
Asian Studies, Yale University Press, 1969.
BOAS, FRANZ, *Primitive Art.* Mangolia, Massachusetts: Smith, Peter,
1962.
BUNZEL, RUTH L., *The Pueblo Potter: A Study of Creative
Imagination in Primitive Art.* New York: Columbia University
Press, 1929.
DARK, PHILIP J. C., 'The Study of Ethno-Aesthetics: The Visual
Arts,' in *Essays on Visual and Verbal Arts: Proceedings of the
American Ethnological Society, Spring Meeting, 1966*, ed. June
Helm. Seattle: University of Washington Press, 1967.
HAUSER, ARNOLD, *The Social History of Art.* 4 vols. New York:
Knopf, 1952.
HENRY, JULES, and Z. *Doll Play of Pilaga Indian Children.* New
York: American Orthopsychiatric Association, 1944.
HUIZINGA, JOHAN, *Homo Ludens: A Study of the Play Element in
Culture.* Boston: Beacon, 1955.
KEIL, CHARLES, *Urban Blues.* Chicago: University of Chicago,
1966.
KROEBER, ALFRED, and RICHARDSON, JANE, 'Three Centuries of
Women's Dress Fashions: a Quantitative Analysis',
Anthropological Records, Vol. 5, No. 2. Berkeley: University
of California Press, 1940.
KURATH, G., *Dances of Anahuac.* New York: Wenner-Gren
Foundation for Anthropological Research, 1964.

LÉVI-STRAUSS, CLAUDE, *Tristes Tropiques*, trans. by John Russell. New York: Atheneum, 1964. (See Ch. 17.)

MCALLESTER, DAVID PARK, *Enemy Way Music: A Study of Social and Aesthetic Values as seen in Navaho Music*. Cambridge, Massachusetts: Papers of the Peabody Museum of American Archaeology and Ethnology, Vol. 41, No. 3. 1965.

MERRIAM, ALAN P., *The Anthropology of Music*. Evanston, Illinois: Northwestern University Press, 1964.

MUNN, NANCY ,'Visual Categories: An Approach to the Study of Representational Systems', *American Anthropologist*, Vol. 68, No. 4, pp. 936–50. 1966.

—, *Walibiri Iconography: Graphic and Cultural Symbolism in a Central Australian Society*. Ithaca: Cornell University Press, 1973.

NETTL, BRUNO, *Music in Primitive Culture*. Cambridge: Harvard University Press, 1956.

NEWCOMB, FRANC, *A Study of Navaho Symbolism*. Cambridge, Massachusetts: Papers of the Peabody Museum of American Archaeology and Ethnology. Vol. 32, No. 7. 1956.

NEWTON, ESTHER. *Mother Camp: Female Impersonators in America*. Englewood Cliffs, New Jersey: Prentice-Hall, 1973.

NORBECK, EDWARD, 'Man at Play', *Natural History Magazine*. Vol. 85, No. 10, pp. 48–75. December 1971.

PANOFSKY, ERWIN, *Meaning in the Visual Arts*. Garden City, New York: Doubleday, 1955.

ROBERTS, JOHN M., SUTTON-SMITH, BRIAN, and KENDON, ADAM, 'Strategy in Games and Folk Tales', *Journal of Social Psychology*, Vol. 61, pp. 185–99. 1963.

SMITH, MARIAN W., ed., *Symposium on the Artist in Tribal Society*. New York: Free Press of Glencoe, 1961.

History as Style

KROEBER, ALFRED, *Style and Civilizations*. Berkeley: University of California Press, n.d.

—, *Configurations of Culture Growth*. Berkeley: University of California Press, 1944.

SCHAPIRO, MEYER, 'Style', *Anthropology Today*. Alfred Kroeber, ed. Chicago: University of Chicago Press, 1953.

SPENGLER, OSWALD, *The Decline of the West*, 2 Vols., trans. by
Charles Atkinson. New York: Knopf, 1932.

Folklore

DORSON, R. M., 'Current Folklore Theories', *Current Anthro-
pology*, pp. 93–112. February 1963.
DUNDES, ALAN, ed., *The Study of Folklore*. Englewood Cliffs,
New Jersey: Prentice-Hall, 1965.
JACOBS, MELVILLE, *The Content and Style of an Oral Literature:
Clackaman's Chinook Myths and Tales*. Chicago: University of
Chicago Press, 1959.
PROPP, VLADIMIR, I., *Morphology of the Folktale*, trans. by
Laurence Scott. American Folklore Society, Bibliographical
and Special Series, Vol. 9. 1958.
THOMPSON, STITH, *The Folktale*. New York: Dryden, 1946.

Symbolism and Interaction

BATESON, GREGORY, 'A Theory of Play and Fantasy', *Psychiatric
Research Reports*, 2, pp. 39–51. December 1955.
BRUNER, EDWARD M., 'The Missing Tins of Chicken: A Symbolic
Interactionist Approach to Culture Change', *Ethos*, Vol. 1,
No. 2, pp. 219–238. 1973.
GOFFMAN, ERVING, *The Presentation of Self in Everyday Life*. New
York: Doubleday, 1959.
—, *Behavior in Public Places*. New York: Free Press of Glencoe,
1963.
HYMES, DELL, 'Toward an Ethnography of Communication'.
American Anthropologist, Vol. 66, No. 6, pp. 1–34, 1964.
HALL, EDWARD T., *The Silent Language*. Greenwich, Connecticut:
Fawcett, 1961.
MEAD, GEORGE HERBERT, *Mind, Self and Society*. Chicago:
University of Chicago Press, 1934.

Glossary

Abangan	Javanese nominal Muslim who is lax in the practice of Islam while continuing to practice non-Islamic religions such as Hinduism, Buddhism, and animism
Akal	Intellect; rationality
Alus	Refined, civilized, spiritual
Antrieb	Impulse, motive, drive
Beruf	Calling, vocation
Geisteswissenschaften	The Humanities
Geistlich	Spiritual, sacred
Gottesfreunde	Friends of God, a medieval mystical movement
Hormat	Politeness, etiquette, manners
Innerweltliche	Concerned with affairs of this world as opposed to the other-world
Kampung	Village; slum neighbourhood; administrative ward of a city
Kasar	Coarse, rude, material as opposed to spiritual
Ludruk	Working-class theater of Java
Modin	Village Muslim official in Indonesia
Naturwissenschaft	Natural science
Pegangan	Something to hold to
Perdjuangan	Struggle, as in a movement or war
Permai	A movement championing the syncretist (abangan) way of life in Java

Pesantren	Muslim boarding school, typically in a remote area and teaching only religious subjects
Rechtsphilosophie	Jurisprudence
Reformasi	Reformation
Religionssoziologie	Sociology of Religion; the study of social aspects of spiritual phenomena
Santri	Pious Muslim (opposite to *abangan*) in Java
Sinn	Meaning
Stimmung	Mood, atmosphere, disposition
Ummat	The Islamic community
Verstehen	Understand, comprehend (in Weber's usage, by empathy as well as analysis)
Wajang	Javanese puppet play
Wanderschaft	Journey, wandering
Weltablehrende	World-denying, otherworldly
Wertrational	The choice of means so as to realize a single value without consideration of cost
Zweckrational	The choice of goals with consideration of the cost of achieving any one as against the others

Subject Index

Author Index